DATA INTERPRETATION TESTS

www.How2Become.com

Get more products for passing any type of test or interview at:

www.how2become.com

Orders: Please contact How2become Ltd, Suite 3, 50 Churchill Square Business Centre, Kings Hill, Kent ME19 4YU. You can also order via the e mail address info@how2become.co.uk.

ISBN: 978-1910202807

First published in 2014 by How2Become Ltd

Copyright © 2014 Richard McMunn. All rights reserved.

All rights reserved. Apart from any permitted use under UK copyright law, no part of this publication may be reproduced or transmitted in any form or by any means, electronic or mechanical, including photocopying, recording, or any information, storage or retrieval system, without permission in writing from the publisher or under licence from the Copyright Licensing Agency Limited. Further details of such licenses (for reprographic reproduction) may be obtained from the Copyright Licensing Agency Ltd, Saffron House, 6-10 Kirby Street, London EC1N 8TS.

Typeset for How2become Ltd by Anton Pshinka.

Printed and bound by CPI Group (UK) Ltd, Croydon, CR0 4YY

CONTENTS

Introduction to your new guide 5
Data interpretation tests part 1 10
Data interpretation tests part 2 47
Data interpretation tests part 3 78
Data interpretation tests part 4 103
Data interpretation tests part 5 134
Data interpretation tests part 6 185
Data interpretation tests part 7 236
Data interpretation tests part 8 266
A few final words 284

As part of this product you have also received FREE access to online tests that will help you to pass data interpretation tests.

To gain access, simply go to:

www.PsychometricTestsOnline.co.uk

INTRODUCTION TO YOUR GUIDE

Dear Sir/Madam,

Welcome to your new guide, Data Interpretation Tests. This guide contains lots of sample test questions that are appropriate for anyone who is required to take a data interpretation test. The key to success in any career or job-related assessment is to try your hardest to get 100% correct answers in the test that you are undertaking. If you aim for 100% in your preparation, then you are far more likely to achieve the trade or career that you want. We have deliberately supplied you with lots of sample questions to assist you. It is crucial that when you get a question wrong, you take the time to find out why you got it wrong. Understanding the question is very important.

Finally, if you want to try out more tests that will prepare you for your assessment then we offer a wide range of products to assist you at **www.how2become.com.**

Good luck and best wishes,

The how2become team

The How2become team

PREFACE BY AUTHOR RICHARD MCMUNN

It's probably important that I start off by explaining a little bit about myself, my background, and also why I'm suitably qualified to help you prepare for test.

At the time of writing I am 43 years old and live in Tunbridge Wells, Kent. I left school at the usual age of 16 and joined the Royal Navy, serving on-board HMS Invincible as part of 800 Naval Air Squadron which formed part of the Fleet Air Arm. There I was, at the age of 16, travelling the world and working as an engineer on Sea Harrier jets! It was fantastic and I loved every minute of it. After four years I left the Royal Navy and joined Kent Fire and Rescue Service as a firefighter.

Over the next 17 years I worked my way up through the ranks to the position of Assistant Divisional Officer. During my time in the Fire Service I spent a lot of time working as an instructor at the Fire Brigade Training Centre. I was also involved in the selection process for assessing candidates who wanted to join the job as a firefighter. Therefore, my knowledge and experience gained so far in life has been invaluable in helping people like you to pass any type of selection process. I am sure you will find this guide an invaluable resource during your preparation for your assessment.

I have always been fortunate in the fact that I persevere at everything I do. I've understood that if I keep working hard in life then I will always be successful; or I will achieve whatever it is that I want to achieve. This is an important lesson that I want you to take on-board straight away. If you work hard and persevere, then success will come your way. It is also very important that you believe in your own abilities. It does not matter if you have no qualifications. It does not matter if you are currently weak in the area of data interpretation tests or psychometric testing. What does matter is self-belief, self-discipline and a genuine desire to improve and become successful.

Finally, as part of this product I want to give you FREE access to online tests that will help you to pass data interpretation tests. To gain access, simply go to:

www.PsychometricTestsOnline.co.uk

Best wishes,

Richard McMunn

Richard McMunn

DISCLAIMER

Every effort has been made to ensure that the information contained within this guide is accurate at the time of publication. How2become Ltd are not responsible for anyone failing any part of any selection process as a result of the information contained within this guide. How2become Ltd and their authors cannot accept any responsibility for any errors or omissions within this guide, however caused. No responsibility for loss or damage occasioned by any person acting, or refraining from action, as a result of the material in this publication can be accepted by How2become Ltd.

The information within this guide does not represent the views of any third party service or organisation.

TIPS FOR PASSING THE TESTS

There's no two ways about it, the most effective way in which you can prepare for the tests is to carry out lots of sample test questions. When I say lots, I mean lots! Before I provide you with a host of test questions for you to try, here are a few important tips for you to consider:

- Variety is the key to success. I recommend that you attempt a variety of different testing questions from a range of areas, such as generic psychometric tests, numerical reasoning, verbal reasoning, fault analysis and spatial reasoning etc. This will undoubtedly improve your overall ability to pass the test that you are required to undertake. If you go to the free tests at **www.PsychometricTestsOnline.co.uk** then you will be able to try all of these free of charge.

- During your preparation for the data interpretation test it is important that you understand why you answered a question incorrectly and how you arrived at your chosen answer. If you take the time to check your answers carefully then this will undoubtedly improve your performance when you sit the real test.

- Confidence is an important part of test preparation. Most people who sit 'timed-tests' find their mind goes blank. Once this happens, they start to panic. This is because their mind is focused on negative thoughts and they end up believing they will fail the test. If you practice plenty of test questions under timed conditions then your confidence will undoubtedly grow. If your confidence is at its peak at the commencement of the test, then there is no doubt that you will actually look forward to sitting it, as opposed to being fearful of the outcome.

- Whilst this is a very basic tip that appears obvious, many people neglect to follow it. Make sure you get a good night's sleep the night prior to your test or assessment. Research has shown that those people who have regular 'good' sleep are far more likely to concentrate better during psychometric tests.

- During the test aim for SPEED as well as ACCURACY. Many test centres want to see how quickly you can work, but they also want to see how accurate your work is, too. Therefore, when tackling the tests you must work as quickly as you can without sacrificing accuracy. Most tests nowadays

INTRODUCTION TO YOUR NEW GUIDE

are designed so that you do not finish them; you will also most probably lose marks for incorrect answers and guessing.

- You are what you eat! In the week prior to the test eat and drink healthily. Avoid cigarettes, alcohol and food with high fat content. The reason for this is that all of these will make you feel sluggish and you will not perform at your peak. On the morning of your assessment eat a healthy breakfast such as porridge and a banana.

- Drink plenty of water, always!

- If you have any special needs that need to be catered for ensure you inform the assessment centre staff prior to the assessment day. I have met people in the past who are fearful of telling the assessment staff that they are dyslexic. You will not be treated negatively; in fact the exact opposite. They will give you extra time in the tests which can only work in your favour.

Now that I have provided you with a number of important tips, take the time to work through the sample test exercises that follow.

Please note: I have deliberately not provided a time constraint to the test sections as it is important that you work through the questions carefully and understand how you have reached your answers.

Calculators are permitted during the practice tests that follow.

DATA INTERPRETATION TESTS

PART 1

DATA INTERPRETATION TESTS PART 1

Q1. Study the following chart before answering the questions that follow.

BMW sales

Country	Jan	Feb	Mar	April	May	June	Total
UK	21	28	15	35	31	20	150
Germany	45	48	52	36	41	40	262
France	32	36	33	28	20	31	180
Brazil	42	41	37	32	35	28	215
Spain	22	26	17	30	24	22	141
Italy	33	35	38	28	29	38	201
Total	195	214	192	189	180	179	1149

The above table shows the sales across 6 countries for the model BMW for a 6 month period. The BMW's are imported to each country from a main dealer. Use the information provided to answer the following questions. Please circle the correct answer.

1. What percentage of the overall total was sold in April?

A	B	C	D	E
17.8	17.2	18.9	16.4	21.6

2. What percentage of the overall total sales were BMW's sold to the French importer?

A	B	C	D	E
15.7	18.2	18.9	25.6	24.5

3. What percentage of total imports is accounted for by the two smallest importers?

A	B	C	D	E
35.6	25.3	22.6	28.1	29.1

4. What is the average number of units per month imported to Brazil over the first 4 months of the year?

A	B	C	D	E
28	24	32	38	40

5. What month saw the biggest increase in total sales from the previous month?

A	B	C	D	E
January	February	March	April	May

6. What percentage of the monthly total was sold to the biggest importer in March?

A	B	C	D	E
27.1	35.6	4.5	12.6	32.8

DATA INTERPRETATION TESTS

Q2. Study the following chart before answering the questions that follow.

NSR500 Motorcycle sales

Country	Jan	Feb	Mar	April	May	June	Total
UK	32	36	28	21	42	46	205
Germany	42	51	53	49	41	35	271
France	12	18	21	15	28	21	115
Belgium	16	18	19	22	21	25	121
Spain	35	31	26	27	31	35	185
Italy	35	38	41	28	36	42	220
Total	172	192	188	162	199	204	1117

The above table shows the sales across 6 European countries for the NSR500 Motorcycle for a 6 month period. The NSR500 Motorcycle is imported to each country from a main dealer. Use the information provided to answer the following questions. Please circle the correct answer.

1. What is average number of units per month imported to Germany over the 6 month period?

A	B	C	D	E
35.6	45.2	52.4	54.6	31.8

2. What percentage of total imports is accounted for by the three smallest importers?

A	B	C	D	E
27.8	31.7	37.7	42.7	37.1

3. What is the difference between the average number of units per month imported by Spain over the first 4 months and the average number of units per month imported by the UK over the first 4 months?

A	B	C	D	E
0.5	1.5	2	4	5.5

4. What percentage of the overall total sales were NSR500's sold to Italian importers?

A	B	C	D	E
18.7	21.7	28.4	21.3	19.7

5. What month saw the biggest increase in total sales from the previous month?

A	B	C	D	E
January	February	March	April	May

6. What percentage of the overall total was sold in February?

A	B	C	D	E
17	17.2	17.4	17.6	17.8

Q3. Study the following chart before answering the questions that follow.

Number of divorces across different countries

Country	Jan	Feb	Mar	April	May	June	Total
UK	356	258	129	352	312	258	1665
Germany	357	325	259	257	329	316	1843
France	201	285	210	285	236	196	1413
Belgium	95	85	109	83	91	108	571
Spain	148	156	201	122	189	175	991
Italy	138	254	169	147	168	96	972
Total	1295	1363	1077	1246	1325	1149	7455

The above table shows the number of divorces across 6 different countries for a 6 month period. Use the information provided to answer the following questions. Please circle the correct answer.

1. What is the average number of divorces per month in Spain over the first 5 months of the year?

A	B	C	D	E
158.3	162.5	163.2	163.9	161.8

2. What percentage of total divorces is accounted for by the three lowest divorce rate countries?

A	B	C	D	E
34	31	28	35	41

3. What is average number of divorces per month for Germany over the 6 month period?

A	B	C	D	E
301.5	303.6	300	306.2	307.2

4. What month saw the biggest increase in total divorces from the previous month?

A	B	C	D	E
January	February	March	April	May

5. In total, what is the average number of divorces across the 6 countries?

A	B	C	D	E
1282.6	1242.5	1422.5	1452.2	1225.5

6. What percentage of the overall divorce rates were from Belgium?

A	B	C	D	E
7.2	7.3	7.5	7.7	7.9

DATA INTERPRETATION TESTS

Q4. Study the following chart before answering the questions that follow.

Number of families from the UK that went on holiday

Country	Jan	Feb	Mar	April	May	June	Total
UK	85	102	96	72	63	56	474
Germany	103	96	92	80	86	73	530
France	205	216	184	112	96	68	881
America	186	197	210	152	109	98	952
Sweden	84	28	16	23	21	19	191
Ireland	234	185	139	208	214	165	1145
Total	897	824	737	647	589	479	4173

The above table shows the number of families from the UK that went on holiday to one of these six countries in a 6 month period. Use the information provided to answer the following questions. Please circle the correct answer.

1. What is the difference between the country that had the lowest number of families that went on holiday there and the country that had the highest number of families that went on holiday there?

A	B	C	D	E
1226	935	954	1663	986

2. What is the average number of family holidays per month to Ireland from January to April?

A	B	C	D	E
190	182.6	119.5	191.5	128.5

3. What percentage of total number of family holidays is accounted for by holidays to America?

A	B	C	D	E
22.8	21.8	18.8	20.8	18.2

4. What percentage of the monthly total was accounted for by the most popular holiday destination in March?

A	B	C	D	E
22	28.5	30.5	32.5	40

5. What is average number of families who had their holiday in France over the 6 month period?

A	B	C	D	E
146.8	150	134.8	136.5	136.8

6. What percentage of the overall total of holidays happened in January?

A	B	C	D	E
15	25	11.6	18	21.5

Q5. Study the following chart before answering the questions that follow.

Number of car accidents in the south east, UK

Year	Jan-Feb	Mar-April	May-Jun	July-Aug	Sept-Oct	Nov-Dec	Total
2008	100	89	85	110	115	168	667
2009	179	165	154	120	169	184	971
2010	149	130	120	75	183	208	865
2011	168	142	135	102	128	147	822
2012	206	198	178	152	168	230	1132
2013	189	146	120	89	108	186	838
Total	991	870	792	648	871	1123	5295

The above table shows the number of car accidents in the south east, UK, in a 12 month period. The table shows data from the years 2008-2013. Use the information provided to answer the following questions. Please circle the correct answer.

1. What percentage of the total number of car accidents happened in Sept-Oct?

A	B	C	D	E
25	16.4	75	52.4	26.4

2. What is the average number of car accidents across the 12 month period for the year 2012?

A	B	C	D	E
94.3	92.8	188.6	175.5	160.3

3. What percentage of the monthly total was accounted for by the highest number of car accidents that occurred in Mar-April?

A	B	C	D	E
30	35.2	22.8	26.8	42.2

4. What is the difference between the year that had the lowest number of car accidents and the year that had the highest number of accidents?

A	B	C	D	E
580	210	385	465	596

5. In total, what is the average number of car accidents across the July-Aug period?

A	B	C	D	E
108	110.5	115	85	121.6

6. What percentage of the total number of car accidents is accounted for by the three years that have the highest number of car accidents?

A	B	C	D	E
60	62.4	51.8	52.6	56.1

16 DATA INTERPRETATION TESTS

Q6. Study the following chart before answering the questions that follow.

Number of births in the south east, UK

Year	Jan-Feb	Mar-April	May-Jun	July-Aug	Sept-Oct	Nov-Dec	Total
2008	352	302	254	216	169	320	1613
2009	310	296	242	241	190	313	1592
2010	286	273	249	214	168	146	1336
2011	234	216	206	165	172	210	1203
2012	196	176	135	167	166	106	946
2013	118	123	185	135	147	109	817
Total	1496	1386	1271	1138	1012	1204	7507

The above table shows the number of births in the south east, UK, in a 12 month period. The table shows data from the years 2008–2013. Use the information provided to answer the following questions. Please circle the correct answer.

1. What is the difference between the year that had the lowest number of births and the year that had the highest number of births?

A	B	C	D	E
721	712	796	769	779

2. What percentage of the total number of births is accounted for by the three years that have the highest number of births?

A	B	C	D	E
75	72.5	61.5	60.5	55.5

3. What percentage of the overall total was the birth rate between Nov-Dec?

A	B	C	D	E
12	14	16	18	20

4. What percentage of the overall total number of births happened in the year 2008?

A	B	C	D	E
21.5	18.5	35	25	17.5

5. What percentage of the monthly total was the highest number of births that occurred between May-Jun?

A	B	C	D	E
18	20	22	24	26

6. What is the mean number of births across the 12 month period for 2010?

A	B	C	D	E
121.3	111.3	120	125	118.5

Q7. Study the following chart before answering the questions that follow.

Jaguar XK car sales

Country	Jan	Feb	Mar	April	May	June	Total
UK	115	85	72	93	116	135	616
Germany	285	214	206	185	147	163	1200
France	86	74	67	101	62	71	461
Belgium	48	46	59	93	82	103	431
Spain	108	139	195	146	127	101	816
Italy	215	189	165	147	256	210	1182
Total	857	747	764	765	790	783	4706

The above table shows the sales across 6 European countries for the Jaguar XK car for a 6 month period. The Jaguar XK is imported to each country from a main dealer. Use the information provided to answer the following questions. Please circle the correct answer.

1. What is average number of units per month imported to Spain over the 6 month period?

A	B	C	D	E
163	136	140	146	121

2. What percentage of total imports is accounted for by the three smallest importers?

A	B	C	D	E
32	12	52	22	17

3. What is the difference between the average number of units per month imported by Germany over the first 4 months and the average number of units per month imported by the UK over the first 4 months?

A	B	C	D	E
180.75	180.25	131.75	150	131.25

4. What percentage of the overall total sales were the Jaguar XK sold to Italian importers?

A	B	C	D	E
75.1	25.1	30.2	40.5	60.5

5. What month saw the biggest increase in total sales from the previous month?

A	B	C	D	E
January	February	March	April	May

6. What percentage of the overall total was sold in March?

A	B	C	D	E
18.9	16.2	25.2	31.4	11.6

18 DATA INTERPRETATION TESTS

Q8. Study the following chart before answering the questions that follow.

Number of people unemployed in the south east, UK

Year	Jan-Feb	Mar-April	May-Jun	July-Aug	Sept-Oct	Nov-Dec	Total
2008	89	106	111	113	125	164	708
2009	92	93	123	127	148	152	735
2010	109	159	176	130	169	162	905
2011	201	194	157	165	138	139	994
2012	253	249	239	258	247	219	1465
2013	213	139	219	243	216	206	1236
Total	957	940	1025	1036	1043	1042	6043.

The above table shows the number of people unemployed in the south east, UK, following a 12 month period. The table shows data from the years 2008 – 2013. Use the information provided to answer the following questions.

1. What is the average number of people unemployed in the 12 month period of 2010?

A	B	C	D	E
75.4	82.2	71.4	80	65.5

2. What is the total mean number of unemployed people between July-Aug?

A	B	C	D	E
156.5	152.7	172.7	182.6	168.2

3. What percentage of the overall total was the unemployment rate between Nov-Dec?

A	B	C	D	E
21.2	28.2	17.2	32.2	40.2

4. What is the difference between the average number of people unemployed in the first 4 months of 2008 and the average number of people unemployed in the first 4 months of 2013?

A	B	C	D	E
101.25	105.5	85.75	98.75	98.25

5. What percentage of the overall unemployment rates were from 2013?

A	B	C	D	E
21.5	18.5	11.5	15.5	20.5

6. What months saw the biggest increase in total unemployment rates from the previous month?

A	B	C	D	E
Jan-Feb	Mar-April	May-Jun	July-Aug	Sept-Oct

Q9. Study the following chart before answering the questions that follow.

Number of West End theatre tickets sold in a London theatre

Year	Jan-Feb	Mar-April	May-Jun	July-Aug	Sept-Oct	Nov-Dec	Total
2008	210	315	345	165	268	167	1470
2009	570	562	763	719	589	345	3548
2010	596	587	526	358	687	348	3102
2011	458	324	459	763	359	368	2731
2012	358	361	206	586	236	695	2442
2013	359	354	469	454	462	523	2621
Total	2551	2503	2768	3045	2601	2446	15,914

The above table shows the number of tickets sold at a West End theatre in London, following a 12 month period. The table shows data from the years 2008 – 2013. Use the information provided to answer the following questions.

1. What percentage of the overall total was the ticket rate between July-Aug?

A	B	C	D	E
15.2	19.1	22	31.5	35

2. What is average number of tickets sold per month in the 12 month period of 2012?

A	B	C	D	E
215.5	210.5	203.5	208.5	212.5

3. What is the total mean number of tickets sold in 2009 in the 12 month period?

A	B	C	D	E
295.7	285.7	265.7	210	125.7

4. What percentage of the total number of tickets sold is accounted for by the three years that sold the highest number of tickets in that year?

A	B	C	D	E
45	50.2	55.5	52.9	58.9

5. What percentage of total number of tickets sold is accounted for by the years 2013 and 2008?

A	B	C	D	E
28.7	25.3	28.3	25.7	30

6. What is the difference between the year that had the lowest number of tickets sold and the year that had the highest number of tickets sold?

A	B	C	D	E
1458	2035	2078	2087	2807

DATA INTERPRETATION TESTS

Q10. Study the following chart before answering the questions that follow.

Civic car sales

Country	Jan	Feb	Mar	April	May	June	Total
UK	68	82	71	106	108	112	547
Germany	142	162	152	136	205	211	1008
France	112	103	96	85	73	109	578
Belgium	68	106	186	150	83	89	682
Spain	103	168	158	103	96	75	703
Italy	110	136	65	76	88	103	578
Total	603	757	728	656	653	699	4096

The above table shows the sales across 6 European countries for the Civic car for a 6 month period. The Civic car is imported to each country from a main dealer. Use the information provided to answer the following questions.

1. What is average number of units per month imported to Germany over the 6 month period?

A	B	C	D	E
168	102	158	121	135

2. What percentage of total imports is accounted for by the smallest importers?

A	B	C	D	E
12.6	13.4	15	16.2	22.2

3. What is the difference between the average number of units per month imported by Italy over the first 4 months and the average number of units per month imported by Belgium over the first 4 months?

A	B	C	D	E
30.15	30.25	30.45	30.75	30.95

4. What percentage of the overall total sales were Civics sold to Italian importers?

A	B	C	D	E
14.1	13.1	12.1	11.1	10.1

5. What month saw the biggest increase in total sales from the previous month?

A	B	C	D	E
January	February	March	April	May

6. What percentage of the overall total was sold in February?

A	B	C	D	E
18.1	18.3	18.5	18.7	18.9

Q11. Study the following chart before answering the questions that follow.

Harley Davidson Motorcycle sales

Country	Jan	Feb	Mar	April	May	June	Total
UK	38	32	28	19	15	29	161
Germany	52	48	36	38	41	45	260
France	21	19	28	17	14	19	118
Brazil	18	21	32	27	21	23	142
Spain	18	35	34	17	15	21	140
Italy	19	21	25	31	28	22	146
Total	166	176	183	149	134	159	967

The above table shows the sales across 6 countries for the model Harley Davidson motorcycle for a 6 month period. The Harley Davidson's are imported to each country from a main dealer. Use the information provided to answer the following questions. Please circle the correct answer.

1. What percentage of the overall total was sold in February?

A	B	C	D	E
32	16.8	15.1	18.2	32.5

2. What percentage of the overall total sales were Harley Davidson's sold to the Brazil importers?

A	B	C	D	E
14.7	22.6	18.5	22	25

3. What percentage of total imports is accounted for by the two smallest importers?

A	B	C	D	E
22.3	26.7	31.8	45	36.7

4. What is the average number of units per month imported to Italy over the first 4 months of the year?

A	B	C	D	E
21	22	23	24	25

5. What month saw the biggest increase in total sales from the previous month?

A	B	C	D	E
February	March	April	May	June

6. What percentage of the monthly total was sold to the biggest importer in March?

A	B	C	D	E
21.3	19.7	8.6	11.2	13.6

DATA INTERPRETATION TESTS

Q12. Study the following chart before answering the questions that follow.

Number of teenage pregnancies in the south west UK

Year	Jan-Feb	Mar-April	May-Jun	July-Aug	Sept-Oct	Nov-Dec	Total
2008	18	12	11	9	13	19	82
2009	21	19	25	26	17	19	127
2010	18	25	23	16	12	21	115
2011	25	32	31	29	35	37	189
2012	42	39	35	41	28	38	223
2013	42	56	63	65	42	36	304
Total	166	183	188	186	147	170	1040

The above table shows the number of teenage pregnancies in the south west, UK, following a 12 month period. The table shows data from the years 2008 – 2013. Use the information provided to answer the following questions.

1. What percentage of the overall total was the pregnancy rate between Mar-April?

A	B	C	D	E
17.6	22.3	31.6	17.1	22.9

2. What is average number of pregnancies per month in the 12 month period of 2010?

A	B	C	D	E
5.5	8.4	9.6	7.2	10.1

3. What is the total mean number of pregnancies in 2013 in the 12 month period?

A	B	C	D	E
25.8	23.5	23.2	25.3	45

4. What percentage of the total number of pregnancies is accounted for by the two years that have the highest number of pregnancies?

A	B	C	D	E
50.7	55	62.5	42.7	42.8

5. What percentage of total number of pregnancies is accounted for by the years 2012 and 2009?

A	B	C	D	E
45	33.7	42.1	27.8	39.4

6. What is the difference between the year that had the lowest pregnancy rate and the year that had the highest number of pregnancies?

A	B	C	D	E
221	212	222	112	121

Q13. Study the following chart before answering the questions that follow.

Number of book sales for a local book company

Year	Jan	Feb	Mar	April	May	June	Total
2008	86	56	76	103	108	72	501
2009	115	136	130	92	86	135	694
2010	93	86	79	108	165	142	673
2011	106	56	134	85	81	138	600
2012	96	76	68	46	69	92	447
2013	106	180	136	106	135	167	830
Total	602	590	623	540	644	746	3745

The above table shows the number book sales for a local book company, following a 6 month period. The table shows data from the years 2008 – 2013. Use the information provided to answer the following questions.

1. What is average number of book sales per month for 2012 over the 6 month period?

A	B	C	D	E
78.5	74.5	82	82.5	81.5

2. What month saw the biggest increase in total book sales from the previous month?

A	B	C	D	E
January	February	March	April	May

3. What percentage of total book sales is accounted for by the year 2010?

A	B	C	D	E
18	21	11	13	26

4. What percentage of the overall total sales were books sold in April?

A	B	C	D	E
26.3	14.4	18.8	21.2	25

5. What percentage of the monthly total was the highest number of book sales that occurred in February?

A	B	C	D	E
30.5	35	31.5	38.5	36.5

6. What is average number of book sales in April over the 6 year period?

A	B	C	D	E
92	85	90	87	65

DATA INTERPRETATION TESTS

Q14. Study the following chart before answering the questions that follow.

Number of single parent households in the UK

Year	Jan-Feb	Mar-April	May-Jun	July-Aug	Sept-Oct	Nov-Dec	Total
2005	86	76	79	59	49	85	434
2006	92	98	85	72	69	62	478
2007	105	120	142	131	95	97	690
2008	136	142	154	120	168	130	850
2009	168	146	165	176	164	94	913
2010	204	167	168	213	236	192	1180
Total	791	749	793	771	781	660	4545

The above table shows the number of single parent households in the UK, following a 12 month period. Use the information provided to answer the following questions. Please circle the correct answer.

1. What is the difference between the year that had the lowest number of single parent households and the year that had the highest number of single parent households?

A	B	C	D	E
476	467	764	746	674

2. What is the overall average number of single parent households in the months May-June?

A	B	C	D	E
154.4	128.4	136.5	129.6	132.2

3. What percentage of total number of single parent households is accounted for the year 2007?

A	B	C	D	E
18.6	21.4	35	29.1	15.2

4. What percentage of the monthly total was accounted for by the highest number of single parent households in July-August time?

A	B	C	D	E
23.2	27.6	56.8	62.4	33.3

5. What is the average number of single parent households in the years 2010 and 2005?

A	B	C	D	E
122.5	136.5	134.5	148.5	150

6. What percentage of the overall total of single parent households was accounted for in January-February?

A	B	C	D	E
18.2	22	26.2	17.4	19.6

Q15. Study the following chart before answering the questions that follow.

Number of cakes sold at a local bakery

Year	Jan	Feb	Mar	April	May	June	Total
2006	234	235	238	168	359	341	1575
2007	165	268	264	214	368	349	1628
2008	435	468	438	514	519	645	3019
2009	465	658	562	573	468	431	3157
2010	648	641	561	468	482	348	3148
2011	397	468	462	531	358	453	2669
Total	2344	2738	2525	2468	2554	2567	15,196

The above table shows the sales of cakes for a local bakery over a time period of 6 years. The table above shows the data collected for the first 6 months in the year. Use the information provided to answer the following questions. Please circle the correct answer.

1. What percentage of the overall total was sold in February?

A	B	C	D	E
21	31	18	6	27

2. What percentage of the overall total sales were cakes sold in 2010?

A	B	C	D	E
25	20.7	33.3	48.5	52.6

3. What percentage of total cakes sold is accounted for by the two highest years for the local bakery?

A	B	C	D	E
22.4	35.5	45	29.6	41.5

4. What is the average number of cakes sold over the first 4 months of the year 2009?

A	B	C	D	E
584.5	564.5	524.5	515.5	563.5

5. What month saw the biggest increase in total sales from the previous month?

A	B	C	D	E
January	February	March	April	May

6. What percentage of the monthly total was the highest number of cakes sold in April?

A	B	C	D	E
23.2	26.1	30.1	30.5	27.8

26 DATA INTERPRETATION TESTS

Q16. Study the following chart before answering the questions that follow.

Number of prison sentences

Country	Jan	Feb	Mar	April	May	June	Total
UK	215	312	165	235	432	132	1491
Germany	354	353	463	452	235	532	2389
France	135	262	135	236	231	291	1290
Brazil	96	166	135	130	138	120	785
Spain	235	235	136	130	135	92	963
Italy	84	76	165	135	131	198	789
Total	1119	1404	1199	1318	1302	1365	7707

The above table shows the number of prison sentences across 6 countries for a 6 month period. Use the information provided to answer the following questions. Please circle the correct answer.

1. What percentage of the overall total was the number of prison sentences in January?

A	B	C	D	E
18.5	16.5	14.5	20.5	22.5

2. What percentage of the overall total sentences came from Spain?

A	B	C	D	E
12.5	11.5	13.5	15.5	18.5

3. What percentage of total number of sentences is accounted for by the two lowest countries?

A	B	C	D	E
25	21.8	20.6	20.4	22.1

4. What is the average number of sentences in France over the first 4 months of the year?

A	B	C	D	E
157	108	66	183	192

5. What month saw the biggest increase in total number of sentences from the previous month?

A	B	C	D	E
January	February	March	April	May

6. What percentage of the monthly total was sentences highest in May?

A	B	C	D	E
33.2	38.6	42.6	42.8	50

Q17. Study the following chart before answering the questions that follow.

Houses put on the market in an area in Kent, UK

Year	Jan	Feb	Mar	April	May	June	Total
2008	135	147	139	132	230	295	1078
2009	289	456	269	364	429	132	1939
2010	314	138	341	463	480	435	2171
2011	419	389	432	487	410	325	2462
2012	132	92	79	125	103	89	620
2013	112	101	98	94	87	106	598
Total	1401	1323	1358	1665	1739	1382	8868

The above table shows the number of houses put on the market in an area in Kent, UK, based on a 6 month period. Use the information provided to answer the following questions.

1. What percentage of the overall total was the house rate in 2010?

A	B	C	D	E
22.5	42	55	24.5	32.5

2. What is the difference between the average number of houses that went on the market in 2008 over the first 3 months and the average number of houses that went on the market in 2013 over the first 3 months?

A	B	C	D	E
32.4	36.6	42.5	42.6	55.5

3. What percentage of the monthly total was accounted for by the highest number of houses put on the market in June?

A	B	C	D	E
31.5	36.8	42.8	42.5	36

4. What is the difference between the year that had the lowest number of houses put on the market and the year that had the highest number of houses put on the market?

A	B	C	D	E
1358	1369	1875	1864	1346

5. What is the total mean number of houses put on the market in 2009 in the 6 month period?

A	B	C	D	E
189.2	323.2	175.2	175.5	165.8

6. What percentage of the overall total was houses put on the market in 2012?

A	B	C	D	E
25	11	12	7	31

DATA INTERPRETATION TESTS

Q18. Study the following chart before answering the questions that follow.

8C Alfa Romeo sales

Country	Jan	Feb	Mar	April	May	June	Total
UK	32	25	27	31	45	54	214
Germany	46	49	51	58	36	45	285
France	36	21	29	31	38	25	180
Brazil	26	34	19	21	25	37	162
Spain	36	25	34	19	17	26	157
Italy	54	59	68	42	39	57	319
Total	230	213	228	202	200	244	1317

The above table shows the sales across 6 countries for the model 8C Alfa Romeo for a 6 month period. The 8C's are imported to each country from a main dealer. Use the information provided to answer the following questions. Please circle the correct answer.

1. What percentage of the overall total was sold in June?

A	B	C	D	E
13.5	21.5	18.5	26.5	30.5

2. What percentage of the overall total sales were Alfa's sold to the Brazilian importers?

A	B	C	D	E
12.3	12.8	13.4	14.6	15

3. What percentage of total imports is accounted for by the two smallest importers?

A	B	C	D	E
28.2	24.2	26.2	22.2	20.2

4. What is the average number of units per month imported to the UK over the first 4 months of the year?

A	B	C	D	E
25.65	25.15	25.5	28.25	28.75

5. What month saw the biggest increase in total sales from the previous month?

A	B	C	D	E
February	April	May	June	January

6. What percentage of the monthly total was sold to the biggest importer in February?

A	B	C	D	E
25.5	30	27.7	32	37.7

Q19. Study the following chart before answering the questions that follow.

Nissan 37oZ sales

Country	Jan	Feb	Mar	April	May	June	Total
UK	15	21	25	28	16	13	118
Germany	42	41	34	31	27	17	192
France	34	36	25	21	42	29	187
Japan	42	58	59	63	42	39	303
Spain	32	39	42	47	45	34	239
Italy	39	34	18	23	27	31	172
Total	204	229	203	213	199	163	1211

The above table shows the sales across 6 countries for the model Nissan 37oZ for a 6 month period. The Nissan's are imported to each country from a main dealer. Use the information provided to answer the following questions. Please circle the correct answer.

1. What percentage of the overall total sales were Nissan's sold to the Italian importers?

A	B	C	D	E
12.2	13.2	14.2	15.2	16.2

2. What month saw the biggest decrease in total sales from the previous month?

A	B	C	D	E
May	February	June	March	January

3. What percentage of the overall total was sold in April?

A	B	C	D	E
17.6	21.5	28.4	13.6	22

4. What percentage of total number of car sales is accounted for by the months January, February and May?

A	B	C	D	E
65	52.2	36.5	75.2	42.6

5. What is the difference between the country that had the lowest car sales and the country that had the highest number of car sales?

A	B	C	D	E
125	155	175	185	165

6. What is the total mean number of car sales in Spain based on the 6 month period?

A	B	C	D	E
32.6	39.8	42.6	48.4	46.8

DATA INTERPRETATION TESTS

Q20. Study the following chart before answering the questions that follow.

Suzuki Motorcycle sales

Country	Jan	Feb	Mar	April	May	June	Total
UK	23	31	24	27	19	16	140
Germany	35	39	41	17	21	26	179
France	25	29	17	16	6	9	102
Belgium	9	11	18	21	27	25	111
Spain	11	13	8	12	15	21	80
Italy	21	25	31	38	42	28	185
Total	124	148	139	131	130	125	797

The above table shows the sales across 6 European countries for the Suzuki Motorcycle for a 6 month period. The Suzuki Motorcycle is imported to each country from a main dealer. Use the information provided to answer the following questions. Please circle the correct answer.

1. What is the average number of units per month imported to France over the 6 month period?

A	B	C	D	E
17	21	25	19	24

2. What percentage of total imports is accounted for by the two smallest importers?

A	B	C	D	E
32.8	32.6	29.5	22.8	45

3. What is the difference between the average number of units per month imported by the UK over the first 4 months and the average number of units per month imported to Belgium over the first 4 months?

A	B	C	D	E
8.5	9.5	10.5	10.75	11.5

4. What percentage of the overall total sales were Suzuki's sold to Italian importers?

A	B	C	D	E
21.8	18.5	9.5	32.6	23.2

5. What month saw the biggest increase in total sales from the previous month?

A	B	C	D	E
January	February	March	April	May

6. What percentage of the overall total was sold in May?

A	B	C	D	E
19.3	16.3	12.3	11.3	5.3

Now check your answers before moving on to the next section of your guide.

PART 1

DATA INTERPRETATIONS PART 1 EXPLANATIONS AND ANSWERS

QUESTION 1

1. D

EXPLANATION: to work out the percentage overall total that was sold in April, divide how many BMW's were sold in April (189) by the total (1149) and then multiply it by 100. (189 / 1149 x 100 = 16.4).

2. A

EXPLANTATION: to work out the percentage overall total that was sold to France, divide how many BMW's were sold to France (180) by the total (1149) and then multiply it by 100. (180 / 1149 x 100 = 15.66). Rounded up to 1 decimal place = 15.7.

3. B

EXPLANTATION: to work out the percentage overall for imports accounted by the two smallest importers, divide the total (1149) by how many BMW's were sold from the two smallest importers (UK and France = 150 + 141 = 291) and then multiply it by 100. (291 / 1149 x 100 = 25.3).

4. D

EXPLANTATION: to work out the average number of units per month imported to Brazil over the first 4 months of the year, you add up the first 4 amounts (Jan-April) and then divide it by how many numbers there are (4). So, (42 + 41 + 37 + 32 = 152 / 4 = 38).

5. B

EXPLANATION: to work out the biggest increase in total sales from the previous month, you work out the difference between the totals for each of the month and work out which has the biggest increase. Between January and February, there was an increase by 19. None of the other months have a bigger increase and therefore February is the correct answer.

6. A

EXPLANATION: to work out the percentage of the monthly total that was sold to the biggest importer in March, you find the biggest number in March (52) and divide it by the monthly total (192) and multiply it by 100. So, (52 / 192 x 100 = 27.08). Rounded up to 1 decimal place = 27.1.

QUESTION 2

1. B

EXPLANATION: to work out the average number of units per month imported to Germany for the 6 month period, add up all the numbers from the Jan-June for Germany (271) and then divide it by how many numbers there were (6). So, (271 / 6 = 45.166) Rounded up to 1 decimal place = 45.2.

DATA INTERPRETATION TESTS

2. C
EXPLANATION: to work out the percentage overall for the imports accounted by the three smallest importers, divide the total (1117) by how many motorcycles were sold from the three smallest importers (France, Belgium and Spain = 115 + 121 + 185 = 421) and then multiply it by 100. So, (421 / 1117 x 100 = 37.690) Rounded up to 1 decimal place = 37.7.

3. A
EXPLANATION: to work out the difference between averages for UK and Spain in the first 4 months, add up first 4 months for the UK (32 + 36 + 28 + 21 = 117), then divide it by how many numbers there are (4). (117 / 4 = 29.25). For Spain (35 + 31 + 26 + 27 = 119), then divide it by 4 = 29.75. So, the difference between UK (29.25) and Spain (29.75) = 0.50.

4. E
EXPLANATION: to work out the percentage overall total that was sold to Italian importers, divide the total (1117) by how many BMW's were sold to Italian importers (220) and then multiply it by 100. So, (220 / 1117 x 100 = 19.69) Rounded up to 1 decimal place = 19.7.

5. E
EXPLANATION: to work out the biggest increase in total sales from the previous month, you work out the difference between the totals for each of the month and work out which has the biggest increase. Between April and May, there was an increase by 37. None of the other months have a bigger increase and therefore May is the correct answer.

6. B
EXPLANATION: to work out the total overall percentage that was sold in February, divide how many motorcycles were sold in February (192) by the total (1117) and then multiply it by 100. So, (192 / 1117 x 100 = 17.188) Rounded up to 1 decimal place = 17.2.

QUESTION 3

1. C
EXPLANATION: to work this out, add up the first 5 months of the number of divorces for Spain (148 + 156 + 201 + 122 + 189 = 816) and then divide this by how many numbers there are (5). So, (816 / 5 = 163.2).

2. A
EXPLANTATION: to work out the percentage overall for imports accounted by the three countries with the lowest divorce rate, divide the lowest three countries total (Belgium, Spain and Italy = 2534) and divide it by the overall total (7455) and multiply it by 100. So, (2534 / 7455 x 100 = 33.99) rounded to the nearest whole number 34.

3. E
EXPLANATION: to work this out, add up the first 6 months of the number of divorces for Germany (1843) and then divide this by how many numbers there are (6). So, (1843 / 6 = 307.16). Rounded up to 1 decimal place = 307.2.

PART 1

4. D

EXPLANATION: to work out the biggest increase in total divorces from the previous month, you work out the difference between the totals for each of the month and work out which has the biggest increase. Between March and April, there was an increase by 169. None of the other months have a bigger increase and therefore April is the correct answer.

5. B

EXPLANATION: to work out the total average of the number of divorces across the 6 countries, you take the total number of divorces (7455) and then divide it by how many countries there are (6). So, (7455 / 6 = 1242.5).

6. D

EXPLANATION: to work out the percentage of the overall divorce rates that were from Belgium, you divide the total of divorces from Belgium (571) by the overall total (7455) and then multiply it by 100. So, (571 / 7455 x 100 = 7.65) Rounded up to 1 decimal place = 7.7.

QUESTION 4

1. C

EXPLANATION: to work out the difference between the country with the lowest amount of families that went on holiday and the country with the highest amount of families that went on holiday, find which country has the lowest amount (Sweden = 191) and the highest amount (Ireland = 1145) and work out the difference by: (1145 – 191 = 954)

2. D

EXPLANATION: to work out the average percentage on families that went on holiday to Ireland between January and April, add up (234 + 185 + 139 + 208 = 766) and then divide it by how many months you were working out (4). So, (766 / 4 = 191.5).

3. A

EXPLANATION: to work out the percentage of the total number of family holidays that were accounted for by holidays to America, you divide the number of holidays to America (952) by the total number of holidays (4173) and then multiply it by 100. So, (952 / 4173 x 100 = 22.8).

4. B

EXPLANATION: to work out the percentage of the monthly total that was accounted for by the most popular holiday destination in March, you find the most popular holiday destination in March (America = 210) and then divide the monthly total (737) and multiply it by 100. So, (210 / 737 x 100 = 28.49) Rounded up to 1 decimal place = 28.5.

5. A

EXPLANATION: to work out the average number of families who had their holiday in France over the 6 month period, you divide the number of holidays to France (881) by the number of months (6). So, (881 / 6 = 146.83).

DATA INTERPRETATION TESTS

6. E
EXPLANATION: to work out the percentage of the overall total of holidays that happened in January, you divide the number of holidays that happened in January (897) and divide it by the total number of holidays (4173) and then multiply it by 100. So, (897 / 4173 x 100 = 21.49).

QUESTION 5

1. B
EXPLANATION: to work out the percentage of the total number of car accidents that happened Sept-Oct, divide the number of car accidents that happened in Sept-Oct (871) by the total number of car accidents (5295) and then multiply it by 100. So, (871 / 5295 x 100 = 16.44).

2. A
EXPLANATION: to work out the average number of car accidents across the 12 month period for the year 2012, divide the number of car accidents that happened in 2012 (1132) by the number of months (12) (Note: you would divide by 12 months and not 6, as the question asks for the average across '12' months) So, (1132 / 12 = 94.3).

3. C
EXPLANATION: to work out the percentage of the monthly total that was accounted for by the highest number of car accidents that occurred in Mar-April, you divide the highest number of car accidents that happened in Mar-April (198) and divide it by the monthly total (870) and multiply it by 100. So, (198 / 870 x 100 = 22.75) Rounded up to 1 decimal place = 22.8.

4. D
EXPLANATION: to work out the difference between the year that had the lowest number of car accidents and the year that had the highest number of accidents, subtract the year with the lowest number of car accidents (667) by the year with the highest (1132). So, (1132 – 667 = 465).

5. A
EXPLANATION: to work out the total average of car accidents across the July-Aug period, divide the number of car accidents that happened in July-Aug (648) by the number of years (6). So, (648 / 6 = 108).

6. E
EXPLANATION: to work out the percentage of the total number of car accidents that accounts for the three years with the highest number of car accidents, add up the three highest years (1132 + 971 + 865 = 2968) and then divide it by the total (5295) and then multiply it by 100. So, (2968 / 5295 x 100 = 56.05) Rounded up to 1 decimal place = 56.1.

PART 1   35

QUESTION 6

1. C

EXPLANATION: to work out the difference between the year with the highest number of births and the year with the lowest number of births, subtract the lowest number of births (817) away from the highest number of births (1613). So, (1613 – 817 = 796).

2. D

EXPLANATION: to work out the percentage of the total number of births that is accounted by the three years with the highest number of births, add up the three highest years (1613 + 1592 + 1336 = 4541) and then divide it by the overall total (7507) and then multiply it by 100. So, (4541 / 7507 x 100 = 60.49) Rounded up to 1 decimal place = 60.5.

3. C

EXPLANATION: to work out the percentage of the overall total of birth rates that occurred between Nov-Dec, divide the number of births in Nov-Dec (1204) by the overall total (7507) and then multiply it by 100. So, (1204 / 7507 x 100 = 16.03).

4. A

EXPLANATION: to work out the percentage of the overall total number of births that happened in the year 2008, divide the number of births that happened in 2008 (1613) by the overall total number of births (7507) and then multiply it by 100. So, (1613 / 7507 x 100 = 21.48) Rounded up to 1 decimal place = 21.5.

5. B

EXPLANATION: to work out the percentage of the monthly total of the number of births that occurred between May-Jun, divide the highest number of births that occurred in May-Jun (254) by the monthly total (1271) and multiply it by 100. So, (254 / 1271 x 100 = 19.98) Rounded up to 1 decimal place = 20.

6. B

EXPLANATION: to work out the mean number of births across the 12 month period for 2010. Add up all the totals for 2010 (1336) and then divide it by the number of months (12). So, (1336 / 12 = 111.33).

QUESTION 7

1. B

EXPLANATION: to work out the average number of units per month imported to Spain over the 6 month period, you divide the total number of cars imported to Spain (816) by the number of months (6). So, (816 / 6 = 136).

2. A

EXPLANATION: to work out the percentage of the total imports accounted for by the three smallest importers, add up the three smallest importers (Belgium, France, UK = 616 + 461

+ 431 = 1508) and then divide it by the overall total (4706) and multiply it by 100. So, (1508 / 4706 x 100 = 32.04).

3. E

EXPLANATION: to work out the difference between the average number of cars sold in the first 4 months in Germany and the number of cars sold in the first 4 months in the UK, add up the first 4 months for Germany (285 + 214 + 206 + 185 = 890) and then divide it by 4 = 222.5. Add up the first 4 months for the UK (115 + 85 + 72 + 93 = 365) and then divide it by 4 = 91.25. So, the difference between 222.5 and 91.25 = 131.25.

4. B

EXPLANATION: to work out the percentage of the overall total sales sold to Italian importers, you divide the number of sales to Italian importers (1182) by the overall total (4706) and multiply it by 100. So, (1182 / 4706 x 100 = 25.11).

5. E

EXPLANATION: to work out the biggest increase in total sales from the previous month, you work out the difference between the totals for each of the month and work out which has the biggest increase. Between April and May, there was an increase by 25. None of the other months have a bigger increase and therefore May is the correct answer.

6. B

EXPLANATION: to work out the percentage of the overall total that was sold in March, divide the number of cars sold in March (764) by the overall total (4706) and multiply it by 100. So, (764 / 4706 x 100 = 16.23) Rounded up to 1 decimal place = 16.2.

QUESTION 8

1. A

EXPLANATION: to work out the average number of people unemployed in the 12 month period of 2010, divide the total number of unemployed people for the year 2010 (905) and divide it by the number of months (12). So, (905 / 12 = 75.41).

2. C

EXPLANATION: to work out the total mean number of people unemployed between July and August, divide the total number of people unemployed in those months (1036) and divide it by the number of years (6). So, (1036 / 6 = 172.66) Rounded up to 1 decimal place = 172.7.

3. C

EXPLANATION: to work out the percentage of the overall total that was unemployed between November and December, divide the number of unemployed people between these months (1042) by the overall total (6043) and multiply it by 100. So, (1042 / 6043 x 100 = 17.24).

PART 1   37

4. D

EXPLANATION: to work out the difference between the average number of people unemployed in the first 4 months of 2008 and the average number of people unemployed in the first 4 months of 2013, add up the first 4 months for 2008 (89 + 106 + 111 + 113 = 419) and then divide it by 4 = 104.75. Add up the first 4 months for 2013 (213 + 139 + 219 + 243 = 814) and then divide it by 4 = 203.5. So, the difference between 104.75 and 203.5 = 98.75.

5. E

EXPLANATION: to work out the overall percentage rates for 2013, divide the number of unemployed people in 2013 (1236) by the overall total (6043) and multiply it by 100. So, (1236 / 6043 x 100 = 20.45) Rounded up to 1 decimal place = 20.5.

6. C

EXPLANATION: to work out the biggest increase in total unemployment rates from the previous month, you work out the difference between the totals for each of the month and work out which has the biggest increase. Between March-April and May-June, there was an increase by 85. None of the other months have a bigger increase and therefore May-June is the correct answer.

QUESTION 9

1. B

EXPLANATION: to work out the percentage of the overall total of tickets that was between July-Aug, divide the number of tickets sold in July-Aug (3045) by the overall total (15,914) and multiply it by 100. So, (3045 / 15,914 x 100 = 19.13) Rounded up to 1 decimal place = 19.1.

2. C

EXPLANATION: to work out the average number of tickets sold per month over the 12 month period of 2012, you divide the total number of tickets sold in 2012 (2442) by the number of months (12). So, (2442 / 12 = 203.5).

3. A

EXPLANATION: to work out the total mean number of tickets sold in the 12 month period of 2009, divide the total number of tickets sold in 2009 (3548) and divide it by the number of months (12). So, (3548 / 12 = 295.66) Rounded up to 1 decimal place = 295.7.

4. E

EXPLANATION: to work out the percentage of the total number of tickets that is accounted for by the three highest years of sold tickets, add up the three highest years (2009, 2010, and 2011 = 3548 + 3102 + 2731 = 9381) and then divide it by the overall total (15,914) and multiply it by 100. So, (9381/ 15,914 x 100 = 58.94). Rounded up to 1 decimal place = 58.9.

5. D

EXPLANATION: to work out the percentage of the total number of tickets sold in 2008 and 2013, divide the number of tickets sold in 2008 and 2013 (1470 + 2621 = 4091) by the overall total (15,914) and then multiply it by 100. So, (4091 / 15,914 x 100 = 25.70).

6. C

EXPLANATION: to work out the difference between the year with the highest number of tickets sold and the year with the lowest number of tickets sold, subtract the year with the lowest number of tickets sold (1470) away from the year with the highest number of tickets sold (3548). So, (3548 – 1470 = 2078).

QUESTION 10

1. A

EXPLANATION: to work out the average number of units per month imported to Germany for the 6 month period, add up all the numbers from the Jan-June for Germany (1008) and then divide it by how many numbers there were (6). So, (1008 / 6 = 168)

2. B

EXPLANATION: to work out the percentage overall for the imports accounted by the smallest importer, divide the total (4096) by how many cars were sold from the smallest importer (UK = 547) and then multiply it by 100. So, (547 / 4096 x 100 = 13.35) Rounded up to 1 decimal place = 13.4.

3. D

EXPLANATION: to work out the difference between averages for Italy and Belgium in the first 4 months, add up first 4 months for Italy (110 + 136 + 65 + 76 = 387), then divide it by how many numbers there are (4). (387 / 4 = 96.75). For Belgium, (68 + 106 + 186 + 150 = 510), then divide it by 4 = 127.5. So, the difference between Italy (96.75) and Belgium (127.5) = 30.75.

4. A

EXPLANATION: to work out the percentage overall total that was sold to Italian importers, divide how many civics were sold to Italian importers (578) by the overall total (4096) and then multiply it by 100. So, (578 / 4096 x 100 = 14.11)

5. B

EXPLANATION: to work out the biggest increase in total sales from the previous month, you work out the difference between the totals for each of the month and work out which has the biggest increase. Between January and February, there was an increase by 154. None of the other months have a bigger increase and therefore February is the correct answer.

6. C

EXPLANATION: to work out the total overall percentage that was sold in February, divide how many cars were sold in February (757) by the total (4096) and then multiply it by 100. So, (757 / 4096 x 100 = 18.48) Rounded up to 1 decimal place = 18.5.

QUESTION 11

1. D

EXPLANATION: to work out the percentage overall total that was sold in February, divide how many Harley Davidson's were sold in February (176) by the total (967) and then multiply it by 100. So, (176 / 967 x 100 = 18.20).

2. A

EXPLANTATION: to work out the percentage overall total that was sold to Brazil, divide how many Harley Davidson's were sold to Brazil (142) by the total (967) and then multiply it by 100. So, (142 / 967 x 100 = 14.68). Rounded up to 1 decimal place = 14.7.

3. B

EXPLANATION: to work out the percentage overall for imports accounted by the two smallest importers, divide the total (967) by how many Harley Davidson's were sold from the two smallest importers (France and Spain = 118 + 140 = 258) and then multiply it by 100. (258 / 967 x 100 = 26.68). Rounded up to 1 decimal place = 26.7

4. D

EXPLANTATION: to work out the average number of units per month imported to Italy over the first 4 months of the year, you add up the first 4 amounts (Jan-April) and then divide it by how many numbers there are (4). So, (19 + 21 + 25 + 31 = 96 / 4 = 24).

5. E

EXPLANATION: to work out the biggest increase in total sales from the previous month, you work out the difference between the totals for each of the month and work out which has the biggest increase. Between May and June, there was an increase by 25. None of the other months have a bigger increase and therefore June is the correct answer.

6. B

EXPLANATION: to work out the percentage of the monthly total that was sold to the biggest importer in March, you find the biggest number in March (36) and divide it by the monthly total (183) and multiply it by 100. So, (36 / 183 x 100 = 19.67). Rounded up to 1 decimal place = 19.7.

QUESTION 12

1. A

EXPLANATION: to work out the percentage of the overall total of teenage pregnancies between Mar-April, divide the number of pregnancies between Mar-April (183) by the overall total (1040) and multiply it by 100. So, (183 / 1040 x 100 = 17.59) Rounded up to 1 decimal place = 17.6.

DATA INTERPRETATION TESTS

2. C
EXPLANATION: to work out the average number of pregnancies per month over the 12 month period of 2010, you divide the total number of pregnancies in 2010 (115) by the number of months (12). So, (115 / 12 = 9.58). Rounded up to 1 decimal place = 9.6.

3. D
EXPLANATION: to work out the total mean number of pregnancies in the 12 month period of 2013, divide the total number of pregnancies in 2013 (304) by the number of months (12). So, (304 / 12 = 25.33)

4. A
EXPLANATION: to work out the percentage of the total number of pregnancies that is accounted for by the two highest years of pregnancies, add up the two highest years (2012 + 2013 = 304 + 223 = 527) and then divide it by the overall total (1040) and multiply it by 100. So, (527 / 1040 x 100 = 50.67). Rounded up to 1 decimal place = 50.7

5. B
EXPLANATION: to work out the percentage of the total number of pregnancies in 2009 and 2012, divide the number of pregnancies in 2009 and 2012 (127 + 223 = 350) by the overall total (1040) and then multiply it by 100. So, (350 / 1040 x 100 = 33.65). Rounded up to 1 decimal place = 33.7

6. C
EXPLANATION: to work out the difference between the year with the highest number of pregnancies and the year with the lowest number of pregnancies, subtract the year with the lowest number of pregnancies (82) away from the year with the highest number of pregnancies (304). So, (304 – 82 = 222)

QUESTION 13

1. B
EXPLANATION: to work out the average number of book sales per month over the 6 month period of 2012, you divide the total number of book sales in 2012 (447) by the number of months (6). So, (447 / 6 = 74.5).

2. E
EXPLANATION: to work out the biggest increase in total sales from the previous month, you work out the difference between the totals for each of the month and work out which has the biggest increase. Between April and May, there was an increase by 104. None of the other months have a bigger increase and therefore May is the correct answer.

3. A
EXPLANATION: to work out the percentage of the total number of books sales that is accounted for by the year 2010, find the total number of books sold in 2010 (673) and then

divide it by the overall total (3745) and multiply it by 100. So, (673 / 3745 x 100 = 17.97). Rounded up to 1 decimal place = 18.

4. B

EXPLANATION: to work out the percentage of the total number of books sales that is accounted for in April, find the total number of books sold in April (540) and then divide it by the overall total (3745) and multiply it by 100. So, (540 / 3745 x 100 = 14.41).

5. A

EXPLANATION: to work out the percentage of the monthly total of the number of book sales that occurred in February, divide the highest number of book sales that occurred in February (180) by the monthly total (590) and multiply it by 100. So, (180 / 590 x 100 = 30.50).

6. C

EXPLANATION: to work out the average number of book sales in April over the 6 year period, you divide the total number of book sales in April (540) by the number of years (6). So, (540 / 6 = 90).

QUESTION 14

1. D

EXPLANATION: to work out the difference between the year with the lowest amount single parent households and the year with the highest amount of single parent households, find which year has the lowest amount (2005= 434) and the highest amount (2010 = 1180) and work out the difference by: (1180 – 434 = 746).

2. E

EXPLANATION: to work out the overall average on single parent households in between May-June, add up the total amount of single parent households in May- June (793) and then divide it by how many months you were working out (6). So, (793 / 6 = 132.16). Rounded up to 1 decimal place = 132.2.

3. E

EXPLANATION: to work out the percentage of the total number of single parent households accounted for the year 2007, you divide the number single parent households in 2007 (690) by the overall total (4545) and then multiply it by 100. So, (690 / 4545 x 100 = 15.18). Rounded up to 1 decimal place = 15.2.

4. B

EXPLANATION: to work out the percentage of the monthly total that was accounted for by highest number of single parent households in between July and August, you find the highest number of single parent households in July-August (213) and then divide the monthly total (771) and multiply it by 100. So, (213 / 771 x 100 = 27.62).

5. C

EXPLANATION: to work out the average number of single parent households in the years 2005 and 2010, you divide the number of single parent households in 2005 and 2010 (434 + 1180 = 1614) by the number of months (12). So, (1614 / 12 = 134.5).

6. D

EXPLANATION: to work out the percentage of the overall total of single parent households that was accounted for in Jan-Feb, you divide the number of single parent households that happened in January-February (791) and divide it by the total number of single parent households (4545) and then multiply it by 100. So, (791 / 4545 x 100 = 17.40).

QUESTION 15

1. C

EXPLANATION: to work out the percentage overall total that was sold in February, divide how many cakes were sold in February (2738) by the total (15,196) and then multiply it by 100. (2738 / 15,196 x 100 = 18.01).

2. B

EXPLANTATION: to work out the percentage overall total that was sold in 2010, divide how many cakes were sold in 2010 (3148) by the total (15,196) and then multiply it by 100. (3148 / 15,196 x 100 = 20.71).

3. E

EXPLANTATION: to work out the percentage overall for cakes sold accounted by the highest years, divide how many cakes were sold from the two highest years (2009 + 2010 = 3157 + 3148 = 6305) by the total (15,196) and then multiply it by 100. (6305 / 15,196 x 100 = 41.49). Rounded up to 1 decimal place = 41.5.

4. B

EXPLANTATION: to work out the average number of cake sales over the first 4 months of the year 2009, you add up the first 4 amounts (Jan-April) of 2009 and then divide it by how many months there are (4). So, (465 + 658 + 562 + 573 = 2258 / 4 = 564.5).

5. B

EXPLANATION: to work out the biggest increase in total sales from the previous month, you work out the difference between the totals for each of the month and work out which has the biggest increase. Between January and February, there was an increase by 394. None of the other months have a bigger increase and therefore February is the correct answer.

6. A

EXPLANATION: to work out the percentage of the monthly total that was sold in April, you find the biggest number in April (573) and divide it by the monthly total (2468) and multiply it by 100. So, (573 / 2468 x 100 = 23.21).

PART 1

QUESTION 16

1. C

EXPLANTATION: to work out the percentage of the overall total that the number of sentences that happened in January, divide how many sentences happened in January (1119) by the total (7707) and then multiply it by 100. (1119 / 7707 x 100 = 14.51).

2. A

EXPLANTATION: to work out the percentage of the overall total that the number of sentences that happened in Spain, divide how many sentences happened in Spain (963) by the total (7707) and then multiply it by 100. (963 / 7707 x 100 = 12.49). Rounded up to 1 decimal place = 12.5.

3. D

EXPLANTATION: to work out the percentage overall number of sentences accounted by the two lowest countries, divide the two countries with lowest number of sentences (Brazil and Italy = 785 + 789 = 1574) by the overall total (7707) and then multiply it by 100. (1574 / 7707 x 100 = 20.42).

4. E

EXPLANTATION: to work out the average number of sentences in France over the first 4 months of the year, add up the first 4 amounts (Jan-April) for France and then divide it by how many months there are (4). So, (135 + 262 + 135 + 236 = 768 / 4 = 192).

5. B

EXPLANATION: to work out the biggest increase in number of sentences from the previous month, you work out the difference between the totals for each of the month and work out which has the biggest increase. Between January and February, there was an increase by 285. None of the other months have a bigger increase and therefore February is the correct answer.

6. A

EXPLANATION: to work out the percentage of the monthly total that sentences was highest in May, you find the biggest number in May (432) and divide it by the monthly total (1302) and multiply it by 100. So, (432 / 1302 x 100 = 33.17). Rounded up to 1 decimal place = 33.2.

QUESTION 17

1. D

EXPLANTATION: to work out the percentage of the overall total that the number of houses that went on the market in 2010, divide how many houses went on the market in 2010 (2171) by the total (8868) and then multiply it by 100. (2171 / 8868 x 100 = 24.48). Rounded up to 1 decimal place = 24.5.

2. B

EXPLANATION: to work out the difference between averages for 2008 and 2013 in the first 3 months, add up first 3 months for 2008 (135 + 147 + 139 = 421), then divide it by how many numbers there are (3). (421 / 3 = 140.3). For 2013, (112 + 101 +98 = 311), then divide it by 3 = 103.7. So, the difference between 2008 (140.3) and 2013 (103.7) = 36.6.

3. A

EXPLANATION: to work out the percentage of the monthly total that houses were the highest in June, you find the biggest number in June (435) and divide it by the monthly total (1382) and multiply it by 100. So, (435 / 1382 x 100 = 31.47). Rounded up to 1 decimal place = 31.5.

4. D

EXPLANATION: to work out the difference between the year with the highest number of houses puts on the market and the year with the lowest number of houses put on the market, subtract the year with the lowest number of houses (598) away from the year with the highest number (2462). So, (2462 − 598 = 1864)

5. B

EXPLANATION: to work out the total mean number of houses put on the market in the 6 month period of 2009, divide the total number of houses put on the market in 2009 (1939) by the number of months (6). So, (1939 / 6 = 323.16) Rounded up to 1 decimal place = 323.2

6. D

EXPLANATION: to work out the percentage of the overall total houses went on the market in 2012, you find the total amount of houses put on the market in 2012 (620) and divide it by the overall total (8868) and multiply it by 100. So, (620 / 8868 x 100 = 6.99). Rounded up to 1 decimal place = 7.

QUESTION 18

1. C

EXPLANATION: to work out the percentage overall total that was sold in June, divide how many Alfa's were sold in June (244) by the total (1317) and then multiply it by 100. (244 / 1317 x 100 = 18.52).

2. A

EXPLANTATION: to work out the percentage overall total that was sold to Brazil, divide how many Alfa's were sold to Brazil (162) by the total (1317) and then multiply it by 100. (162 / 1317 x 100 = 12.30).

3. B

EXPLANTATION: to work out the percentage overall for imports accounted by the two smallest importers, divide the total (1317) by how many Alfa's were sold from the two smallest importers (Brazil and Spain = 162 + 157 = 319) and then multiply it by 100. (319 / 1317 x 100 = 24.22).

PART 1   45

4. E

EXPLANTATION: to work out the average number of units per month imported to the UK over the first 4 months of the year, you add up the first 4 amounts (Jan-April) and then divide it by how many numbers there are (4). So, (32 + 25 + 27 + 31 = 115 / 4 = 28.75).

5. D

EXPLANATION: to work out the biggest increase in total sales from the previous month, you work out the difference between the totals for each of the month and work out which has the biggest increase. Between May and June, there was an increase by 44. None of the other months have a bigger increase and therefore June is the correct answer.

6. C

EXPLANATION: to work out the percentage of the monthly total that was sold to the biggest importer in February, you find the biggest number in February (59) and divide it by the monthly total (213) and multiply it by 100. So, (59 / 213 x 100 = 27.69). Rounded up to 1 decimal place = 27.7.

QUESTION 19

1. C

EXPLANATION: to work out the percentage of the overall sales that were imported to Italy, divide how many Nissan's were sold to Italy (172) by the total (1211) and then multiply it by 100. (172 / 1211 x 100 = 14.20).

2. C

EXPLANATION: to work out the biggest decrease in total sales from the previous month, you work out the difference between the totals for each of the month and work out which has the biggest decrease. Between May and June, there was a decrease by 36. None of the other months have a bigger decrease and therefore June is the correct answer.

3. A

EXPLANTATION: to work out the percentage overall total that was sold in April, divide how many Nissan's were sold in April (213) by the total (1211) and then multiply it by 100. (213 / 1211 x 100 = 17.58). Rounded up to 1 decimal place = 17.6.

4. B

EXPLANATION: to work out the percentage of the total number of car sales that is accounted for in January, February and May, find the total number of cars sold in January, February and May (204 + 229 + 199 = 632) and then divide it by the overall total (1211) and multiply it by 100. So, (632 / 1211 x 100 = 52.18). Rounded up to 1 decimal place = 52.2.

5. D

EXPLANATION: to work out the difference between the country with the highest number of car sales and the country with the lowest number of car sales, subtract the country with the lowest number of houses (118) away from the country with the highest number (303). So, (303 – 118 = 185).

6. B

EXPLANATION: to work out the total mean number of car sales based on the 6 month period for Spain, divide the total number of car sales in Spain (239) by the number of months (6). So, (239 / 6 = 39.83).

QUESTION 20

1. A

EXPLANATION: to work out the average number of units per month imported to France for the 6 month period, add up all the numbers from the Jan-June for France (102) and then divide it by how many numbers there were (6). So, (102 / 6 = 17).

2. D

EXPLANATION: to work out the percentage overall for the imports accounted by the two smallest importers, divide the total (797) by how many motorcycles were sold to the two smallest importers (Spain and France = 102 + 80 = 182) and then multiply it by 100. So, (182 / 797 x 100 = 22.83).

3. E

EXPLANATION: to work out the difference between averages for UK and Belgium in the first 4 months, add up first 4 months for the UK (23 + 31 + 24 +27 =105), then divide it by how many numbers there are (4). (105 / 4 = 26.25). For Belgium (9 + 11 + 18 + 21 = 59), then divide it by 4 = 14.75. So, the difference between UK (26.25) and Belgium (14.75) = 11.5.

4. E

EXPLANATION: to work out the percentage overall total that was sold to Italian importers, divide the total (797) by how many Suzuki's were sold to Italian importers (185) and then multiply it by 100. So, (185 / 797 x 100 = 23.21).

5. B

EXPLANATION: to work out the biggest increase in total sales from the previous month, you work out the difference between the totals for each of the month and work out which has the biggest increase. Between January and February, there was an increase by 24. None of the other months have a bigger increase and therefore February is the correct answer.

6. B

EXPLANATION: to work out the total overall percentage that was sold in May, divide how many motorcycles were sold in May (130) by the total (797) and then multiply it by 100. So, (130 / 797 x 100 = 16.31).

Now move on to the next section of the guide.

DATA INTERPRETATION TESTS

PART 2

DATA INTERPRETATION TESTS PART 2

Q1.

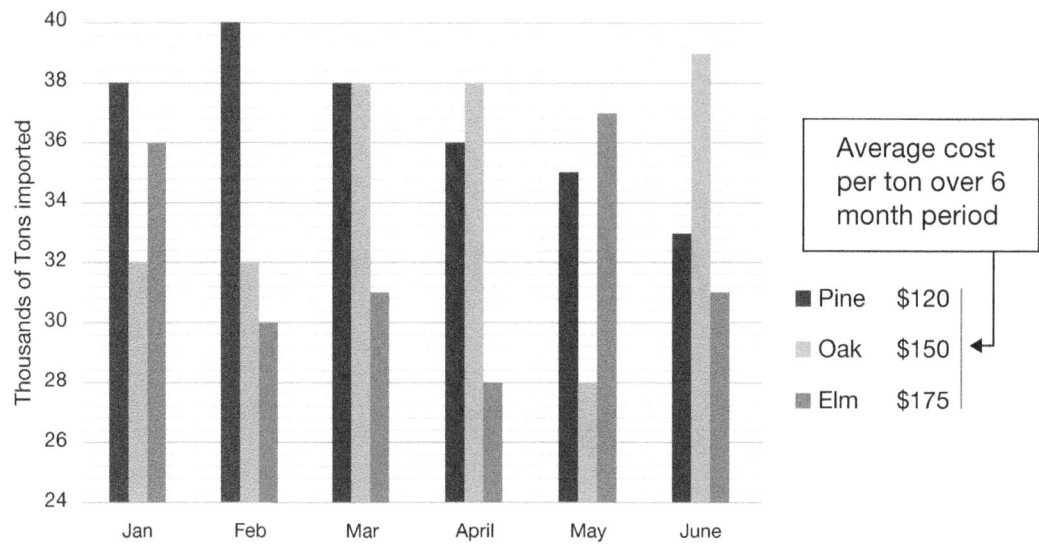

The above table shows imports for three types of wood over a 6 month period. Use this information to answer the following questions. Please circle the correct answer.

1. What was the difference in thousands of tons between oak wood and elm wood imports in the first 3 months of the year?

A	B	C	D	E
2	5	4	9	11

2. What was the ratio of pine wood and oak wood imports in the first 3 months of the year?

A	B	C	D	E
15:4	12:3	58:51	16:3	18:9

3. What was the total value of oak wood ($) imported over the 6 month period?

A	B	C	D	E
31,050	42,550	32,500	30,050	36,550

4. Which month showed the largest total decrease in imports over the previous month?

A	B	C	D	E
March	January	June	February	April

5. What was the percentage of elm wood imported over the 6 month period?

A	B	C	D	E
33.1	32.2	35.5	31.2	40.5

PART 2

Q2.

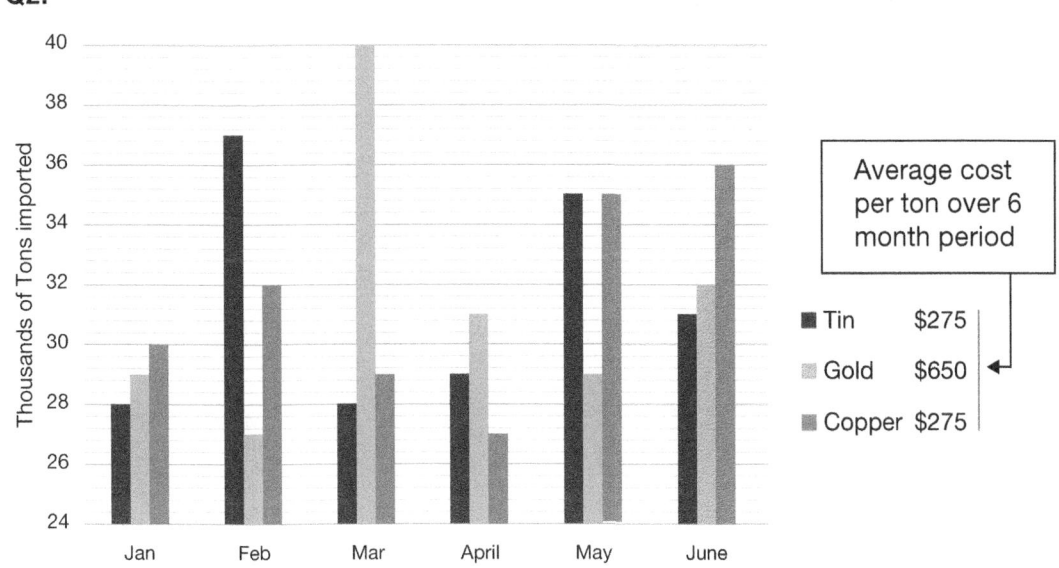

The above table shows imports for three types of metal over a 6 month period. Use this information to answer the following questions. Please circle the correct answer.

1. What was the percentage of gold imported over the 6 month period?

A	B	C	D	E
35.8	28.7	31.5	33.3	42.5

2. What was the difference in thousands of tons between gold and copper metal imports in the first 4 months of the year?

A	B	C	D	E
12	9	17	19	3

3. What was the total value ($) of tin and copper combined that was imported over the 6 month period?

A	B	C	D	E
95,585	103,675	120,750	135,975	128,850

4. Which month showed the largest total increase in imports over the previous month?

A	B	C	D	E
June	February	May	January	April

5. What is the mean total (thousands) for gold metal over the 6 month period?

A	B	C	D	E
52.6	58.4	63.2	24.5	31.3

DATA INTERPRETATION TESTS

Q3.

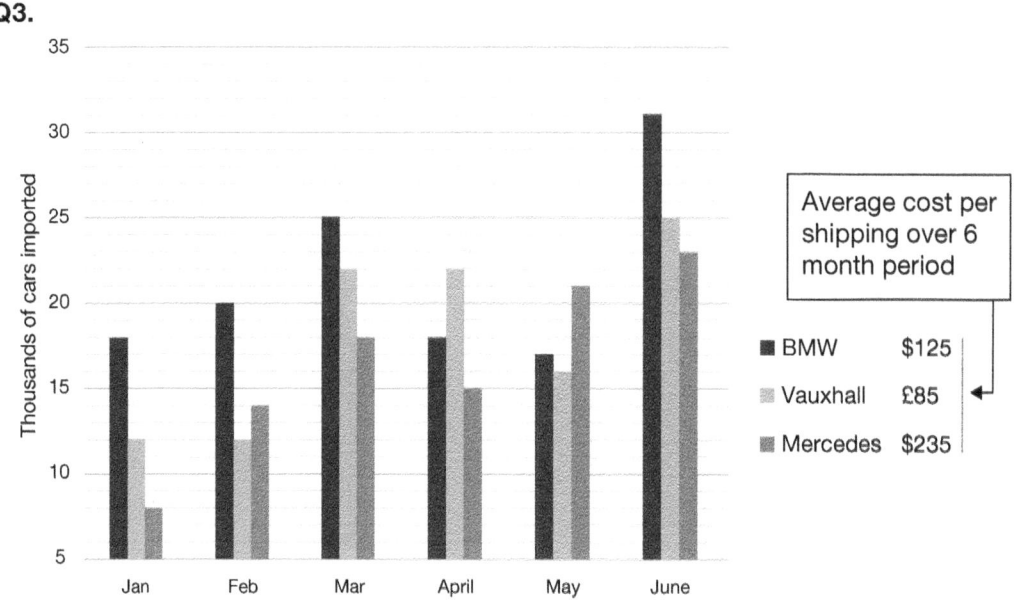

The above table shows imports for three types of cars over a 6 month period. Use this information to answer the following questions. Please circle the correct answer.

1. What is the range for Mercedes cars to be imported across the 6 month period?

A	B	C	D	E
18	15	23	32	51

2. What is the mean value for Vauxhall cars to be imported across the 6 month period?

A	B	C	D	E
18.2	15.3	11.1	8.5	30.2

3. What was the total value ($) of shipping costs for BMW's that was imported over the 6 month period?

A	B	C	D	E
12,550	11,050	16,125	21,250	25,000

4. What was the ratio of BMW and Mercedes imports in the first 3 months of the year?

A	B	C	D	E
61:40	31:40	15:50	21:41	63:40

5. Which month showed the largest total decrease in imports over the previous month?

A	B	C	D	E
April	January	June	May	February

Q4.

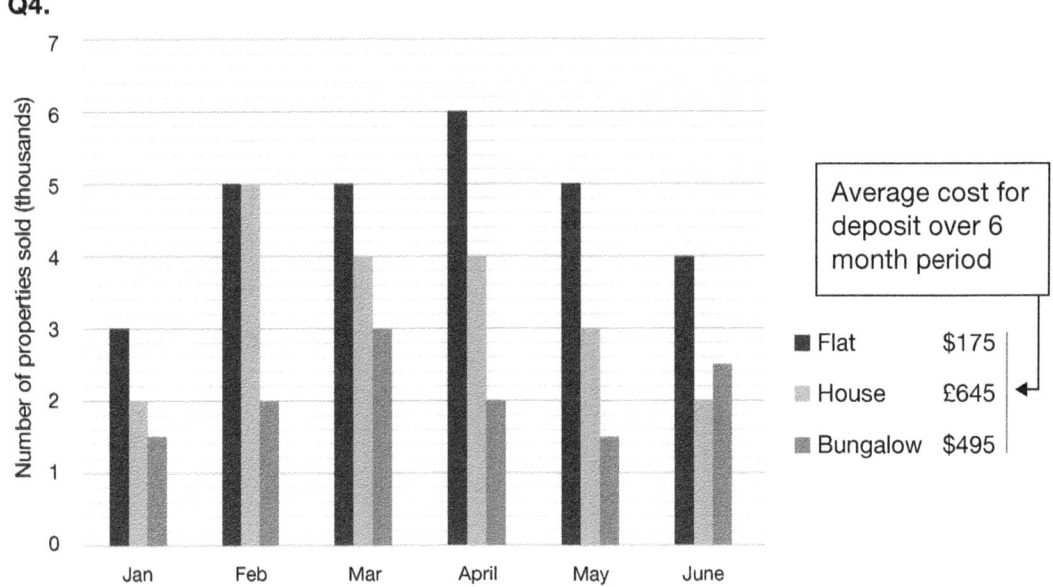

The above table shows imports for three types of properties over a 6 month period. Use this information to answer the following questions. Please circle the correct answer.

1. What is the difference between the number of properties sold in February and the number of properties sold in May?

A	B	C	D	E
950	250	1,500	2,500	1,795

2. Which month showed the largest total increase in the number of properties sold over the 6 month period?

A	B	C	D	E
May	March	February	January	June

3. What is the range for houses sold (thousands) across the 6 month period?

A	B	C	D	E
2	3	5	1	7

4. What was the approximate ratio of flat to house sales in the first 3 months of the year?

A	B	C	D	E
9:3	13:11	12:3	17:8	15:6

5. Which property sold the most in the 6 month period?

A	B	C	D	E
Flats	Houses	Bungalows	Bungalows+ flats	Flats + houses

DATA INTERPRETATION TESTS

Q5.

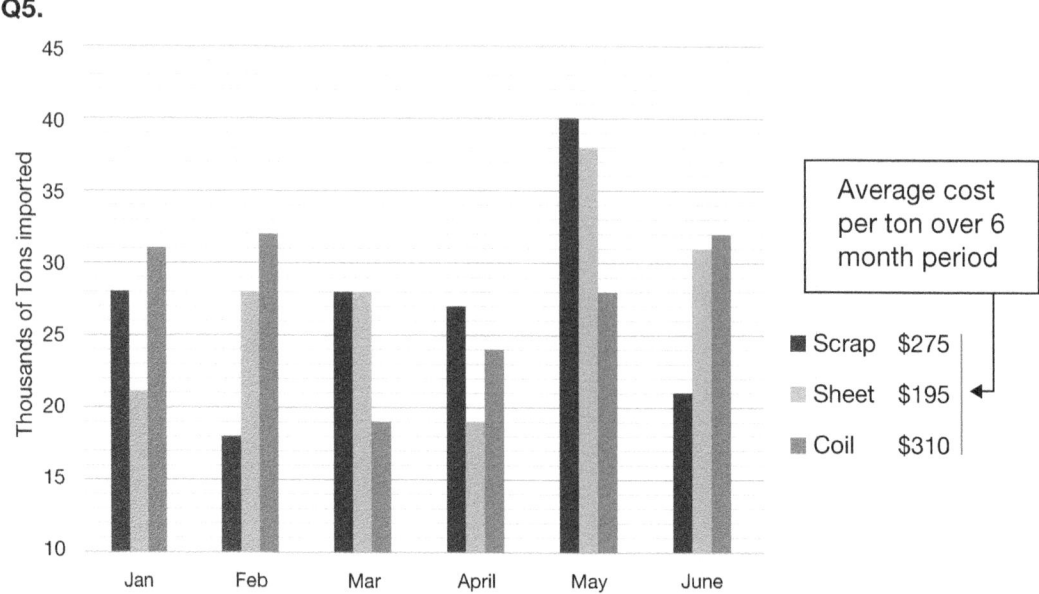

The above table shows imports for three types of steel over a 6 month period. Use this information to answer the following questions. Please circle the correct answer.

1. What is the range for sheet imports (thousands) across the 6 month period?

A	B	C	D	E
19	21	35	42	9

2. What was the difference in thousands of tons between scrap steel and coil steel imports in the first 4 months of the year?

A	B	C	D	E
7	23	25	5	11

3. What was the total value ($) of scrap steel imported over the first 4 months?

A	B	C	D	E
27,775	25,755	57,255	27,252	27,722

4. What is the mean value for coil steel imported across the 6 month period?

A	B	C	D	E
12.8	25.7	27.7	32.7	29.3

5. What was the percentage of sheet steel imported over the 6 month period?

A	B	C	D	E
21.9	33.5	42.5	55.5	62.5

Q6.

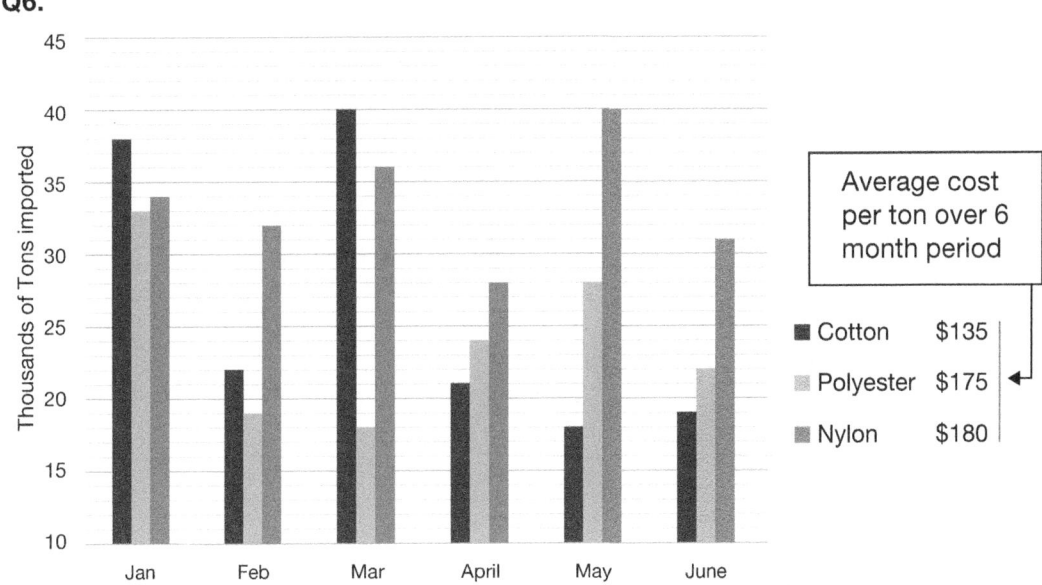

The above table shows imports for three different materials. Use this information to answer the following questions. Please circle the correct answer.

1. What is the mean value for nylon imported over the 6 month period?

A	B	C	D	E
42.5	18.5	33.5	49.5	37.5

2. What is the range for polyester imports across the 6 month period?

A	B	C	D	E
15	21	23	52	51

3. What was the difference in thousands of tons between cotton material and nylon material imports in the first 3 months of the year?

A	B	C	D	E
5	15	24	17	2

4. What was the ratio of polyester and nylon material imports in the first 4 months of the year?

A	B	C	D	E
12:3	47:65	17:13	11:7	9:5

5. Which month showed the largest total increase in imports over the previous month?

A	B	C	D	E
June	February	April	March	January

DATA INTERPRETATION TESTS

Q7.

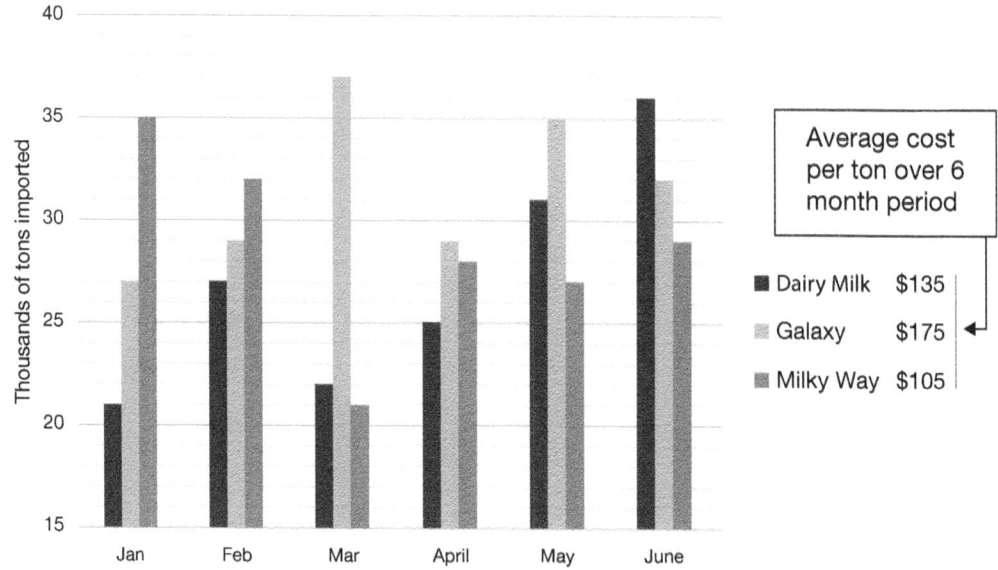

The above table shows the imports for three different chocolate brands. Use this information to answer the following questions. Please circle the correct answer.

1. What was the difference in thousands of tons between Dairy Milk and Milky Way imports in the first 3 months of the year?

A	B	C	D	E
9	18	21	25	32

2. What is the range for Galaxy imports (thousands) across the 6 month period?

A	B	C	D	E
11	13	4	10	22

3. What is the mean value for Milky Way imported over the 6 month period?

A	B	C	D	E
35.4	45.5	28.7	18.5	11.6

4. Which month showed the largest total increase in imports over the previous month?

A	B	C	D	E
January	May	February	June	March

5. What was the total value of Dairy Milk ($) imported over the 6 month period?

A	B	C	D	E
24,800	22,550	19,750	21,870	15,500

Q8.

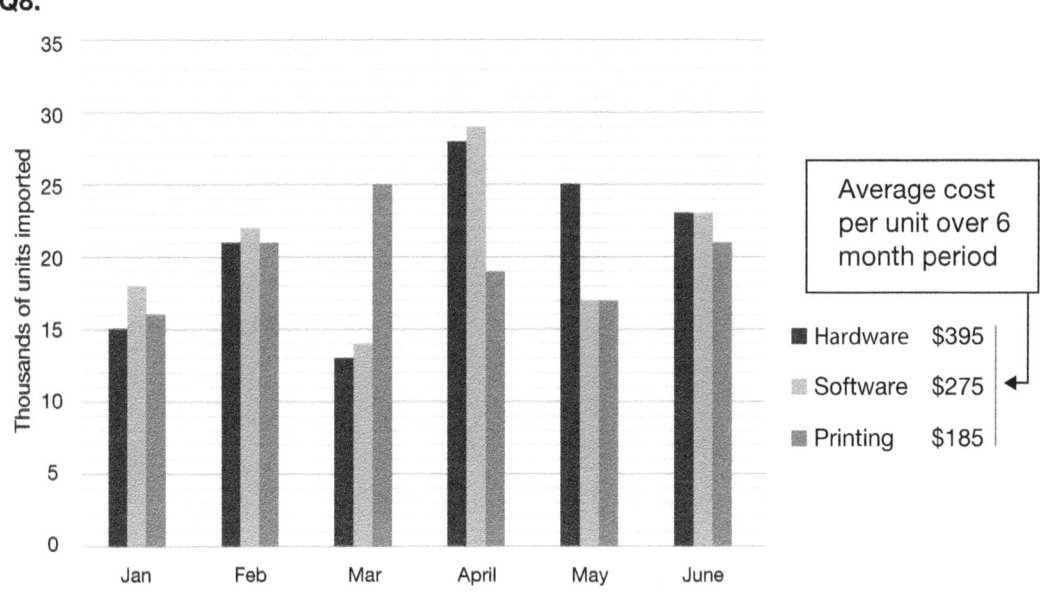

The above table shows the imports for three different computing services. Use this information to answer the following questions. Please circle the correct answer.

1. What is the mean value for printing imported over the 6 month period?

A	B	C	D	E
19.8	12.5	11.7	5.8	8.5

2. What is the range for software imports across the 6 month period?

A	B	C	D	E
21	28	11	7	15

3. What was the difference in thousands of units between hardware service and software service imports in the first 3 months of the year?

A	B	C	D	E
1	2	3	4	5

4. Which month showed the largest total decrease in imports over the previous month?

A	B	C	D	E
March	January	June	May	April

5. What was the percentage of printing imported over the 6 month period?

A	B	C	D	E
45.5	18.6	32.4	11.2	21.8

DATA INTERPRETATION TESTS

Q9.

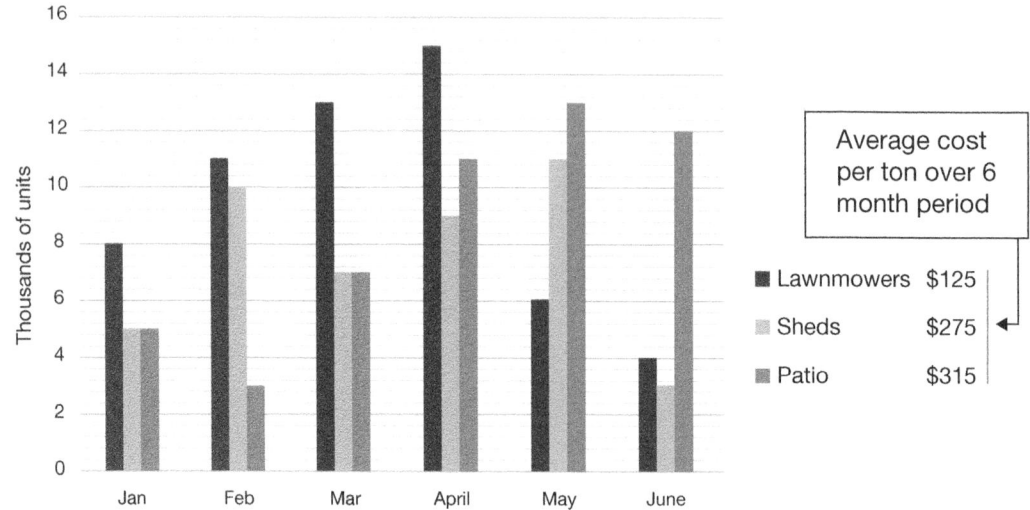

The above table shows imports for three types of garden equipment over a 6 month period. Use this information to answer the following questions. Please circle the correct answer.

1. What was the difference in thousands of units between sheds and patio imports in the first 3 months of the year?

A	B	C	D	E
7	9	8	15	21

2. What is the ratio of sheds and patio imports in the first 4 months of the year?

A	B	C	D	E
27:7	31:26	31:18	29:19	26:17

3. What was the total value for lawnmowers ($) imported over the 6 month period?

A	B	C	D	E
9,125	7,125	8,750	10,950	11,250

4. Which month showed the largest total decrease in imports over the previous month?

A	B	C	D	E
January	March	June	April	February

5. What was the percentage of patios imported over the 6 month period?

A	B	C	D	E
21.3	29.3	18.3	8.3	33.3

Q10.

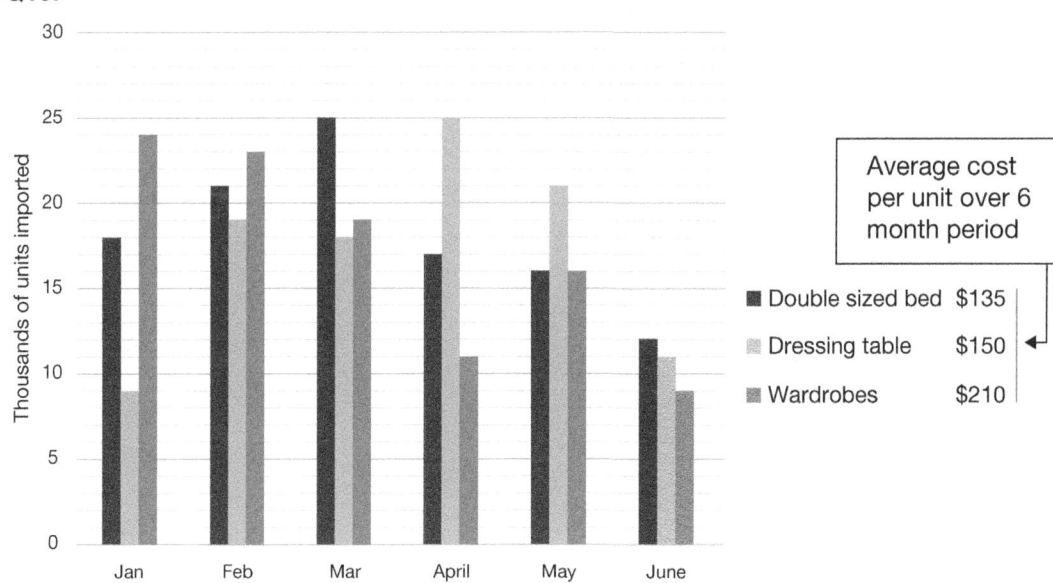

The above table shows imports for three types of bedroom furniture over a 6 month period. Use this information to answer the following questions. Please circle the correct answer.

1. What is the range for dressing table imports (thousands) across the 6 month period?

A	B	C	D	E
11	16	8	25	21

2. What was the difference in thousands of units between dressing tables and wardrobes imported in the first 4 months of the year?

A	B	C	D	E
18	11	9	22	6

3. What was the average value for double sized beds imported over the 6 month period?

A	B	C	D	E
18.2	11.5	19.3	8.5	17.5

4. What is the mean value for wardrobes imported across the 6 month period?

A	B	C	D	E
18.5	12.5	17	12	10

5. What was the percentage of wardrobes imported over the 6 month period?

A	B	C	D	E
38.5	32.5	25.5	21.5	18.5

DATA INTERPRETATION TESTS

Q11.

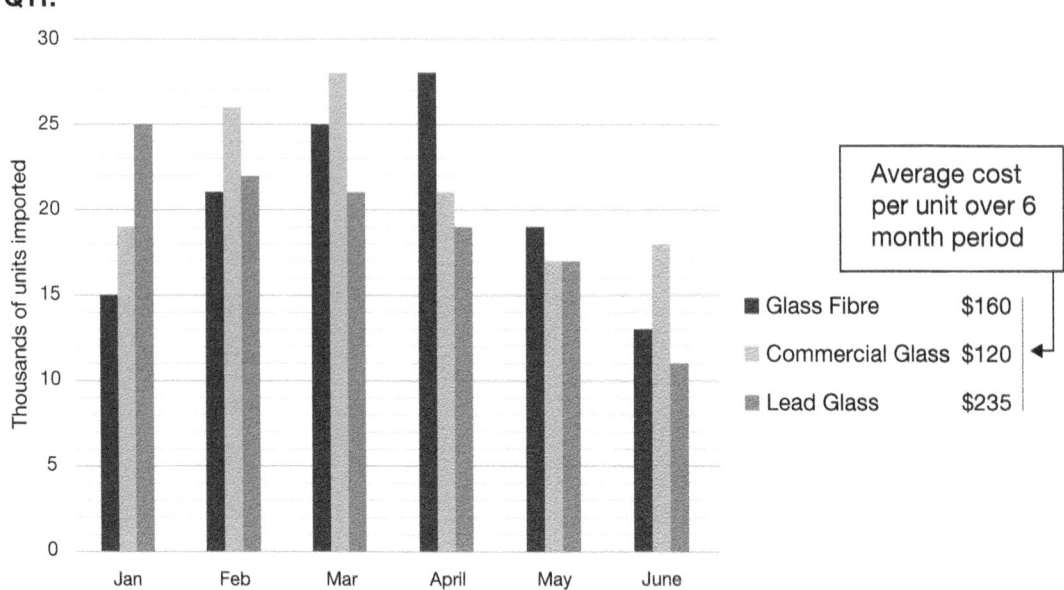

The above table shows imports for three types of glass over a 6 month period. Use this information to answer the following questions. Please circle the correct answer.

1. What was the ratio of glass fibre and lead glass imports in the first 3 months of the year?

A	B	C	D	E
30:35	61:70	61:68	32:33	41:47

2. What was the total value of commercial glass ($) imported over the 6 month period?

A	B	C	D	E
15,480	16,120	18,250	22,500	19,760

3. What is the range for lead glass imports (thousands) across the 6 month period?

A	B	C	D	E
8	5	14	17	19

4. What is the mean value for glass fibre imported over the 6 month period?

A	B	C	D	E
18.4	20.2	19.5	17.3	11.6

5. Which month showed the largest total increase in imports over the previous month?

A	B	C	D	E
March	June	January	April	February

PART 2   59

Q12.

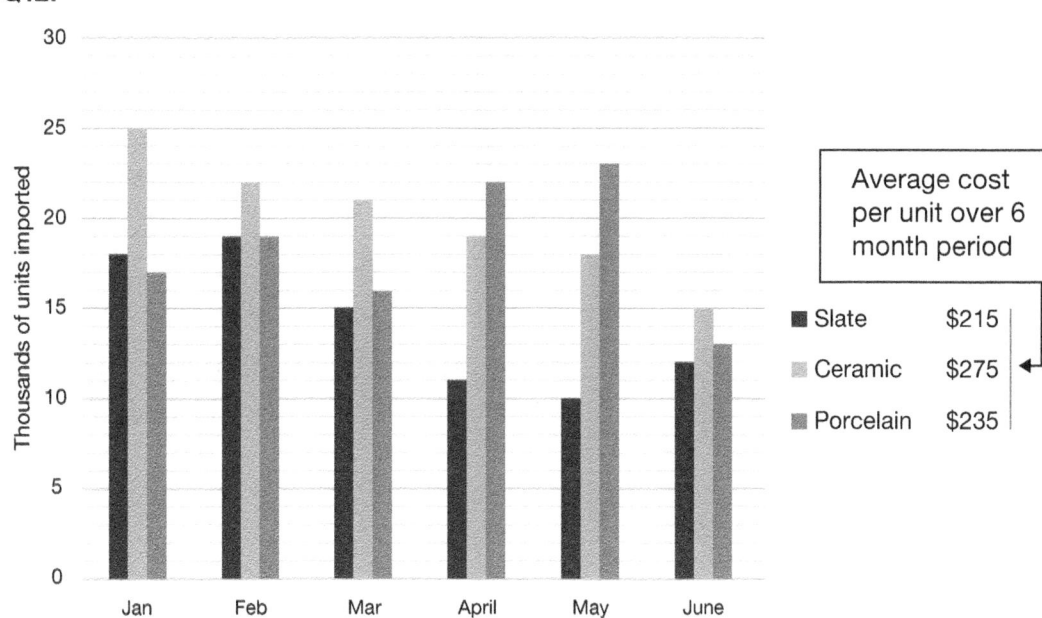

The above table shows imports for three types of tiles over a 6 month period. Use this information to answer the following questions. Please circle the correct answer.

1. What is the range for slate imports (thousands) across the 6 month period?

A	B	C	D	E
6	9	18	27	32

2. What was the difference in thousands of units between ceramic tiles and porcelain tiles imported in the first 4 months of the year?

A	B	C	D	E
11	17	21	13	29

3. What was the total value ($) of ceramic tiles imported over the 6 month period?

A	B	C	D	E
33,000	38,000	32,500	34,150	37,350

4. What is the mean value for slate tiles imported across the 6 month period?

A	B	C	D	E
14.5	14.2	14.3	14.4	14.6

5. What was the percentage of porcelain tiles imported over the 6 month period?

A	B	C	D	E
22.4	19.8	36.2	34.9	50.5

Q13.

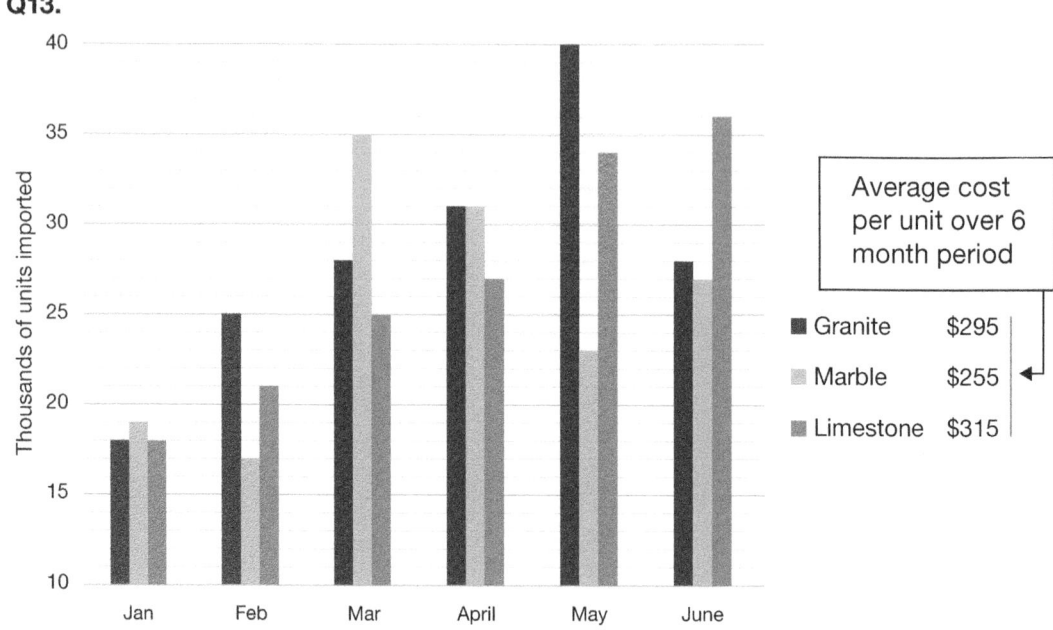

The above table shows imports for three types of stone over a 6 month period. Use this information to answer the following questions. Please circle the correct answer.

1. What was the difference in thousands of units between granite stone and marble stone imported in the first 5 months of the year?

A	B	C	D	E
11	13	15	17	19

2. Which month showed the largest total increase in the number of units (thousands) over the 6 month period?

A	B	C	D	E
January	February	March	April	May

3. What is the range for marble stone (thousands) across the 6 month period?

A	B	C	D	E
18	31	36	25	29

4. What was the ratio of marble and limestone for the 6 month period?

A	B	C	D	E
152:161	90:105	31:37	5:7	9:11

5. What was the percentage of granite stone imported over the 6 month period?

A	B	C	D	E
40.5	42.2	35.2	38.7	39

Q14.

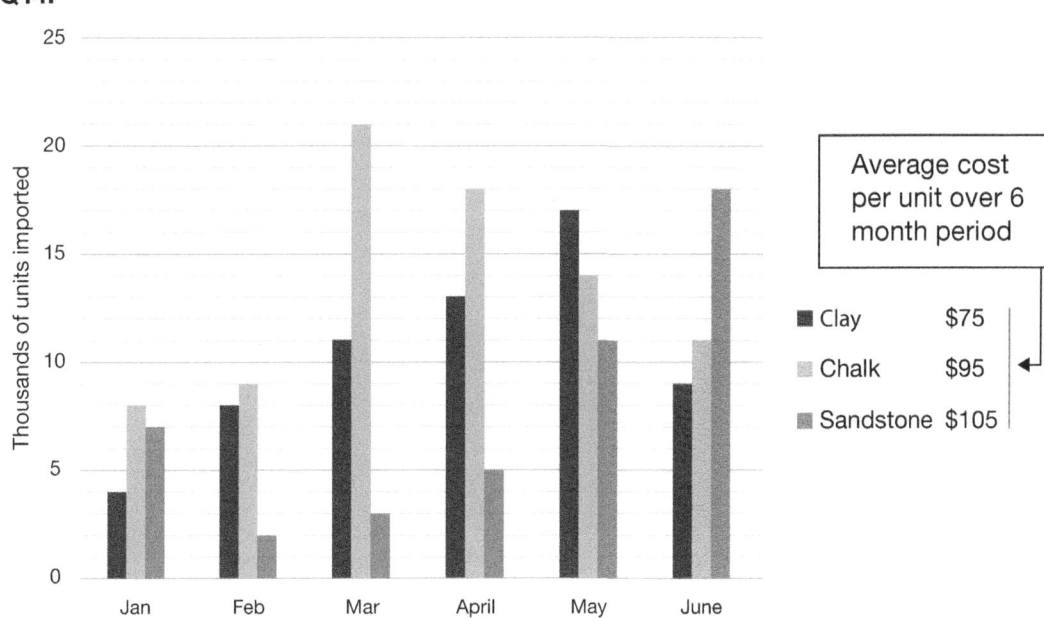

The above table shows imports for three types of rock over a 6 month period. Use this information to answer the following questions. Please circle the correct answer.

1. What is the range for clay rock to be imported across the 6 month period?

A	B	C	D	E
7	13	21	28	35

2. What is the mean value for chalk to be imported across the 6 month period?

A	B	C	D	E
18.5	20.5	14.5	9.5	13.5

3. What was the total value ($) of thousands of units for sandstone that was imported over the 6 month period?

A	B	C	D	E
5,190	4,830	4,350	3,890	8,430

4. What was the ratio of clay and chalk imported in the first 4 months of the year?

A	B	C	D	E
5:11	6:13	9:14	9:18	6:17

5. Which month showed the largest total increase in imports over the previous month?

A	B	C	D	E
April	January	June	March	February

Q15.

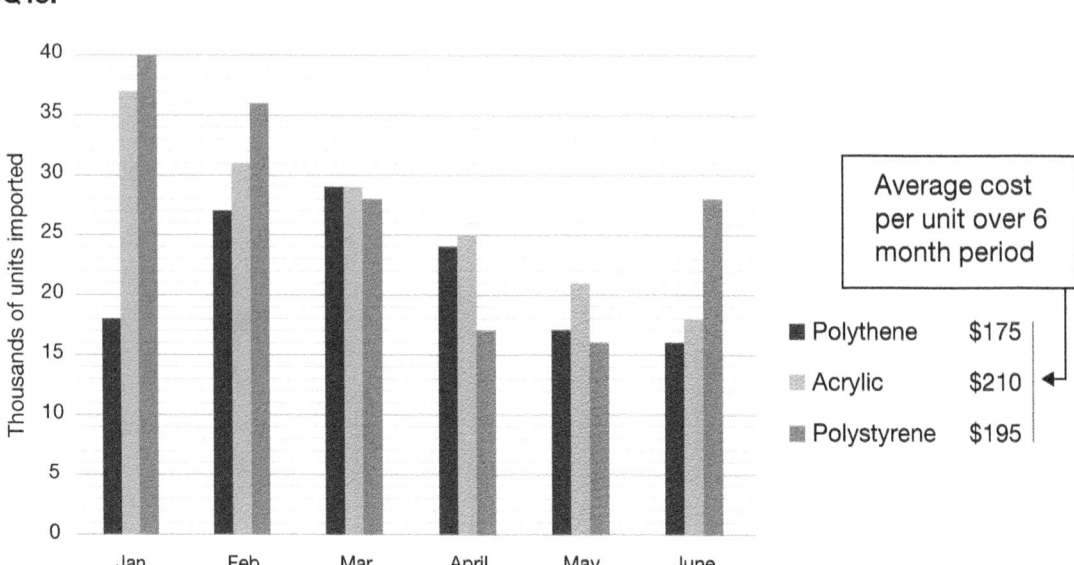

The above table shows imports for three types of plastics over a 6 month period. Use this information to answer the following questions. Please circle the correct answer.

1. What is the range for acrylic imports (thousands) across the 6 month period?

A	B	C	D	E
27	26	7	13	19

2. What was the difference in thousands of units between polythene and polystyrene imports in the first 4 months of the year?

A	B	C	D	E
31	23	37	25	5

3. What was the average value ($) for polystyrene imported over the first 3 months?

A	B	C	D	E
20,180	20,280	20,380	20,480	20,580

4. What is the mean value for polythene imported across the 6 month period?

A	B	C	D	E
21.8	25.8	32.8	40.8	11.8

5. What was the percentage of acrylics imported over the 6 month period?

A	B	C	D	E
45	45.5	35.2	35.5	38

Q16.

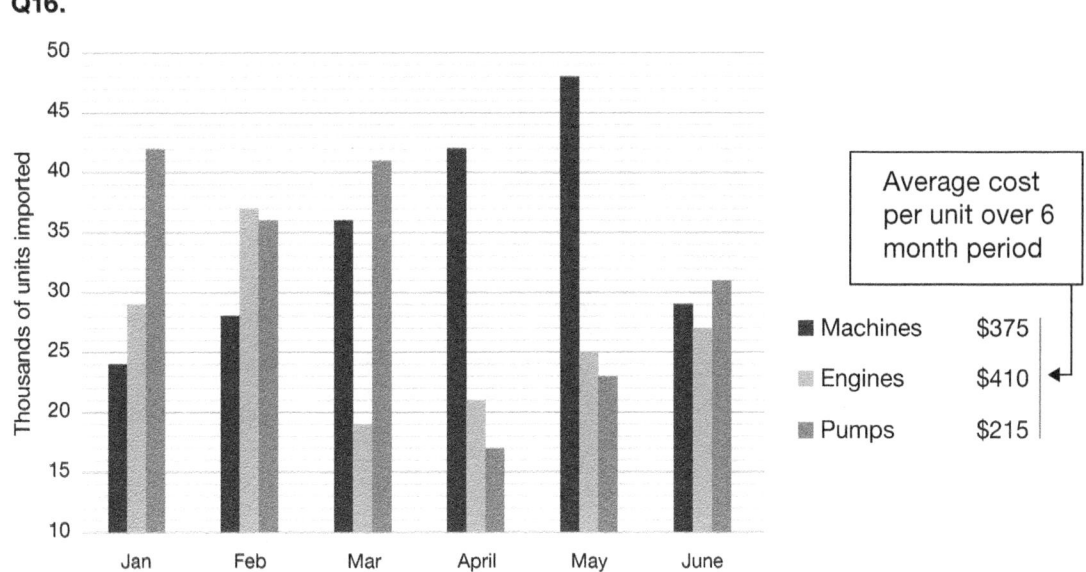

The above table shows imports for three types of technological equipment over a 6 month period. Use this information to answer the following questions. Please circle the correct answer.

1. What was the difference in thousands of tons between engines and machine imports in the first 3 months of the year?

A	B	C	D	E
1	2	3	4	5

2. What was the approximate ratio of engines to pump imports in the first 3 months of the year?

A	B	C	D	E
1:7	2:7	3:7	4:7	5:7

3. What was the total value of pumps ($) imported over the 6 month period?

A	B	C	D	E
20,220	30,150	50,500	40,850	25,750

4. Which month showed the largest total decrease in imports over the previous month?

A	B	C	D	E
January	February	March	April	May

5. What was the percentage of machines imported over the 6 month period?

A	B	C	D	E
28.4	16.4	37.3	32.4	25.4

Q17.

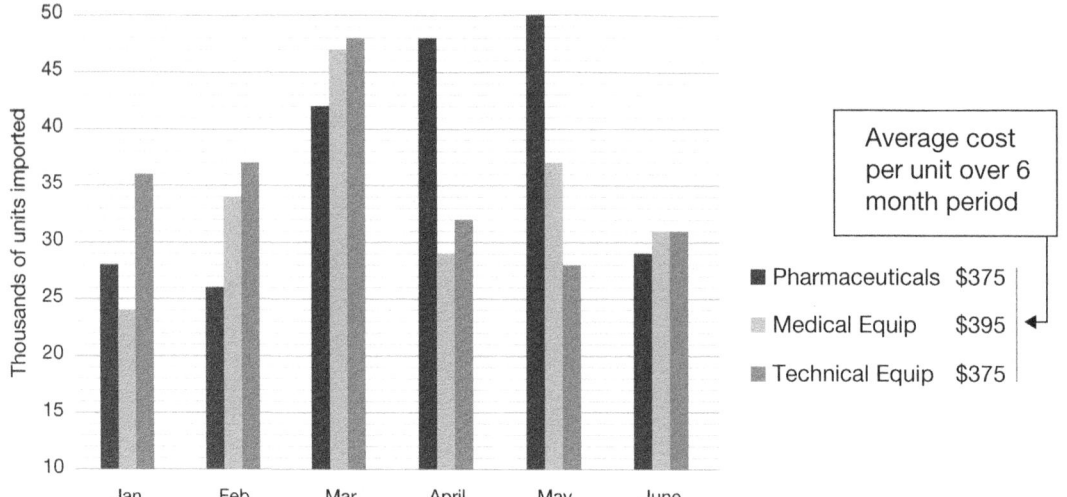

The above table shows imports for three types of medical gear over a 6 month period. Use this information to answer the following questions. Please circle the correct answer.

1. What was the difference in thousands of tons between medical and technical equipment imported in the first 3 months of the year?

A	B	C	D	E
2	3	5	7	16

2. What was the ratio of medical to technical equipment imports in the first 3 months of the year?

A	B	C	D	E
5:9	5:11	103:113	105:121	105:97

3. Which month showed the largest total decrease in imports over the previous month?

A	B	C	D	E
January	February	March	April	May

4. What was the percentage of pharmaceuticals imported over the 6 month period?

A	B	C	D	E
42.5	35	18.6	62.8	55.5

5. What is the range for pharmaceutical imports (thousands) across the 6 month period?

A	B	C	D	E
18	12	8	24	28

Q18.

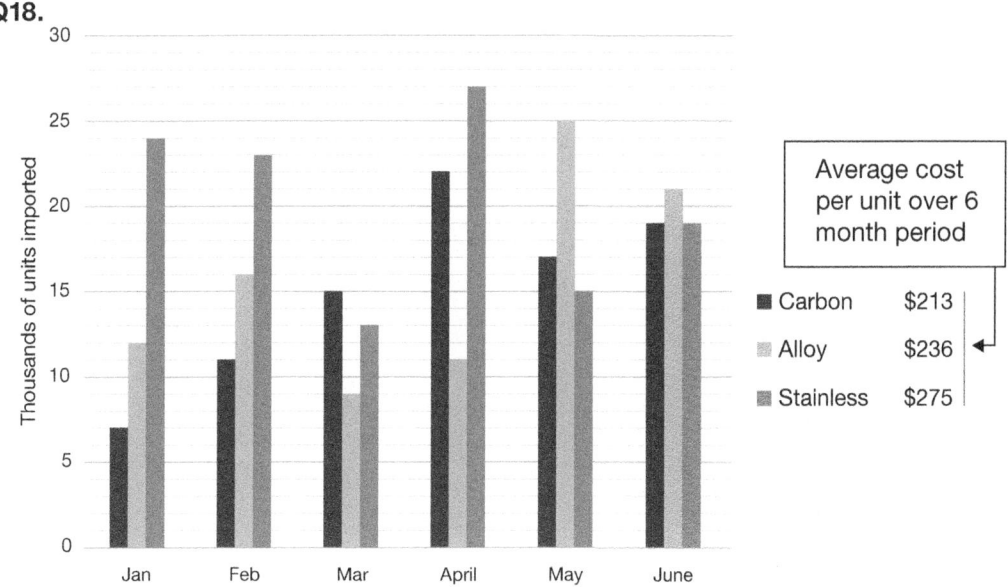

The above table shows imports for three types of steels over a 6 month period. Use this information to answer the following questions. Please circle the correct answer.

1. What is the range for carbon imports (thousands) across the 6 month period?

A	B	C	D	E
11	13	15	17	19

2. What was the difference in thousands of units between alloy steel and stainless steel imported in the first 4 months of the year?

A	B	C	D	E
23	17	29	42	39

3. What was the total value ($) of carbon steel imported over the 6 month period?

A	B	C	D	E
23,587	19,383	21,259	18,315	11,952

4. What is the mean value for stainless steel imported across the 6 month period?

A	B	C	D	E
20.2	18.5	11.4	25.8	27.3

5. What was the percentage of alloy steel imported over the 6 month period?

A	B	C	D	E
55.5	30.7	15.5	13.8	28.8

DATA INTERPRETATION TESTS

Q19.

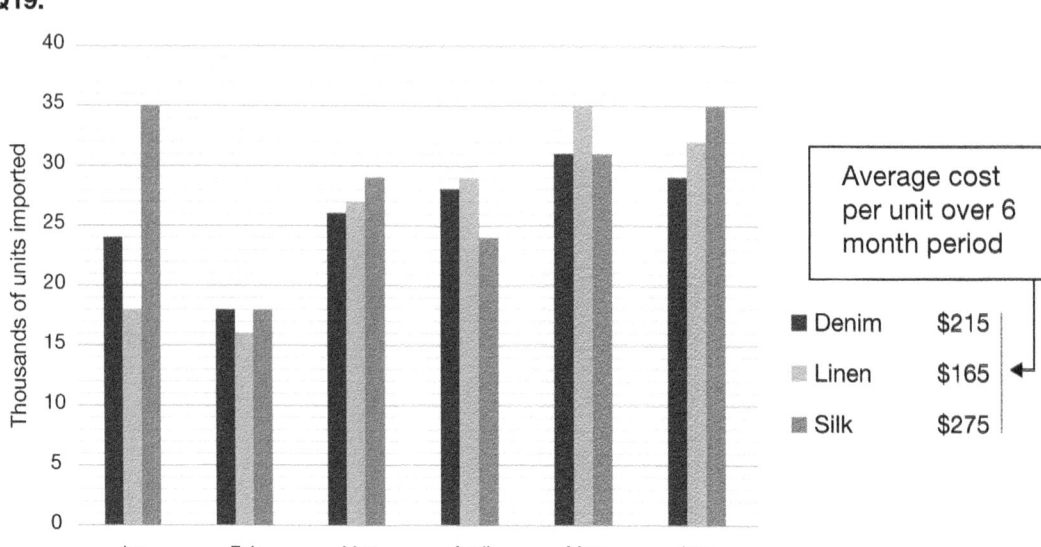

The above table shows imports for three types of fabrics over a 6 month period. Use this information to answer the following questions. Please circle the correct answer.

1. What was the percentage of silk imported over the 6 month period?

A	B	C	D	E
40.5	30.5	45.5	35.5	20.5

2. What was the difference in thousands of tons between denim and linen fabric imports in the first 3 months of the year?

A	B	C	D	E
7	6	5	4	3

3. What was the total value ($) of silk and linen combined that was imported over the 6 month period?

A	B	C	D	E
71,305	73,205	74,405	78,605	79,805

4. Which month showed the largest total increase in imports over the previous month?

A	B	C	D	E
January	February	March	April	May

5. What is the mean total (thousands) for linen fabrics over the 6 month period?

A	B	C	D	E
28.3	26.2	20.5	24.1	27.4

PART 2

Q20.

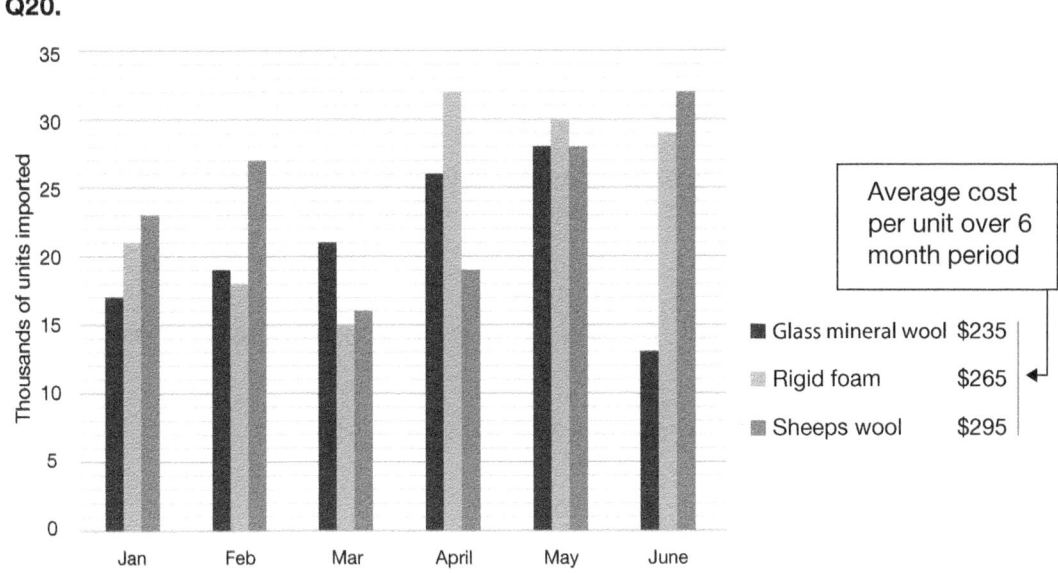

The above table shows imports for three types of insulation over a 6 month period. Use this information to answer the following questions. Please circle the correct answer.

1. What was the difference in thousands of tons between rigid foam and sheep's wool imports in the first 3 months of the year?

A	B	C	D	E
10	8	6	12	14

2. What was the ratio of glass mineral wool and sheep's wool imports in the first 3 months of the year?

A	B	C	D	E
1:4	19:22	1:7	15:22	18:21

3. What was the total value of rigid foam ($) imported over the 6 month period?

A	B	C	D	E
41,125	38,225	41,395	35,500	38,425

4. Which month showed the largest total increase in imports over the previous month?

A	B	C	D	E
January	February	March	April	May

5. What was the percentage of sheep's wool imported over the 6 month period?

A	B	C	D	E
31	32	33	34	35

DATA INTERPRETATIONS PART 2 EXPLANATIONS AND ANSWERS

QUESTION 1

1. B

EXPLANATION: to work out the difference, add up the first 3 months for Oak (32 + 32 + 38 = 102). Add up the first 3 months for Elm (36 + 30 + 31 = 97). So, the difference between Oak and Elm = 5 (thousands).

2. C

EXPLANATION: 116,000:102,000. Divide both numbers by 2000 to give you 58:51.

3. A

EXPLANATION: (32 + 32 + 38 + 38 + 28 + 39 = 207 x 150 = 31,050).

4. E

EXPLANATION: the highest decrease was between March and April, March's total = 107, April's total = 102. The difference is 5, no other months have a higher decreased number.

5. D

EXPLANATION: 193 / 618 x 100 = 31.2.

QUESTION 2

1. D

EXPLANATION: 188 / 565 x 100 = 33.27.

2. B

EXPLANATION: to work out the difference, add up the first 4 months for Gold (29 + 27 + 40 + 31 = 127). Add up the first 4 months for Copper (30 + 32 + 29 + 27 = 118). So, the difference between Gold and Oak = 9 (thousands).

3. B

EXPLANATION:
For tin = (28 + 37 + 28 + 29 + 35 + 31 = 188) 188 x 275 = 51,700.
For copper (30 + 32 + 29 + 27 + 35 + 36 = 189) 189 x 275 = 51, 975.
51,700 + 51,975 = 103,675.

4. C

EXPLANATION: the highest increase was between April and May. April's total = 87, May's total = 99. The difference is 12, no other months have a higher increased number.

5. E

EXPLANATION: gold = 29 + 27 + 40 + 31 + 29 + 32 = 188. 188 / 6 = 31.33.

PART 2

QUESTION 3

1. B

EXPLANATION: to work out the range, find the smallest and highest number of Mercedes. (8) and (23). So, 23 – 8 = 15 (thousands).

2. A

EXPLANATION: Vauxhall cars = 12 12 + 22 +22 + 16 + 25 = 109 / 6 = 18.16. Rounded up to 1 decimal place = 18.2.

3. C

EXPLANATION: (18 + 20 + 25 + 18 + 17+ 31 = 129 x 125 = 16,125).

4. E

EXPLANATION: 63,000:40,000. Divide both numbers by 1,000 to give you 63:40.

5. A

EXPLANATION: the highest decrease was between March and April, March's total = 65, April's total = 55. The difference is 10, no other months have a higher decreased number.

QUESTION 4

1. D

EXPLANATION: Number of properties sold in February = 12,000. Number of properties sold in May = 9,500. So, the difference = 12,000 – 9,500 = 2,500.

2. C

EXPLANATION: the highest increase was between January and February. January's total = 6,500, February's total = 12,000. The difference is 5,500, no other months have a higher increased number.

3. B

EXPLANATION: to work out the range, find the smallest and highest number of houses. (2) and (5). So, 5 – 2 = 3 (thousands) .

4. B

EXPLANATION: 13,000:11,000. Divide both numbers by 1000 to give you 13:11.

5. A

EXPLANATION: flat sales = 28,000. House sales = 20,000. Bungalow sales = 12,500.

QUESTION 5

1. A

EXPLANATION: to work out the range, find the smallest and highest number of sheet imports (19) and (38). So, 38 − 19 = 19 (thousands).

2. D

EXPLANATION: to work out the difference, add up the first 4 months for scrap steel (28 + 18 + 28 + 27 = 101). Add up the first 4 months for coil steel (31 + 32 + 19 + 24 = 106). So, the difference between scrap and coil = 5 (thousands).

3. A

EXPLANATION: (28 + 18 + 28 + 27 = 101 x 275 = 27,775).

4. C

EXPLANATION: coil steel = 31 + 32 + 19 + 24 + 28 + 32 = 166 / 6 = 27.66 Rounded up to 1 decimal place = 27.7.

5. B

EXPLANATION: 165 / 493 x 100 = 33.46. Rounded up to 1 decimal place = 33.5.

QUESTION 6

1. C

EXPLANATION: nylon material = 34 + 32 + 36 + 28 + 40 + 31 = 201 / 6 = 33.5.

2. A

EXPLANATION: to work out the range, find the smallest and highest number of polyester imports (18) and (33). So, 33 − 18 = 15 (thousands).

3. E

EXPLANATION: to work out the difference, add up the first 3 months for cotton (38 + 22 + 40 = 100). Add up the first 3 months for nylon (34 + 32 + 36 = 102). So, the difference between cotton and nylon = 2 (thousands).

4. B

EXPLANATION: 94,000:130,000. Divide both numbers by 2000 to give you 47:65.

5. D

EXPLANATION: the highest increase was between February and March. February's total = 73, March's total = 94. The difference is 21, no other months have a higher increased number.

PART 2

QUESTION 7

1. B

EXPLANATION: to work out the difference, add up the first 3 months for Dairy Milk (21 + 27 + 22 = 70). Add up the first 3 months for Milky Way (35 + 32 + 21 = 88). So, the difference between dairy milk and Milky Way = 18 (thousands).

2. D

EXPLANATION: to work out the range, find the smallest and highest number of Galaxy imports (27) and (37) So, 37 – 27 = 10 (thousands).

3. C

EXPLANATION: Milky Way = 35 + 32 + 21 + 28 + 27 + 29 = 172 / 6 = 28.66. Rounded up to 1 decimal place = 28.7.

4. B

EXPLANATION: the highest increase was between April and May. April's total = 82, May's total = 93. The difference is 11, no other months have a higher increased number.

5. D

EXPLANATION: (21 + 27 + 22 + 25 + 31 + 36 = 162 x 135 = 21,870).

QUESTION 8

1. A

EXPLANATION: printing = 16 + 21 + 25 + 19 + 17 + 21 = 119 / 6 = 19.83.

2. E

EXPLANATION: to work out the range, find the smallest and highest number of software imports (14) and (29). So, 29 – 14 = 15 (thousands).

3. E

EXPLANATION: to work out the difference, add up the first 3 months for hardware (15 + 21 + 13 = 49). Add up the first 3 months for software (18 + 22 + 14 = 54). So, the difference between hardware and software imports = 5 (thousands).

4. D

EXPLANATION: the highest decrease was between April and May. April's total = 76, May's total = 59. The difference is 17, no other months have a higher decreased number.

5. C

EXPLANATION: 119 / 367 x 100 = 32.4.

QUESTION 9

1. A

EXPLANATION: to work out the difference, add up the first 3 months for sheds (5 + 10 + 7 = 22). Add up the first 3 months for patios (5 + 3 + 7 = 15). So, the difference between sheds and patio imports = 7 (thousands).

2. B

EXPLANATION: 31:26. For the exact ratio, you need to find a number that goes in to both of these numbers. No other numbers (apart from 1 and itself can go into it). So, the answer would be 31:26.

3. B

EXPLANATION: (8 + 11 + 13 + 15 + 6 + 4 = 57 x 125 = 7,125).

4. C

EXPLANATION: the highest decrease was between May and June. May's total = 30, June's total = 19. The difference is 11, no other months have a higher decreased number.

5. E

EXPLANATION: 51 / 153 x 100 = 33.33.

QUESTION 10

1. B

EXPLANATION: to work out the range, find the smallest and highest number of dressing table imports (9) and (25) So, 25 – 9 = 16 (thousands).

2. E

EXPLANATION: to work out the difference, add up the first 3 months for dressing tables (9 + 19 + 18 + 25 = 71). Add up the first 3 months for wardrobes (24 + 23 + 19 + 11 = 77). So, the difference between dressing table and wardrobe imports = 6 (thousands).

3. A

EXPLANATION: Double sized bed = 18 + 21 + 25 + 17 + 16 + 12 = 109 / 6 = 18.16. Rounded up to 1 decimal place = 18.2.

4. C

EXPLANATION: Wardrobes = 24 + 23 + 19 + 11 + 16 + 9 = 102 / 6 = 17.

5. B

EXPLANATION: 102 / 314 x 100 = 32.48. Rounded up to 1 decimal place = 32.5.

PART 2   73

QUESTION 11

1. C

EXPLANATION: 61:68. For the exact ratio, you need to find a number that goes in to both of these numbers. No other numbers (apart from 1 and itself can go into it). So, the answer would be 61:68.

2. A

EXPLANATION: (19 + 26 + 28 + 21 + 17 + 18 = 129 x 120 = 15,480).

3. C

EXPLANATION: to work out the range, find the smallest and highest number for lead glass imports (11) and (25). So, 25 − 11 = 14 (thousands).

4. B

EXPLANATION: glass fibre =15 + 21 + 25 + 28 + 19 + 13 = 121 / 6 = 20.16. Rounded up to 1 decimal place = 20.2.

5. E

EXPLANATION: the highest increase was between January and February. January's total = 59, February's total = 69. The difference is 10, no other months have a higher increased number.

QUESTION 12

1. B

EXPLANATION: to work out the range, find the smallest and highest number for slate tiles imports (10) and (19). So, 19 − 10 = 9 (thousands).

2. D

EXPLANATION: to work out the difference, add up the first 4 months for ceramic tiles (25 + 22 + 21 + 19 = 87). Add up the first 4 months for porcelain tiles (17 + 19 + 16 + 22 = 74). So, the difference between ceramic tile and porcelain tile imports = 13 (thousands).

3. A

EXPLANATION: (25 + 22 + 21 + 19 + 18 + 15 = 120 x 275 = 33,000).

4. B

EXPLANATION: slate tiles = 18 + 19 + 15 + 11 + 10 + 12 = 85 / 6 = 14.16. Rounded up to 1 decimal place = 14.2.

5. D

EXPLANATION: 110 / 315 x 100 = 34.92.

QUESTION 13

1. D

EXPLANATION: to work out the difference, add up the first 5 months for granite stone (18 + 25 + 28 + 31 + 40 = 142). Add up the first 5 months for marble stone (19 + 17 + 35 + 31 + 23 = 125). So, the difference between granite stone and marble stone imports = 17 (thousands).

2. C

EXPLANATION: the highest increase was between February and March. February's total = 63, March's total = 88. The difference is 25, no other months have a higher increased number.

3. A

EXPLANATION: to work out the range, find the smallest and highest number for marble stone imports (17) and (35). So, 35 – 17 = 18 (thousands).

4. A

EXPLANATION: 152:161. For the exact ratio, you need to find a number that goes in to both of these numbers. No other numbers (apart from 1 and itself can go into it). So, the answer would be 152:161.

5. C

EXPLANATION: 170 / 483 x 100 = 35.19. Rounded up to 1 decimal place = 35.2.

QUESTION 14

1. B

EXPLANATION: to work out the range, find the smallest and highest number for clay rock imports (4) and (17). So, 17 – 4 = 13 (thousands).

2. E

EXPLANATION: chalk rock = 8 + 9 + 21 + 18 + 14 + 11 = 81 / 6 = 13.5.

3. B

EXPLANATION: (7 + 2 + 3 + 5 + 11 + 18 = 46 x 105 = 4,830).

4. C

EXPLANATION: 36:56. Divide both numbers by 4 to give you 9:14.

5. D

EXPLANATION: the highest increase was between February and March. February's total = 19, March's total = 35. The difference is 16, no other months have a higher increased number.

PART 2   75

QUESTION 15

1. E

EXPLANATION: to work out the range, find the smallest and highest number for acrylic imports (18) and (37). So, 37 – 18 = 19 (thousands).

2. B

EXPLANATION: to work out the difference, add up the first 4 months for polythene (18 + 27 + 29 + 24 = 98). Add up the first 4 months for polystyrene (40 + 36 + 28 + 17 = 121). So, the difference between polythene and polystyrene imports = 23 (thousands).

3. B

EXPLANATION: (40 + 36 + 28 = 104 x 195 = 20,280).

4. A

EXPLANATION: polythene = 18 + 27 + 29 + 24 + 17 + 16 = 131 / 6 = 21.83.

5. C

EXPLANATION: 161 / 457 x 100 = 35.22.

QUESTION 16

1. C

EXPLANATION: to work out the difference, add up the first 3 months for engines (29 + 37 + 19 = 85). Add up the first 3 months for machines (24 + 28 + 36 = 88). So, the difference between engines and machine imports = 3 (thousands).

2. E

EXPLANATION: 85:119. Divide both numbers by 17 to give you 5:7.

3. D

EXPLANATION: (42 + 36 + 41 + 17 + 23 + 31 = 190 x 215 = 40,850).

4. D

EXPLANATION: the highest decrease was between March and April. March's total = 96, April's total = 80. The difference is 16, no other months have a higher decreased number.

5. C

EXPLANATION: 207 / 555 x 100 = 37.29. Rounded up to 1 decimal place = 37.3.

DATA INTERPRETATION TESTS

QUESTION 17

1. E

EXPLANATION: to work out the difference, add up the first 3 months for medical equipment (24 + 34 + 47 = 105). Add up the first 3 months for technical equipment (36 + 37 + 48 = 121). So, the difference between medical and technical equipment imports = 16 (thousands).

2. D

EXPLANATION: 105:116. For the exact ratio, you need to find a number that goes in to both of these numbers. No other numbers (apart from 1 and itself can go into it). So, the answer would be 105:121.

3. D

EXPLANATION: the highest decrease was between March and April. March's total = 137, April's total = 109. The difference is 28, no other months have a higher decreased number.

4. B

EXPLANATION: 223 / 637 x 100 = 35.00. Rounded up to 1 decimal place = 35.

5. D

EXPLANATION: to work out the range, find the smallest and highest number for pharmaceuticals imports (26) and (50). So, 50 – 26 = 24 (thousands).

QUESTION 18

1. C

EXPLANATION: to work out the range, find the smallest and highest number for carbon imports (7) and (22). So, 22 – 7 = 15 (thousands).

2. E

EXPLANATION: to work out the difference, add up the first 4 months for alloy steel (12 + 16 + 9 + 11 = 48). Add up the first 4 months for stainless steel (24 + 23 + 13 + 27 = 87). So, the difference between alloy and stainless steel imports = 39 (thousands).

3. B

EXPLANATION: (7 + 11 + 15 + 22 + 17 + 19 = 91 x 213 = 19,383).

4. A

EXPLANATION: stainless steel = 24 + 23 + 13 + 27 + 19 + 15 = 121 / 6 = 20.2.

5. B

EXPLANATION: 94 / 306 x 100 = 30.71. Rounded up to 1 decimal place = 30.7.

PART 2   77

QUESTION 19

1. D

EXPLANATION: 172 / 485 x 100 = 35.46. Rounded up to 1 decimal place = 35.5.

2. A

EXPLANATION: to work out the difference, add up the first 3 months for denim (24 + 18 + 26 = 68). Add up the first 3 months for linen (18 + 16 + 27 = 61). So, the difference between denim and linen fabric imports = 7 (thousands).

3. B

EXPLANATION: For silk = (35 + 18 + 29 + 24 + 31 + 35 = 172) 172 x 275 = 47,300. For linen (18 + 16 + 27 + 29 + 35 + 32 = 157) 157 x 165 = 25,905.

47,300 + 25,905 = 73,205.

4. C

EXPLANATION: the highest increase was between February and March. February's total = 52, March's total = 82. The difference is 30, no other months have a higher increased number.

5. B

EXPLANATION: linen fabrics = 18 + 16 + 27 + 29 + 35 + 32 = 157 / 6 = 26.16. Rounded up to 1 decimal place = 26.2.

QUESTION 20

1. D

EXPLANATION: to work out the difference, add up the first 3 months for rigid foam (21 + 18 + 15 = 54). Add up the first 3 months for sheep's wool (23 + 27 + 16 = 66). So, the difference between rigid foam and sheep's wool = 12 (thousands).

2. B

EXPLANATION: 19:22. For the exact ratio, you need to find a number that goes in to both of these numbers. Both numbers can be divided by 3. So, the answer would be 19:22.

3. E

EXPLANATION: (21 + 18 + 15 + 32 + 30 + 29 = 145 x 265 = 38,425)

4. D

EXPLANATION: the highest increase was between March and April. March's total = 52, April's total = 77. The difference is 25, no other months have a higher increased number.

5. E

EXPLANATION: 145 / 414 x 100 = 35.02. Rounded up to 1 decimal place = 35.

Now move on to the next section of the guide.

DATA INTERPRETATION TESTS

PART 3

PART 3

DATA INTERPRETATION TESTS PART 3

Q1.

The table above shows the number of English papers published by top UK universities over a six year period. Use the information to answer the following questions. Please circle the correct answers.

1. Which university published the second lowest number of papers over the six year period?

A	B	C	D	E
Oxford	Cambridge	Kings College	Imperial College	East Anglia

2. In what year did researchers at Cambridge publish most papers?

A	B	C	D	E
2000	2001	2002	2003	2004

3. How many papers were published by Imperial College in 2004?

A	B	C	D	E
70	60	55	35	50

4. In what year did East Anglia College publish the lowest number of papers?

A	B	C	D	E
2001	2002	2003	2004	2005

5. How many papers were published by Cambridge University over the six year period?

A	B	C	D	E
275	285	235	245	280

DATA INTERPRETATION TESTS

Q2.

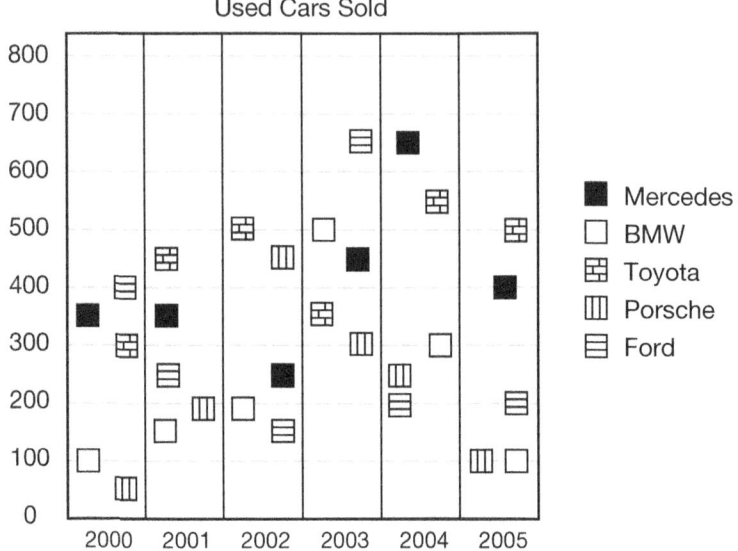

The table above shows the number of used cars sold over a six year period. Use the information to answer the following questions. Please circle the correct answers.

1. In what year did Toyota's sell the most?

A	B	C	D	E
2001	2002	2003	2004	2005

2. Approximately, how many more cars did Ford's sell as opposed to Toyota's in the year 2003?

A	B	C	D	E
150	200	250	300	350

3. How many Porches' were sold over the six year period?

A	B	C	D	E
1500	1350	1150	900	750

4. In what year were the least amount of cars sold?

A	B	C	D	E
2000	2001	2002	2003	2004

5. Approximately, how many cars were sold in 2001 and 2002 combined?

A	B	C	D	E
1870	1920	2580	2780	2950

Q3.

The table shows the number of animals sold from a local store over a six month period. Use the information to answer the following questions. Please circle the correct answers.

1. How many animals were sold in March?

A	B	C	D	E
55	42	64	28	86

2. In what month were the highest number of rabbits sold?

A	B	C	D	E
January	February	March	April	May

3. In what month sold the same amount of hamsters and guinea pigs?

A	B	C	D	E
January	February	March	April	May

4. In what month did hamsters sell more than cats?

A	B	C	D	E
January	February	March	April	May

5. In what month did the most animals got sold overall?

A	B	C	D	E
May	February	April	June	January

Q4.

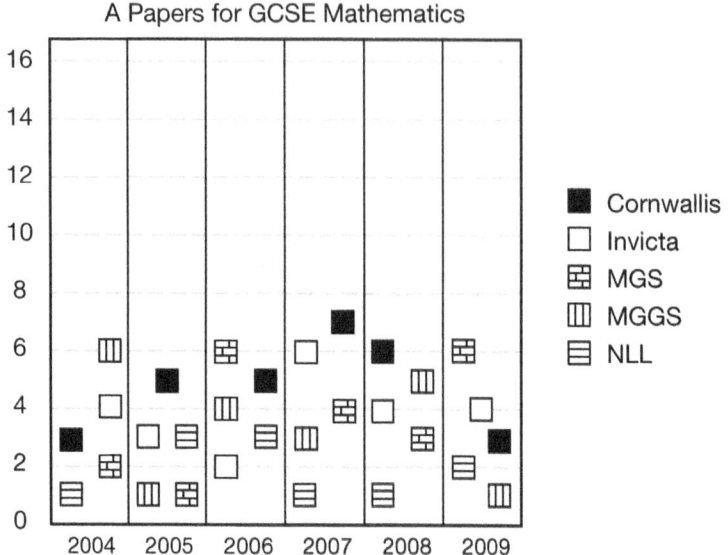

A Papers for GCSE Mathematics

- Cornwallis
- Invicta
- MGS
- MGGS
- NLL

The table shows the number of Grade A papers for GCSE Mathematics over a six year period. Use the information to answer the following questions. Please circle the correct answers.

1. How many times over the six year period did NLL receive only one Grade A Maths paper?

A	B	C	D	E
1	2	3	4	5

2. In what year did Invicta and NLL receive the same number of Grade A Maths papers?

A	B	C	D	E
2004	2005	2006	2007	2008

3. How many Grade A Maths papers did Cornwallis receive overall?

A	B	C	D	E
18	21	27	29	32

4. What school received the least number of Grade A Maths paper across the six year period?

A	B	C	D	E
Cornwallis	Invicta	MGS	MGGS	NLL

5. In what year were the most Grade A Maths papers achieved for Invicta?

A	B	C	D	E
2004	2005	2006	2007	2008

Q5.

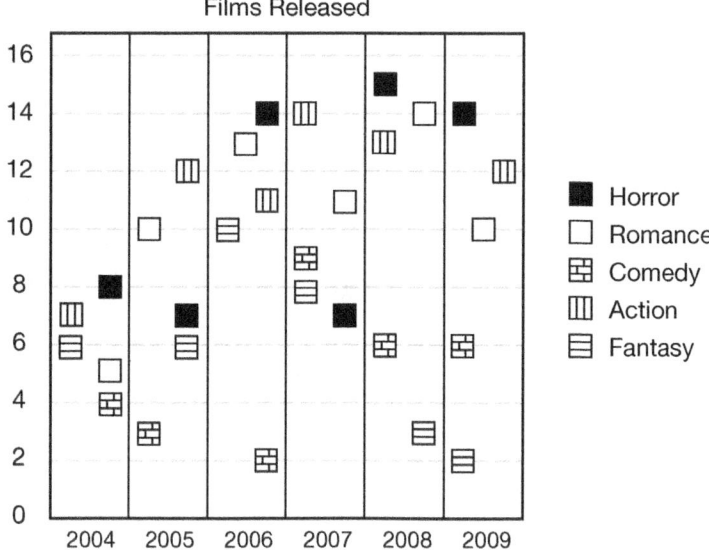

The table shows the number of films released over a six year period. Use the information to answer the following questions. Please circle the correct answers.

1. In what year were the highest amount of Romance films released?

A	B	C	D	E
2004	2005	2006	2007	2008

2. How many Horror films were released across the six month period?

A	B	C	D	E
85	75	65	55	45

3. In what years did Romance films get released more than Horror films? Circle TWO.

A	B	C	D	E
2004	2005	2006	2007	2008

4. Which genre released the second highest number of films over the period?

A	B	C	D	E
Horror	Romance	Comedy	Action	Fantasy

5. How many films were released overall?

A	B	C	D	E
213	262	284	273	758

DATA INTERPRETATION TESTS

Q6.

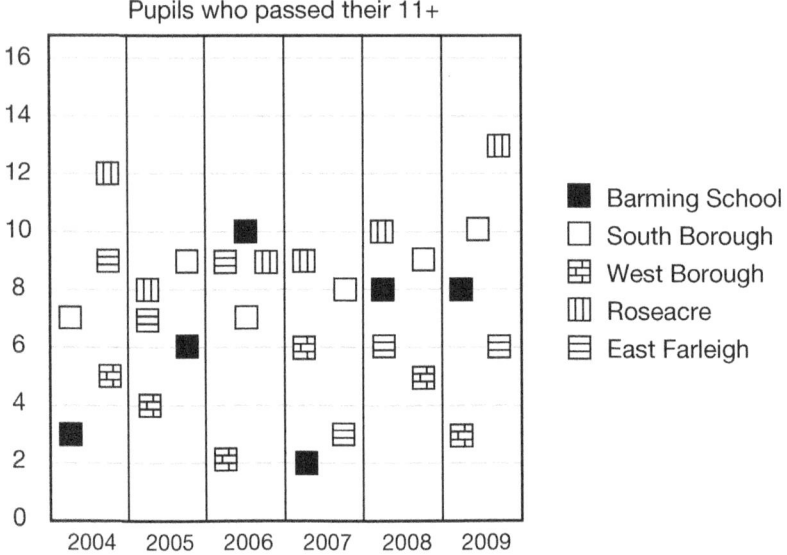

The table shows the number of pupils who passed their 11+ over a six year period. Use the information to answer the following questions. Please circle the correct answers.

1. How many pupils achieved their 11+ by South Borough in 2008?

A	B	C	D	E
5	10	7	9	12

2. In what year did pupils at Barming achieve the most passes for their 11+?

A	B	C	D	E
2004	2005	2006	2007	2008

3. In what year did pupils at East Farleigh and Roseacre achieve the same number of passes for the 11+?

A	B	C	D	E
2004	2005	2006	2007	2008

4. In what year did pupils receive a higher pass rate at South Borough as opposed to Roseacre?

A	B	C	D	E
2004	2005	2006	2007	2008

5. Which school achieved the second highest pass rate over the period?

A	B	C	D	E
Barming	S. Borough	W. Borough	Roseacre	E. Farleigh

Q7.

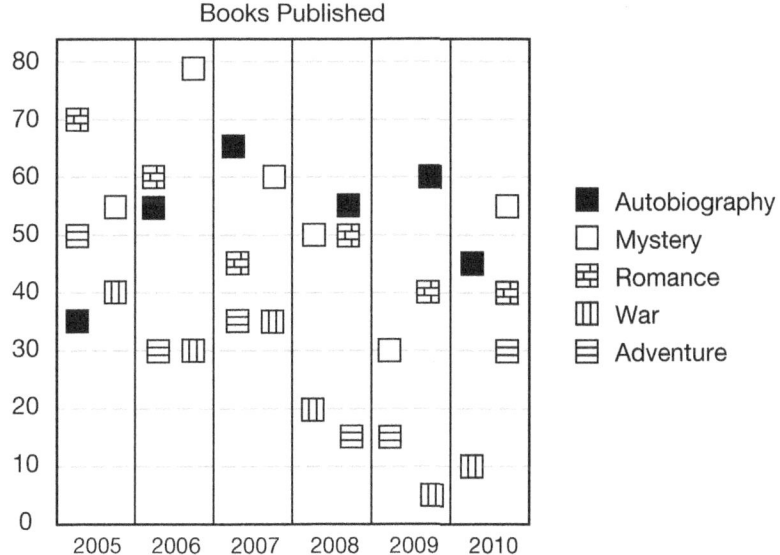

The table shows the number of books published over a six year period. Use the information to answer the following questions. Please circle the correct answers.

1. Which genre was published the second highest over the six year period?

A	B	C	D	E
Autobiography	Mystery	Romance	War	Adventure

2. In what year did Romance novels get published the most?

A	B	C	D	E
2005	2006	2007	2008	2009

3. How many books were published in 2008?

A	B	C	D	E
150	170	190	210	230

4. In what year were Autobiographies published the least?

A	B	C	D	E
2005	2006	2007	2008	2009

5. In what year were the same amount of Mystery novels and Romance novels published?

A	B	C	D	E
2005	2006	2007	2008	2009

Q8.

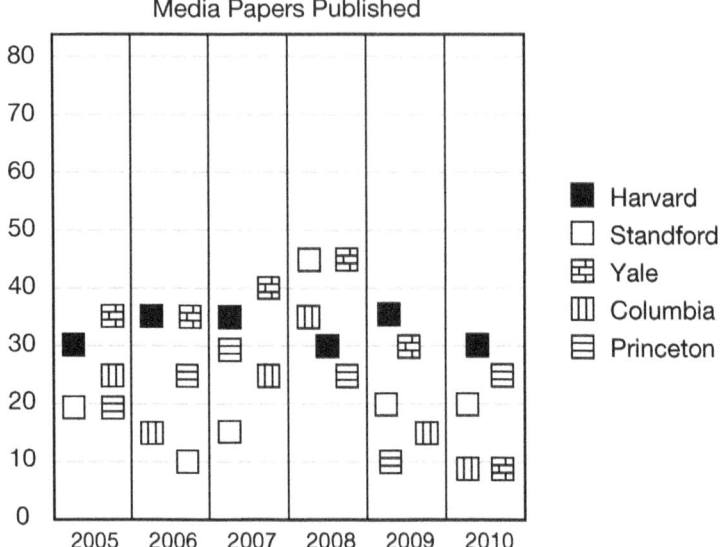

The table shows the number of Media papers published over a six year period. Use the information to answer the following questions. Please circle the correct answers.

1. How many papers were published by Columbia University in 2006?

A	B	C	D	E
10	15	20	25	30

2. In what years did researchers at Harvard University publish the most papers? Circle THREE.

A	B	C	D	E
2005	2006	2007	2008	2009

3. In what years did researchers at Harvard and Yale publish the same number of papers?

A	B	C	D	E
2005	2006	2007	2008	2009

4. How many papers did Yale University publish over the period?

A	B	C	D	E
125	175	105	205	195

5. Which University published the lowest number of papers in 2008?

A	B	C	D	E
Harvard	Stanford	Yale	Columbia	Princeton

Q9.

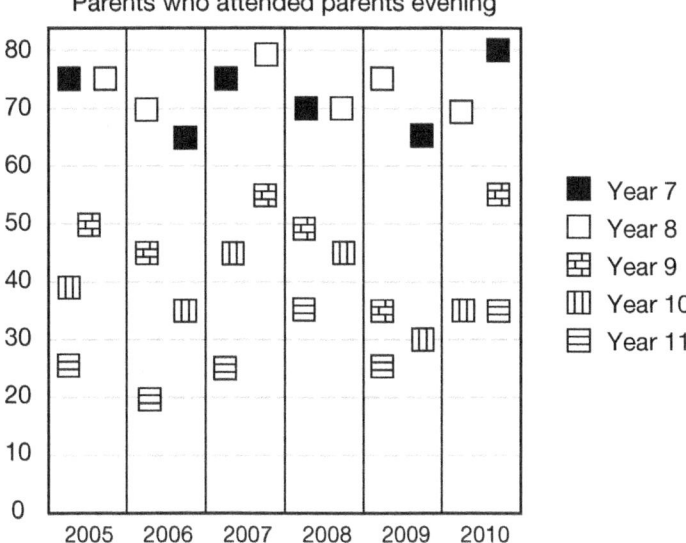

The table shows the number of parents who attended parent's evening at a local school over a six year period. Use the information to answer the following questions. Please circle the correct answers.

1. How many parents attended parents evening for Year 8 in 2009?

A	B	C	D	E
80	55	40	60	75

2. In what year for years 7 and 8 did the same number of parents attend parent's evening? Circle TWO.

A	B	C	D	E
2005	2006	2007	2008	2009

3. How many parents attended parent's evening in 2005?

A	B	C	D	E
215	295	265	245	275

4. Which school year did the least number of parents attend in 2009?

A	B	C	D	E
Year 7	Year 8	Year 9	Year 10	Year 11

5. What is the average number of parents that attended parent's evening for year 7 over the 6 year period? Rounded up to the nearest whole number

A	B	C	D	E
70	71	72	73	76

Q10.

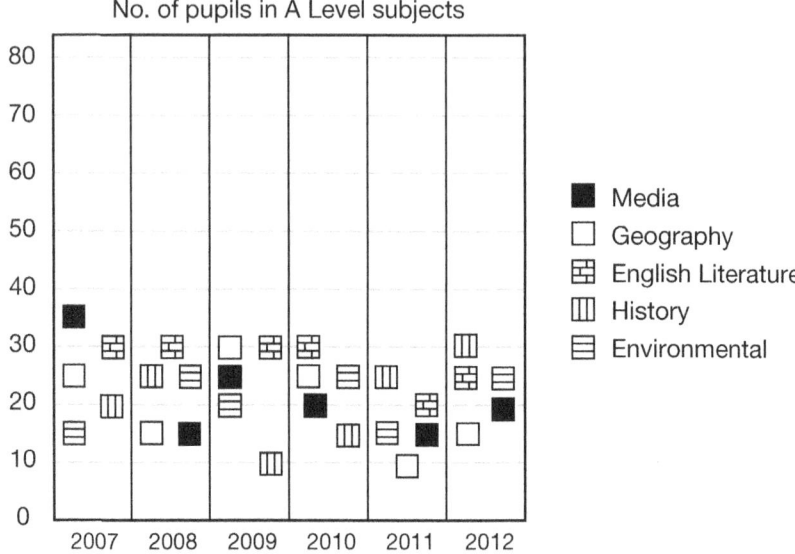

The table shows the number of pupils in A Level subjects over a six year period. Use the information to answer the following questions. Please circle the correct answers.

1. How many pupils were in A Level English Literature in 2009?

A	B	C	D	E
10	15	20	30	35

2. From 2007 to 2012, what was the average number of students in A Level Environmental Studies? Rounded to the nearest whole number.

A	B	C	D	E
18	19	20	21	22

3. Which subject had the most number of pupils in 2012?

A	B	C	D	E
Media	Geography	History	Environmental	English Lit

4. In which year were there the same number of pupils in Environmental as there was in Media?

A	B	C	D	E
2007	2008	2009	2010	2011

5. In what year were there more students in Media as opposed to English Literature?

A	B	C	D	E
2007	2008	2009	2010	2011

PART 3

Q11.

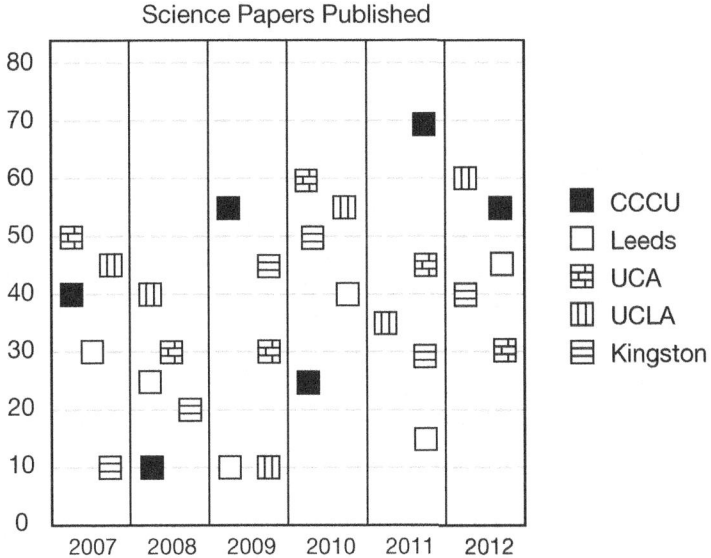

The table above shows the number of Science papers published by universities over a six year period. Use the information to answer the following questions. Please circle the correct answers.

1. Which university published the second lowest number of papers over the six year period?

A	B	C	D	E
CCCU	Leeds	UCA	UCLA	Kingston

2. In what year did researchers at UCLA publish 35 papers?

A	B	C	D	E
2007	2008	2009	2010	2011

3. In what year did researchers at Leeds and UCLA publish the same number of papers?

A	B	C	D	E
2007	2008	2009	2010	2011

4. In what year did researchers at UCA publish the most papers?

A	B	C	D	E
2012	2011	2010	2009	2008

5. How many papers were published by CCCU in 2011?

A	B	C	D	E
40	20	10	70	60

Q12.

The table shows the number of jewellery items sold over a six month period. Use the information to answer the following questions. Please circle the correct answer.

1. How many necklaces were sold in April?

A	B	C	D	E
18	24	28	24	20

2. In what month were the most bracelets sold?

A	B	C	D	E
March	June	January	April	February

3. In what month were bracelets and necklaces sold the same amount?

A	B	C	D	E
June	January	March	May	April

4. Which item of jewellery sold the second highest amount over the six month period?

A	B	C	D	E
Bracelets	Necklaces	Earrings	Rings	Other

5. What was the average number of bracelets sold across the six month period? Rounded up to the nearest whole number.

A	B	C	D	E
16	19	21	28	32

Q13.

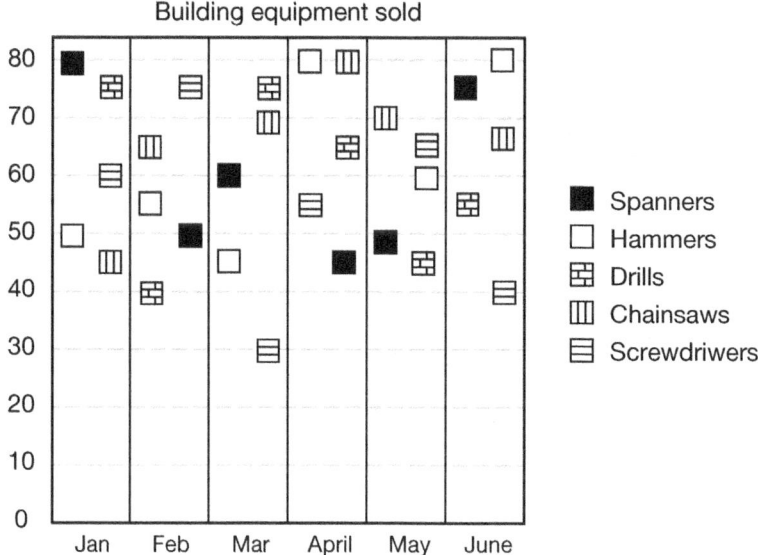

The table shows the number of items sold for building equipment over a six month period. Use the information to answer the following questions. Please circle the correct answer.

1. What item was sold the least amount in May?

A	B	C	D	E
Spanners	Hammers	Drills	Chainsaws	Screwdrivers

2. How many spanners were sold in March?

A	B	C	D	E
45	80	75	60	25

3. In what month did hammers and chainsaws sell the same amount?

A	B	C	D	E
January	February	March	April	May

4. How many hammers were sold in total?

A	B	C	D	E
220	195	340	290	370

5. An item was sold 65 times in May. What item was it?

A	B	C	D	E
Spanners	Hammers	Drills	Chainsaws	Screwdrivers

Q14.

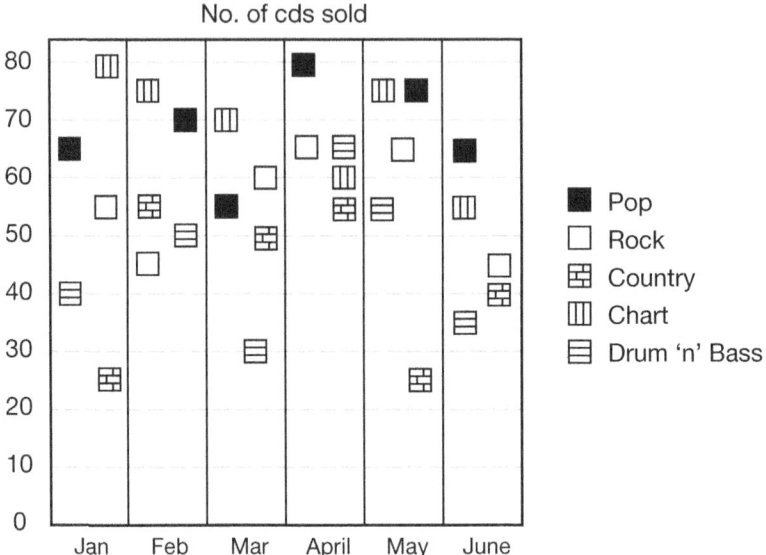

The table shows the number of CD's sold over a six month period. Use the information to answer the following questions. Please circle the correct answer.

1. In what month did Pop sell the least?

A	B	C	D	E
January	February	March	April	May

2. How many Chart CD's were sold in February?

A	B	C	D	E
80	60	55	30	75

3. In what month did Chart Cd's and Pop CD's sell the same amount?

A	B	C	D	E
May	June	February	January	March

4. In what month did Drum 'n' Bass Cd's sell the most?

A	B	C	D	E
May	April	January	June	February

5. How many CD's were sold in June?

A	B	C	D	E
240	280	160	120	310

Q15.

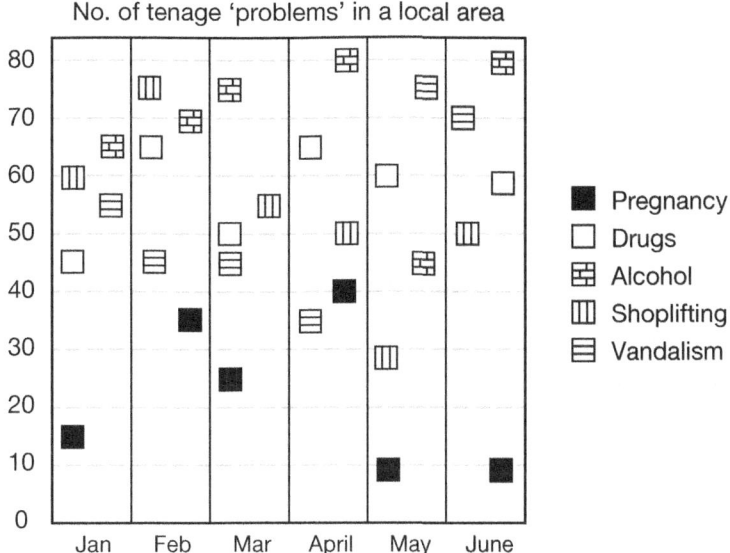

The table shows the number of teenage 'problems' in a local area over a six month period. Use the information to answer the following questions. Please circle the correct answer.

1. What 'problem' occurred 10 times for two months?

A	B	C	D	E
Pregnancy	Drugs	Alcohol	Shoplifting	Vandalism

2. How many alcohol related problems occurred over the six month period?

A	B	C	D	E
385	325	475	415	425

3. What problem occurred the least in in April?

A	B	C	D	E
Pregnancy	Drugs	Alcohol	Shoplifting	Vandalism

4. In what month did vandalism become more of a problem than alcohol?

A	B	C	D	E
February	May	January	June	April

5. How many drug related 'problems' occurred in June?

A	B	C	D	E
45	60	75	80	55

Q16.

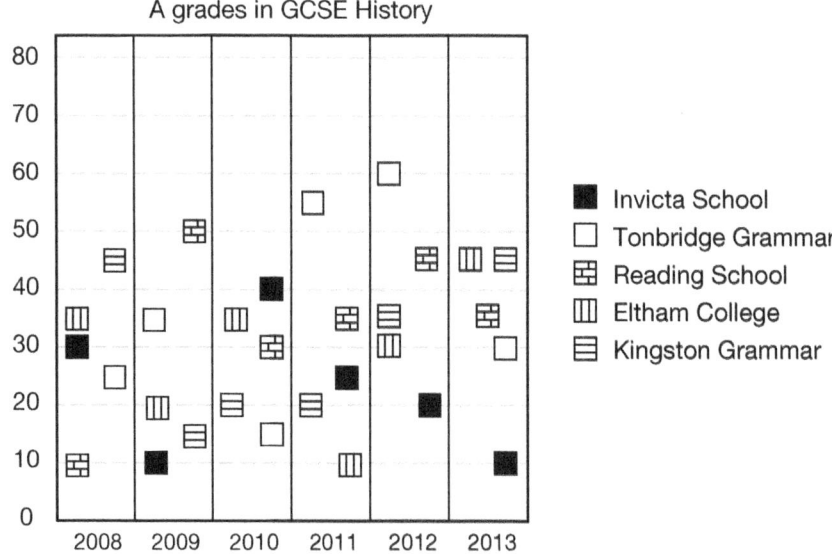

The table shows the number of A grades in GCSE History over a six year period. Use the information to answer the following questions. Please circle the correct answer.

1. How many students achieved an A grade at Tonbridge Grammar in 2011?

A	B	C	D	E
60	80	55	75	40

2. In what year did pupils at Eltham College achieve the most A grades?

A	B	C	D	E
2013	2012	2011	2010	2009

3. In what year did pupils at Eltham College and Kingston Grammar achieve the same number of A grades?

A	B	C	D	E
2011	2013	2008	2010	2009

4. Which school achieved the second highest number of A grades for GCSE History over the six year period?

A	B	C	D	E
Invicta	Tonbridge	Reading	Eltham	Kingston

5. How many A grades were achieved in 2012?

A	B	C	D	E
130	210	270	190	110

Q17.

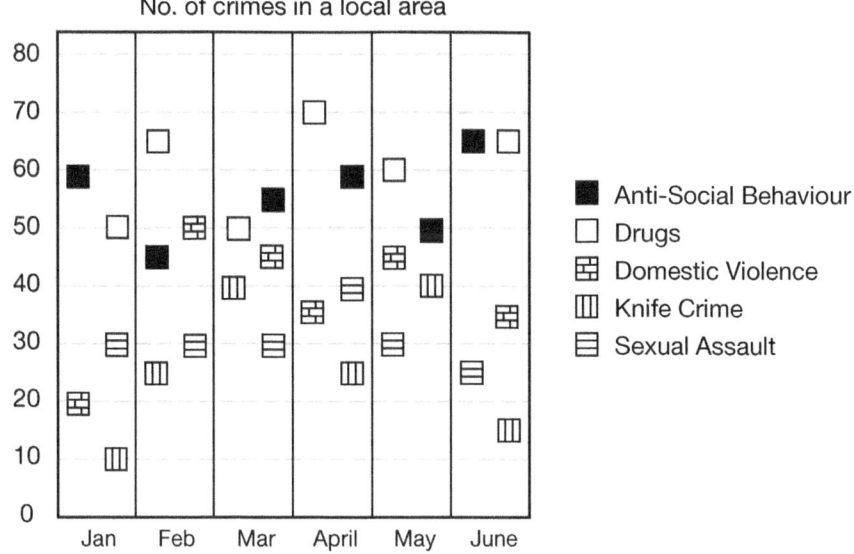

The table shows the number of crimes in a local area over a six month period. Use the information to answer the following questions. Please circle the correct answer.

1. What crime was at the lowest in March?

A	B	C	D	E
ASB	Drugs	Domestic Violence	Knife	Sexual Assault

2. What month was drug related crime at its highest?

A	B	C	D	E
January	February	March	April	May

3. Which crime was the second highest over the six month period?

A	B	C	D	E
ASB	Drugs	Domestic Violence	Knife	Sexual Assault

4. How many knife crimes occurred in June?

A	B	C	D	E
15	30	45	60	80

5. In what month were Anti-Social Behaviour and Drug crime at the same number?

A	B	C	D	E
June	May	April	March	February

Q18.

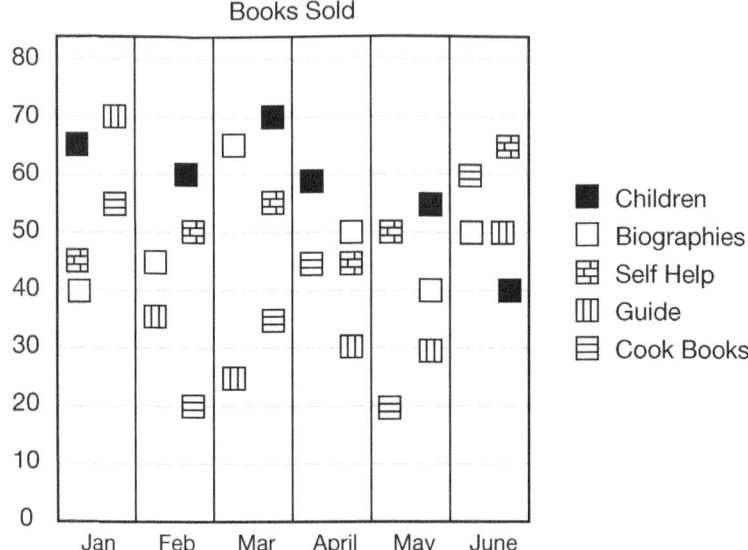

The table shows the number of books released over a six month period. Use the information to answer the following questions. Please circle the correct answer.

1. How many self-help books were sold in April?

A	B	C	D	E
25	15	30	45	65

2. What month did cook books sell the most?

A	B	C	D	E
June	May	April	March	February

3. How many books were sold in April?

A	B	C	D	E
180	230	130	270	250

4. Which type of book sold the second highest of books over the six month period?

A	B	C	D	E
Children	Biographies	Self Help	Guide	Cook Books

5. In what month did cook books and self-help books sell the same amount?

A	B	C	D	E
January	February	March	April	May

Q19.

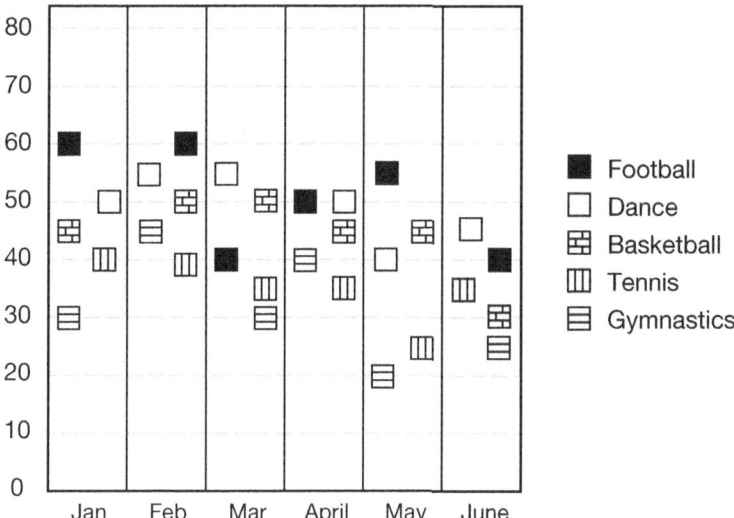

The table shows the number of pupils who are members of an afterschool team over a six month period. Use the information to answer the following questions. Please circle the correct answer.

1. How many pupils were in the football team in April?

A	B	C	D	E
45	60	50	25	30

2. In what month were the least number of pupils in a basketball team?

A	B	C	D	E
June	May	April	March	February

3. Which sport had the least number of members in the afterschool team over the six month period?

A	B	C	D	E
Football	Dance	Basketball	Tennis	Gymnastics

4. Which months did gymnastics have more people in the team as opposed to members of the tennis team? Circle TWO.

A	B	C	D	E
January	February	March	April	May

5. How many pupils were part of the dance team from January to June?

A	B	C	D	E
275	295	215	195	175

Q20.

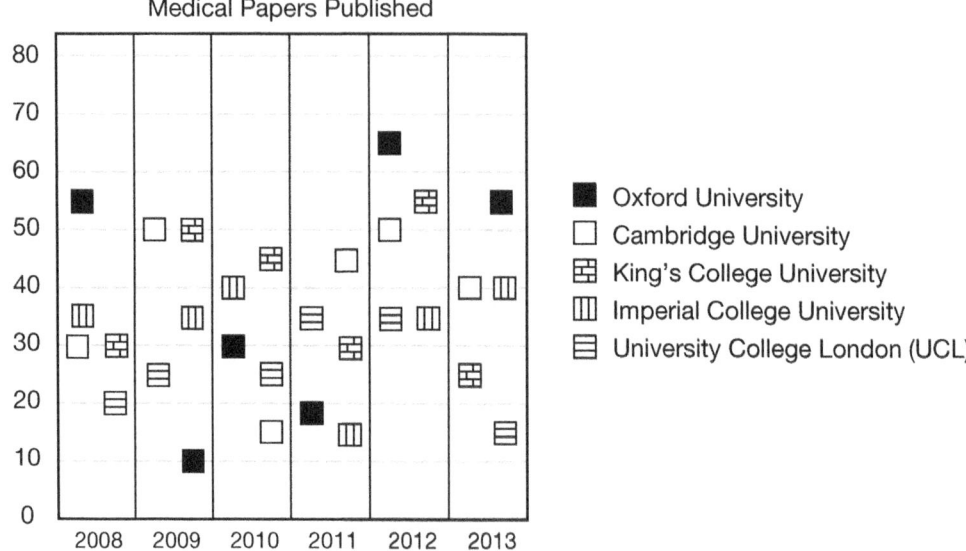

The table shows the number of medical papers published over a six year period. Use the information to answer the following questions. Please circle the correct answer.

1. In what year did researchers at Cambridge University and Imperial College University publish the same number of papers?

A	B	C	D	E
2013	2012	2011	2010	2009

2. In what year did researchers at King's College University publish the most papers?

A	B	C	D	E
2008	2009	2010	2011	2012

3. How many papers were published by University College London (UCL) in 2011?

A	B	C	D	E
65	35	80	70	15

4. In what years did researchers at University College London publish more papers than those from Oxford University? Circle TWO.

A	B	C	D	E
2008	2009	2010	2011	2012

5. Which university published the second lowest number of papers over the six year period?

A	B	C	D	E
Oxford	Cambridge	King's College	Imperial College	UCL

Now check your answers before moving on to the next section of the guide.

DATA INTERPRETATIONS PART 3 ANSWERS

QUESTION 1

1. D
2. B
3. D
4. B
5. C

QUESTION 2

1. D
2. D
3. B
4. A
5. E

QUESTION 3

1. C
2. E
3. A
4. B
5. D

QUESTION 4

1. C
2. B
3. D
4. E
5. D

QUESTION 5

1. E
2. C
3. B + D
4. D
5. B

QUESTION 6

1. D
2. C
3. C
4. B
5. B

QUESTION 7

1. A
2. A
3. C
4. A
5. D

QUESTION 8

1. B
2. C + E + B
3. B
4. E
5. E

QUESTION 9

1. E
2. A + D
3. C
4. E
5. C

QUESTION 10

1. D
2. D
3. C
4. E
5. A

QUESTION 11

1. E
2. E
3. C
4. C
5. D

QUESTION 12

1. D
2. B
3. A
4. A
5. B

QUESTION 13

1. C
2. D
3. D
4. E
5. E

QUESTION 14

1. C
2. E
3. A
4. B
5. A

QUESTION 15

1. A
2. D
3. E
4. B
5. B

QUESTION 16

1. C
2. A
3. B
4. C
5. D

QUESTION 17

1. E
2. D
3. B
4. A
5. A

QUESTION 18

1. D
2. A
3. B
4. C
5. D

QUESTION 19

1. C
2. A
3. E
4. B + D
5. B

QUESTION 20

1. A
2. E
3. B
4. B + D
5. D

Once you have checked your answers move on to the next section of the guide.

DATA INTERPRETATION TESTS

PART 4

DATA INTERPRETATION TESTS PART 4

Q1.

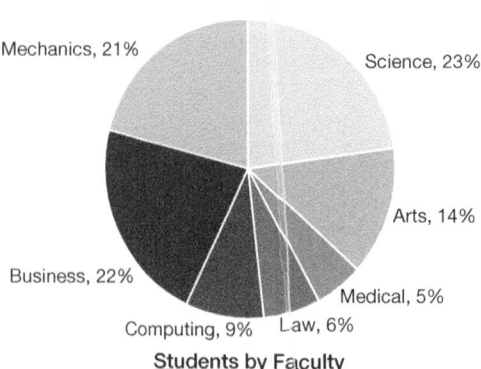

Students by Faculty

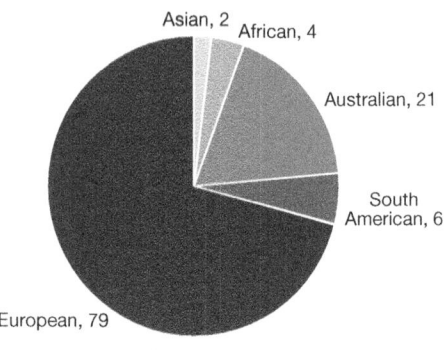

Business students (Non-US)

The pie chart above shows the percentages of students in each faculty at Grove University and the number of non-US students in the Business faculty. These percentages have been rounded to the nearest whole number. There are a total of 1247 students in the Business faculty. Use this information to answer the following questions.

1. What percentage of students in the Business faculty are non-US students?

A	B	C	D	E
11%	13%	9%	7%	8%

2. How many students are there at the university?

A	B	C	D	E
5558	5668	5685	5585	5686

3. How many students are there in the Law faculty?

A	B	C	D	E
310	290	380	340	270

4. If 7 per cent of Mechanic students are Australian, how many Australian students are there studying Mechanics?

A	B	C	D	E
71	76	55	89	83

5. There are 32 South American Arts students. What percentage of the faculty does this represent?

A	B	C	D	E
14%	18%	4%	8%	15%

Q2.

Job sectors | Non-US

The pie chart above shows the percentage of candidates who applied for a job in a particular job sector and the number of non-US candidates for Retail. These percentages have been rounded to the nearest whole number. There are a total of 2856 candidates who applied in the Retail Industry. Use this information to answer the following questions.

1. How many candidates applied for a job in any of the job sectors?

A	B	C	D	E
9,800	10,400	12,500	10,200	12,700

2. What percentage of candidates who applied for a job in the Retail Industry are Non-US?

A	B	C	D	E
1%	4%	9%	16%	22%

3. There are 486 European Media candidates. What percentage of the Media job sector does this represent?

A	B	C	D	E
72%	55%	61%	49%	43%

4. If 22 per cent of Medicine candidates are Asian, how many Asian candidates are there applying for a Medical role?

A	B	C	D	E
296	692	269	226	219

5. How many candidates applied for a job in the Media sector?

A	B	C	D	E
1212	1122	2112	2211	1112

Q3.

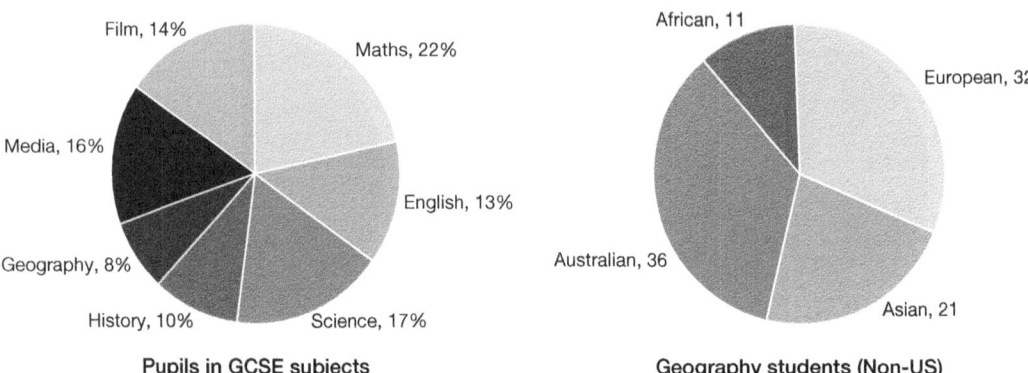

Pupils in GCSE subjects   Geography students (Non-US)

The pie chart above shows the percentage of students in each GCSE subject at a local secondary school and the number of non-US students in the subject of Geography. These percentages have been rounded to the nearest whole number. There are a total of 118 students in Geography. Use this information to answer the following questions.

1. How many students are there studying these GCSE's?

A	B	C	D	E
1475	1495	1325	1675	1435

2. There are 33 European History students. What percentage of the subject does this represent?

A	B	C	D	E
19%	21%	27%	22%	15%

3. If 17% of English students are Australian, how many Australian students are there studying English?

A	B	C	D	E
32	38	41	52	60

4. What percentage of students in the Geography subject are non-US?

A	B	C	D	E
21%	85%	62%	45%	54%

5. How many students are there in the subject of Media?

A	B	C	D	E
219	226	247	255	236

Q4.

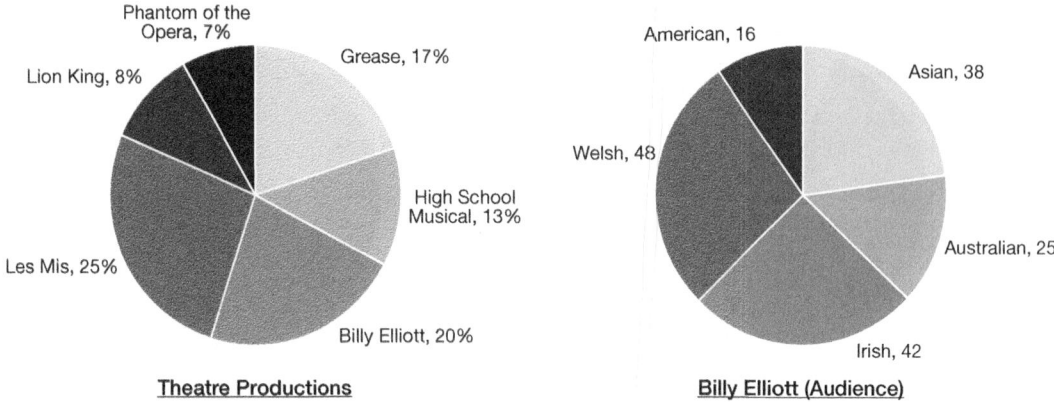

Theatre Productions | Billy Elliott (Audience)

The pie chart above shows the percentage of the most popular theatre productions in London and the audience in relation to ethnicity for the production of Billy Elliot. These percentages have been rounded to the nearest whole number. There are a total of 1118 people in the audience for the production of Billy Elliot. Use this information to answer the following questions.

1. How many members of the audience are there to watch a musical production?

A	B	C	D	E
8975	4650	5590	6650	7890

2. What percentage of the audience for Billy Elliot were not British?

A	B	C	D	E
28%	10%	25%	30%	15%

3. How many people were in the audience for Les Mis?

A	B	C	D	E
1397	1428	1118	2015	1564

4. If 13 per cent of the audience for Grease are Welsh, how many Welsh members of the audience are watching Grease?

A	B	C	D	E
111	123	127	131	136

5. There are 63 Irish people watching The Lion King, What percentage of the total audience for The Lion King does this represent?

A	B	C	D	E
23%	8%	14%	17%	26%

Q5.

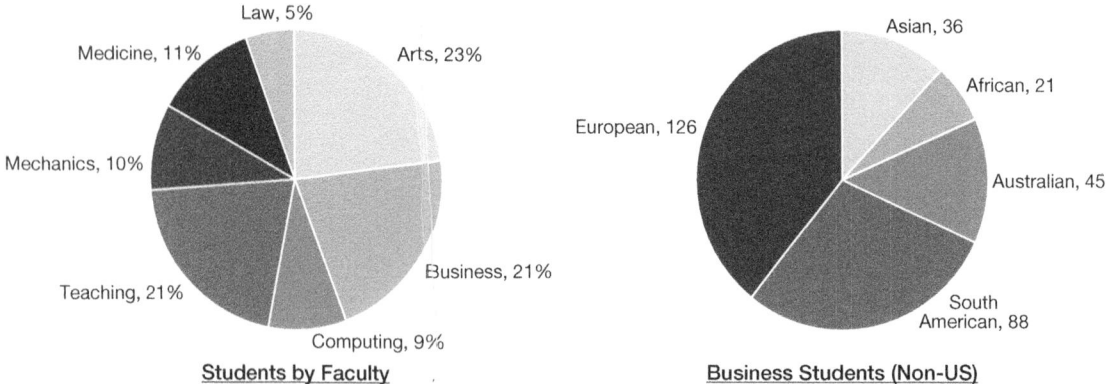

Students by Faculty — Business Students (Non-US)

The pie chart above shows the percentage of students in each faculty at West Gate University and the number of non-US students in the Business faculty. These percentages have been rounded to the nearest whole number. There are a total of 1098 students in the Business faculty. Use this information to answer the following questions.

1. How many students are there at the university?

A	B	C	D	E
2258	5258	5528	5228	5822

2. What percentage of students in the Business faculty are non-US students?

A	B	C	D	E
25%	29%	28%	24%	30%

3. If 23 per cent of Mechanic students are Australian, how many Australian students are there studying Mechanics?

A	B	C	D	E
20	130	125	50	120

4. There are 145 South American Arts students. What percentage of the faculty does this represent?

A	B	C	D	E
21%	25%	12%	30%	7%

5. How many students are there in the Teaching faculty?

A	B	C	D	E
998	1208	1043	1097	1197

Q6.

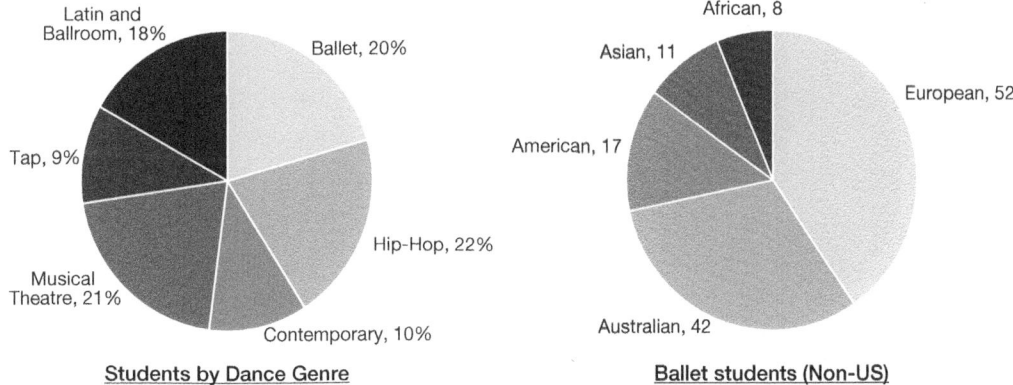

Students by Dance Genre | Ballet students (Non-US)

The pie chart above shows the percentage of students in each dance genre at a Performing Arts College in London and the number of non-US students in the Ballet dance genre. These percentages have been rounded to the nearest whole number. There are a total of 1658 students in the Ballet genre. Use this information to answer the following questions.

1. What percentage of students in the Ballet dance genre are non-US students?

A	B	C	D	E
8%	11%	9%	7%	5%

2. How many students are in the Latin and Ballroom genre?

A	B	C	D	E
1924	1492	1249	1942	1224

3. How many students are there at the Performing Arts College in London?

A	B	C	D	E
8140	8370	8250	8490	8290

4. If 16 per cent of the Musical Theatre students are American, how many American students are there studying Musical Theatre?

A	B	C	D	E
278	268	215	219	276

5. There are 68 American Latin and Ballroom students. What percentage of this dance genre does this represent?

A	B	C	D	E
6%	10%	5%	7%	8%

Q7.

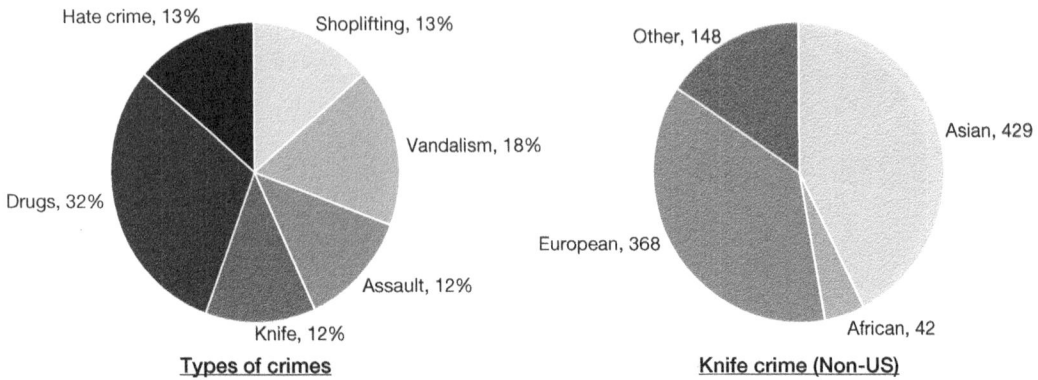

Types of crimes | Knife crime (Non-US)

The pie chart above shows the percentage of teenagers that were convicted of a crime and the number of non-US teenagers that committed a Knife crime offence. These percentages have been rounded to the nearest whole number. There are a total of 1036 teenagers that were convicted of a Knife crime offence. Use this information to answer the following questions.

1. What percentage of teenagers that were convicted of Knife crime are non-US?

A	B	C	D	E
25%	50%	75%	95%	80%

2. How many teenagers were convicted for Drugs?

A	B	C	D	E
2136	2267	2762	6722	2627

3. How many teenagers were convicted of a crime?

A	B	C	D	E
8633	6833	6383	8368	6688

4. If 18 per cent of Assaults are Asian, how many Asian's are there convicting Assaults?

A	B	C	D	E
123	186	195	172	165

5. There are 123 European teenagers convicted of Shoplifting. What percentage of the crime does this represent?

A	B	C	D	E
9%	13%	22%	7%	11%

Q8.

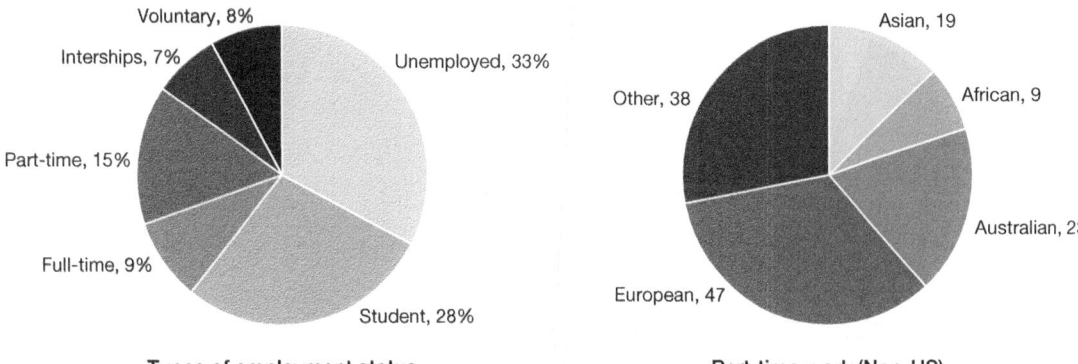

Types of employment status

Part-time work (Non-US)

The pie chart above shows the percentage of teenagers in different employment statuses and the number of non-US part time workers. These percentages have been rounded to the nearest whole number. There are a total of 982 teenagers in part time work. Use this information to answer the following questions.

1. How many teenagers are there altogether?

A	B	C	D	E
6654	6546	5465	4456	4654

2. What percentage of teenagers in Part Time work are non-US teenagers?

A	B	C	D	E
14%	18%	20%	22%	24%

3. There are 64 European Interns. What percentage of the employment status does this represent?

A	B	C	D	E
11%	14%	15%	16%	19%

4. If 48 per cent of students are European, how many European students are there?

A	B	C	D	E
822	813	867	897	879

5. How many teenagers are in Full Time employment?

A	B	C	D	E
521	536	589	571	542

Q9.

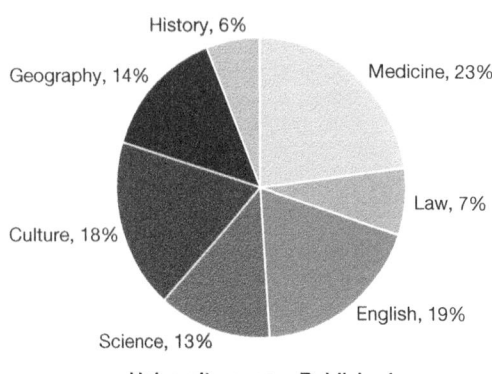

University papers Published

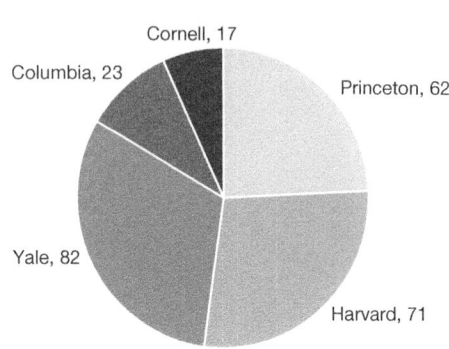

Science papers Published (Ivy League)

The pie chart above shows the percentage of the number of university papers published and the number of Ivy League Science papers that were published. These percentages have been rounded to the nearest whole number. There are a total of 873 Science papers that were published. Use this information to answer the following questions.

1. How many university papers were published?

A	B	C	D	E
6135	6715	6327	6957	6175

2. How many papers were published for Geography?

A	B	C	D	E
940	910	980	970	930

3. There are 103 Harvard Law papers. What percentage of the Law papers does this represent?

A	B	C	D	E
27%	22%	13%	18%	9%

4. If 62 per cent of Medical papers were published by Yale, how many Yale Medical papers were published?

A	B	C	D	E
364	298	1003	957	873

5. What percentage of Science papers are from Ivy League schools?

A	B	C	D	E
41%	15%	76%	29%	58%

Q10.

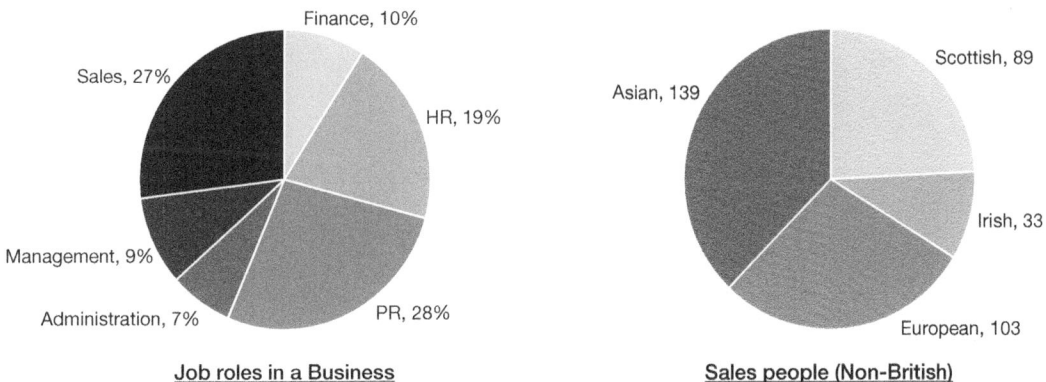

Job roles in a Business   Sales people (Non-British)

The pie chart above shows the percentage of the number of job roles in a local business and the number of Non-British sales people. These percentages have been rounded to the nearest whole number. There are a total of 407 sales people in the Business. Use this information to answer the following questions.

1. How many employees are there at the Business?

A	B	C	D	E
1306	1500	1507	1300	1950

2. There are 236 Asian PR employees. What percentage of that particular job role does this represent?

A	B	C	D	E
23%	71%	44%	56%	20%

3. If 27 per cent of Administration employees are European, how many European Administration employees are there?

A	B	C	D	E
31	28	17	63	45

4. How many employees are there in HR department?

A	B	C	D	E
128	169	248	236	286

5. What percentage of employees in the Sales department are non-British?

A	B	C	D	E
13%	74%	89%	88%	79%

Q11.

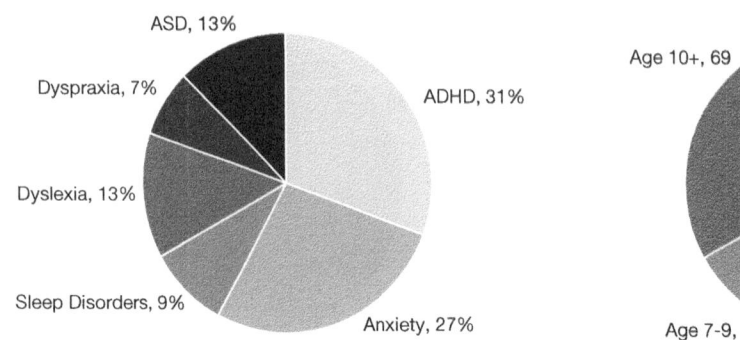

Behavioural Problems at School

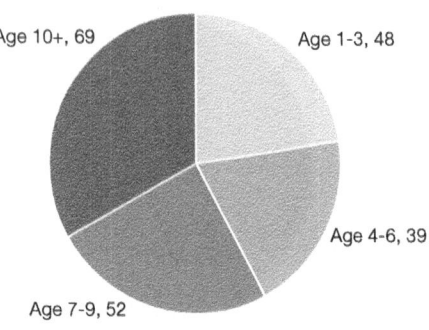

ADHD (Not clinically proven)

The pie chart above shows the percentage of the number of children with signs of behavioural problems and the number of children with signs of ADHD that have not been clinically proven. These percentages have been rounded to the nearest whole number. There are a total of 289 children with signs of ADHD. Use this information to answer the following questions.

1. How many children are in this study?

A	B	C	D	E
912	972	952	932	942

2. What percentage of children with signs of ADHD have not been clinically proven?

A	B	C	D	E
63%	72%	74%	64%	36%

3. There are 21 children aged 4-6 with Dyslexia. What percentage of this behaviour problem does this represent?

A	B	C	D	E
19%	21%	35%	32%	17%

4. If 11 per cent of Sleep Disorders are found in age 7-9 year olds, how many children that age has a sleep disorder?

A	B	C	D	E
10	11	7	9	5

5. How many children have Anxiety issues?

A	B	C	D	E
250	251	252	253	254

Q12.

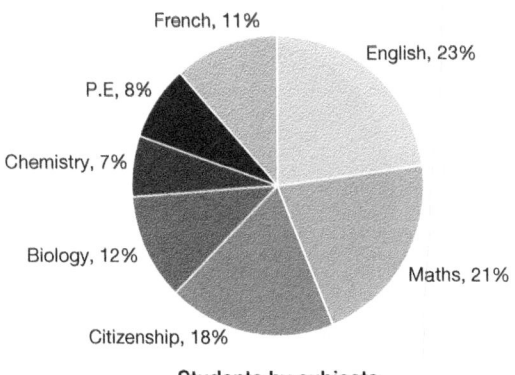

Students by subjects

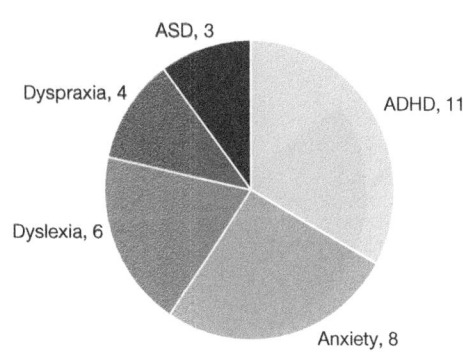

Students with learning difficulties in Citizenship

The pie chart above shows the percentage of the number of students by subjects at a local Secondary School and the number of students with learning difficulties in Citizenship. These percentages have been rounded to the nearest whole number. There are a total of 93 students studying Citizenship. Use this information to answer the following questions.

1. What percentage of students in Citizenship have learning difficulties?

A	B	C	D	E
33%	34%	35%	36%	37%

2. How many students are studying English?

A	B	C	D	E
112	131	138	118	100

3. How many students are there at the Secondary School?

A	B	C	D	E
516	519	521	523	525

4. If 19 per cent of Biology students have Anxiety issues, how many Biology students are there that have anxiety issues?

A	B	C	D	E
9	10	11	12	13

5. There are 17 ASD Chemistry students. What percentage of the subject does this represent?

A	B	C	D	E
32%	47%	16%	8%	71%

DATA INTERPRETATION TESTS

Q13.

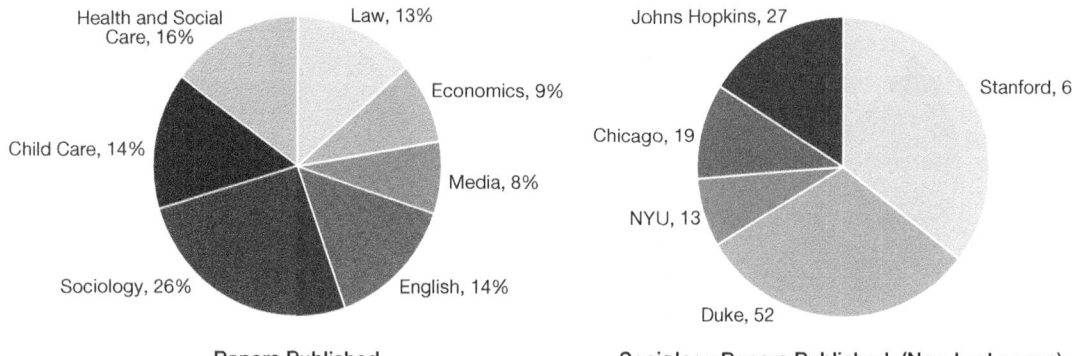

Papers Published | Sociology Papers Published (Non-Ivy League)

The pie chart above shows the percentages of papers published by universities and the number of sociology papers published from Non-Ivy League universities. These percentages have been rounded to the nearest whole number. There are a total of 298 Sociology papers published. Use this information to answer the following questions.

1. How many papers were published altogether?

A	B	C	D	E
1046	1460	1146	1604	146

2. What percentage of Sociology papers were published by non-Ivy League schools?

A	B	C	D	E
58%	27%	33%	75%	61%

3. There are 64 English papers published by Duke University. What percentage of this subject are does this represent?

A	B	C	D	E
35%	40%	41%	45%	48%

4. If 29 per cent of Economic papers were published by NYU, how many Economic papers were published by NYU?

A	B	C	D	E
33	55	29	61	8

5. How many papers were published on Health and Social Care?

A	B	C	D	E
172	132	170	183	195

Q14.

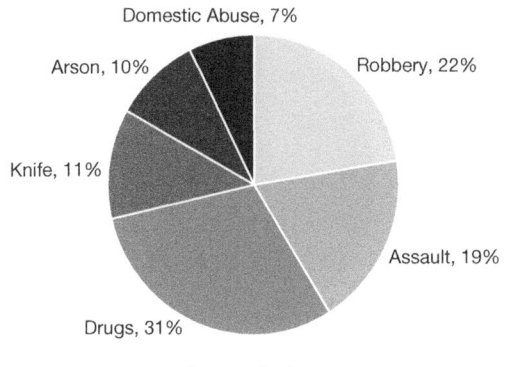

Types of crime

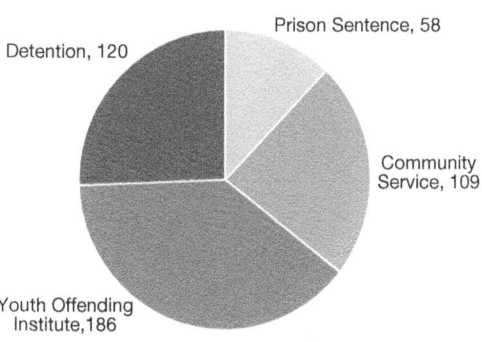

Number of Convictions for Arson

The pie chart above shows the percentage of the types of crimes committed in a local area and the number of convictions for Arson. These percentages have been rounded to the nearest whole number. There are a total of 718 of Arson crimes that have been committed. Use this information to answer the following questions.

1. How many crimes have been committed in the local area?

A	B	C	D	E
7810	8710	1780	1087	7180

2. How many Knife crimes took place in the local area?

A	B	C	D	E
997	998	789	887	879

3. What percentage of crimes committed for Arson were people convicted?

A	B	C	D	E
45%	55%	80%	66%	34%

4. There are 103 drug related crimes that were sent to Youth Offending Institutes. What percentage of this type of crime does this represent?

A	B	C	D	E
5%	10%	11%	8%	13%

5. If 33 per cent of Domestic Abuse crimes served a Prison Sentence, how many people served a Prison Sentence for Domestic Abuse?

A	B	C	D	E
164	165	166	167	168

DATA INTERPRETATION TESTS

Q15.

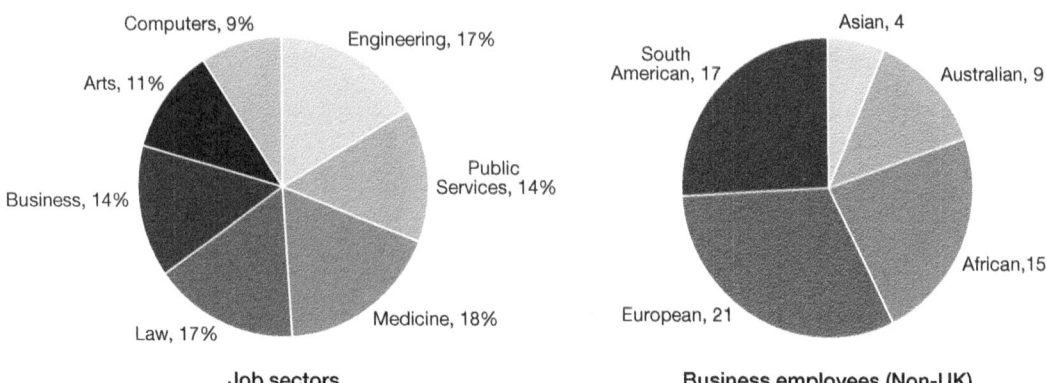

Job sectors | Business employees (Non-UK)

The pie chart above shows the percentage of the number of employees in each job sector and the number of Business employees that are non-UK. These percentages have been rounded to the nearest whole number. There are a total of 458 employees in the Business sector. Use this information to answer the following questions.

1. What percentage of employees in the Business sector are non-UK employees?

A	B	C	D	E
14%	16%	21%	25%	30%

2. How many employees are there altogether?

A	B	C	D	E
3172	3721	3271	3217	2137

3. If 31 per cent of Law employees are European, how many European Law employees are there?

A	B	C	D	E
134	172	186	103	147

4. There are 103 Asian employees in the Medical profession. What percentage of the job sector does this represent?

A	B	C	D	E
13%	21%	26%	18%	31%

5. How many employees are there in the Public Service sector?

A	B	C	D	E
497	455	457	417	437

Q16.

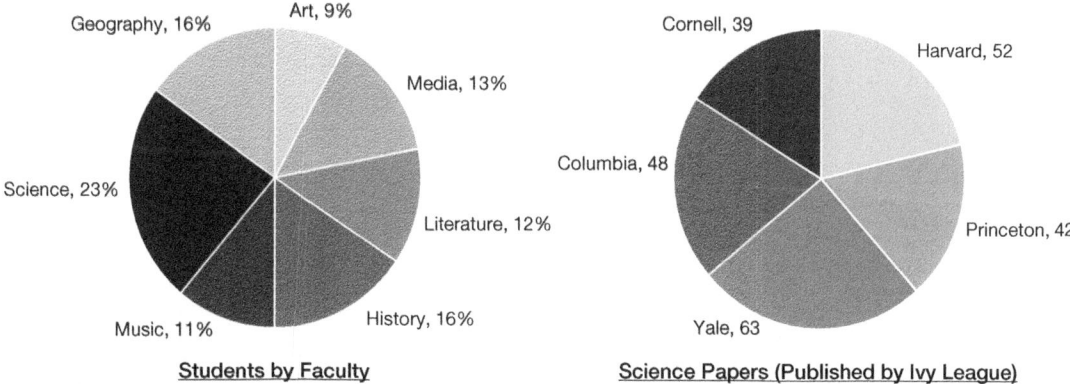

Students by Faculty

Science Papers (Published by Ivy League)

The pie chart above shows the percentage of students by faculty and the number of Science papers published by the Ivy League universities. These percentages have been rounded to the nearest whole number. There are a total of 1369 Science papers published across American universities. Use this information to answer the following questions.

1. How many students are there in the Geography faculty?

A	B	C	D	E
559	639	918	592	952

2. How many students are there in this survey?

A	B	C	D	E
5592	5292	5952	5529	2559

3. What percentage of students who published Science papers were published from an Ivy League school?

A	B	C	D	E
25%	18%	33%	71%	52%

4. There are 64 Media papers published by Cornell University. What percentage of the faculty does this represent?

A	B	C	D	E
8%	9%	10%	11%	12%

5. If 27 per cent of Literature students published there paper from Princeton University, how many Princeton Literature papers were published?

A	B	C	D	E
191	192	193	194	195

DATA INTERPRETATION TESTS

Q17.

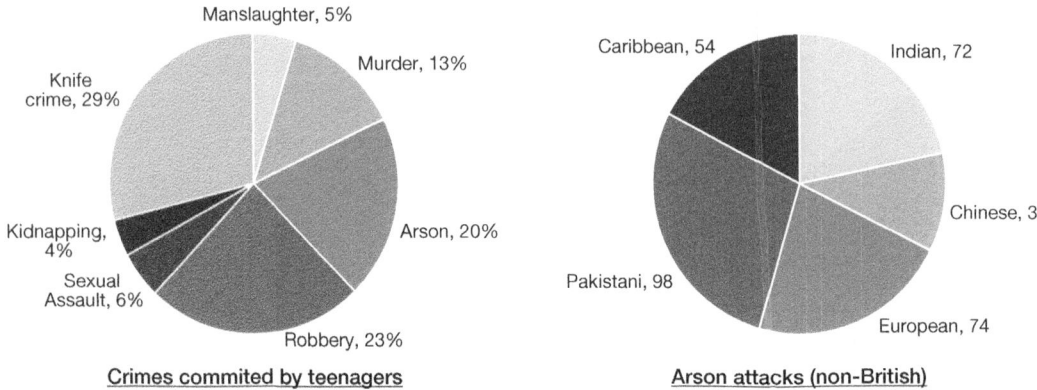

Crimes commited by teenagers   Arson attacks (non-British)

The pie chart above shows the percentage of the types of crimes committed by teenagers and the number of Arson attacks committed by non-British citizens. These percentages have been rounded to the nearest whole number. There are a total of 917 Arson attacks committed by teenagers. Use this information to answer the following questions.

1. How many people are there that have committed a crime?

A	B	C	D	E
4558	4585	5884	5854	4855

2. How many people have committed a Robbery offence?

A	B	C	D	E
954	1034	1074	1054	1094

3. If 41 per cent of people that committed a Knife crime are European, how European people committed a Knife crime offence?

A	B	C	D	E
554	544	524	454	455

4. There are 31 Pakistani citizens that have committed Manslaughter. What percentage of this type of crime does this represent?

A	B	C	D	E
14%	18%	21%	8%	35%

5. What percentage of Arson attacks were committed by non-British citizens?

A	B	C	D	E
32%	33%	34%	35%	36%

Q18.

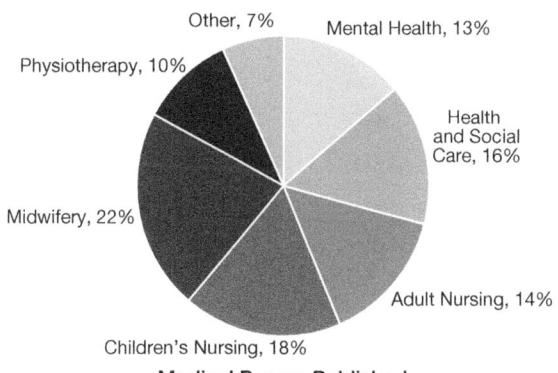

Medical Papers Published

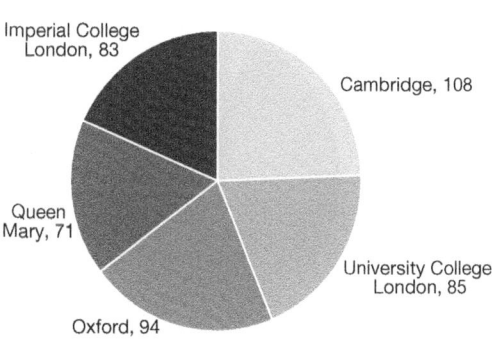

Physiotherapy Papers Published
(Top London Universities)

The pie chart above shows the percentage of Medical papers published in an academic year and the number of Physiotherapy papers published by the Top London universities. These percentages have been rounded to the nearest whole number. There are a total of 1576 Physiotherapy papers published across the UK. Use this information to answer the following questions.

1. How many papers were published for Mental Health?

A	B	C	D	E
408	1088	2018	2048	880

2. What percentage of Physiotherapy papers were published by the Top London universities?

A	B	C	D	E
21%	33%	28%	39%	72%

3. How many papers were published overall?

A	B	C	D	E
15670	15770	15660	15760	15150

4. There are 108 Midwifery papers published by Queen Mary University. What percentage of midwifery papers does this represent?

A	B	C	D	E
14%	23%	3%	33%	43%

5. If 22 per cent of Children's Nursing papers were published by Oxford University, how many Children's Nursing papers were published by Oxford?

A	B	C	D	E
362	316	613	236	623

DATA INTERPRETATION TESTS

Q19.

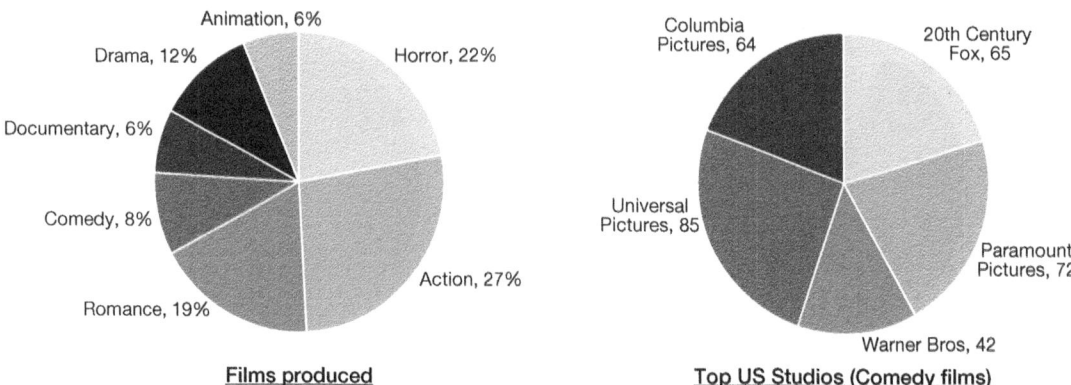

Films produced | Top US Studios (Comedy films)

The pie chart above shows the percentage of different genres of films produced and the number of Comedy films that Top US film studios have produced. These percentages have been rounded to the nearest whole number. There are a total of 508 Comedy films that have been produced in America. Use this information to answer the following questions.

1. How many films have been produced?

A	B	C	D	E
9580	7320	6350	7550	4650

2. If 33 per cent of Action films were produced by 20th Century Fox, how many Action films were produced by 20th Century Fox?

A	B	C	D	E
525	565	585	605	615

3. There are 217 Horror films produced by Columbia Pictures. What percentage of the horror genre does this represent?

A	B	C	D	E
21%	6%	33%	16%	25%

4. What percentage of comedy films are produced by Top US studios?

A	B	C	D	E
25%	50%	85%	15%	65%

5. How many Documentary films were produced?

A	B	C	D	E
375	381	318	388	311

Q20.

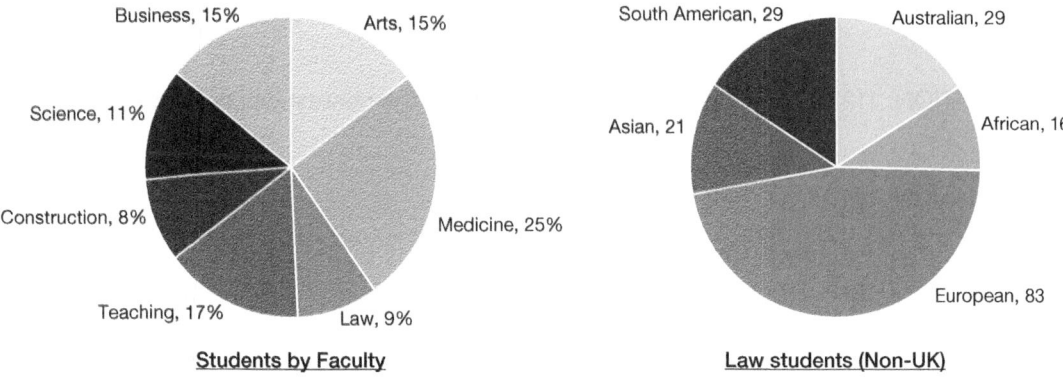

Students by Faculty   Law students (Non-UK)

The pie chart above shows the percentage of students in each faculty at a University and the number of non-UK students in the Law faculty. These percentages have been rounded to the nearest whole number. There are a total of 889 students in the Law faculty. Use this information to answer the following questions.

1. How many students are there at the university?

A	B	C	D	E
8977	8979	9879	9788	9877

2. What percentage of the students in the Law faculty are Non-UK students?

A	B	C	D	E
15%	35%	20%	40%	70%

3. How many students are there in the Medicine faculty?

A	B	C	D	E
2964	2449	2649	2469	2929

4. If 14 per cent of Construction students are European, how many European students are there studying Construction?

A	B	C	D	E
95	110	135	150	170

5. There are 364 European students studying business. What percentage of the faculty does this represent?

A	B	C	D	E
5%	15%	50%	35%	25%

Now check your answers before moving on to the next section of the guide.

DATA INTERPRETATIONS PART 4 ANSWERS

QUESTION 1

1. C

EXPLANATION: 112 / 1247 x 100 = 8.98. Rounded up to the nearest whole number = 9%

2. B

EXPLANATION: 1247 x 100 / 22 = 5668

3. D

EXPLANATION: 5668 / 100 x 6 = 340

4. E

EXPLANATION: 5668 / 100 x 21 = 1190. 1190 / 100 x 7 = 83

5. C

EXPLANATION: 32 / 794 x 100 = 4.03% rounded to the nearest whole number = 4%

QUESTION 2

1. D

EXPLANATION: 2856 x 100 / 28 = 10,200

2. B

EXPLANATION: 111 / 2856 x 100 = 3.88% rounded to the nearest whole number = 4%

3. E

EXPLANATION: 486 / 1122 x 100 = 43.31% rounded to the nearest whole number = 43%

4. C

EXPLANATION: 1224 / 100 x 22 = 269

5. B

EXPLANATION: 10200 / 100 x 11 = 1122

PART 4   125

QUESTION 3

1. A
EXPLANATION: 118 x 100 / 8 = 1475

2. D
EXPLANATION: 33 / 148 x 100 = 22.29% rounded to the nearest whole number = 22%

3. A
EXPLANATION: 192 / 100 x 17 = 32

4. B
EXPLANATION: 100 / 118 x 100 = 84.74% rounded to the nearest whole number = 85%

5. E
EXPLANATION: 1475 / 100 x 16 = 236

QUESTION 4

1. C
EXPLANATION: 1118 x 100 / 20 = 5590

2. E
EXPLANATION: 169 / 1118 x 100 = 15.11% rounded to the nearest whole number = 15%

3. A
EXPLANATION: 5590 / 100 x 25 = 1397

4. B
EXPLANATION: 950 / 100 x 13 = 123

5. C
EXPLANATION: 63 / 447 x 100 = 14.09% rounded to the nearest whole number = 14%

QUESTION 5

1. D

EXPLANATION: 1098 x 100 / 21 = 5228

2. B

EXPLANATION: 316 / 1098 x 100 = 28.77% rounded to the nearest whole number = 29%

3. E

EXPLANATION: 522 / 100 x 23 = 120.06. Rounded to the nearest whole number = 120.

4. C

EXPLANATION: 145 / 1202 x 100 = 12.06% rounded to the nearest whole number = 12%

5. D

EXPLANATION: 5228 / 100 x 21 = 1097

QUESTION 6

1. A

EXPLANATION: 130 / 1658 x 100 = 7.84% rounded to the nearest whole number = 8%

2. B

EXPLANATION: 8290 / 100 x 18 = 1492

3. E

EXPLANATION: 1658 x 100 / 20 = 8290

4. A

EXPLANATION: 1740 / 100 x 16 = 278

5. C

EXPLANATION: 68 / 1492 x 100 = 4.55% rounded to the nearest whole number = 5%

QUESTION 7

1. D

EXPLANATION: 987 / 1036 x 100 = 95.27% rounded to the nearest whole number = 95%

2. C

EXPLANATION: 8633 / 100 x 32 = 2762

3. A

EXPLANATION: 1036 x 100 / 12 = 8633

4. B

EXPLANATION: 1035 / 100 x 18 = 186

5. E

EXPLANATION: 123 / 1122 x 100 = 10.96% rounded to the nearest whole number = 11%

QUESTION 8

1. B

EXPLANATION: 982 x 100 / 15 = 6546

2. A

EXPLANATION: 136 / 982 x 100 = 13.84% rounded to the nearest whole number = 14%

3. B

EXPLANATION: 64 / 458 x 100 = 13.97% rounded to the nearest whole number = 14%

4. E

EXPLANATION: 1832 / 100 x 48 = 879

5. C

EXPLANATION: 6546 / 100 x 9 = 589

DATA INTERPRETATION TESTS

QUESTION 9

1. B
EXPLANATION: 873 x 100 / 13 = 6715

2. A
EXPLANATION: 6715 / 100 x 14 = 940

3. B
EXPLANATION: 103 / 470 x 100 = 21.91% rounded to the nearest whole number = 22%

4. D
EXPLANATION: 1544 / 100 x 62 = 957

5. D
EXPLANATION: 255 / 873 x 100 = 29.20% rounded to the nearest whole number = 29%

QUESTION 10

1. C
EXPLANATION: 407 x 100 / 27 = 1507

2. D
EXPLANATION: 236 / 421 x 100 = 56.05% rounded to the nearest whole number = 56%

3. B
EXPLANATION: 105 / 100 x 27 = 28

4. E
EXPLANATION: 1507 / 100 x 19 = 286

5. C
EXPLANATION: 364 / 407 x 100 = 89.43% rounded to the nearest whole number = 89%

PART 4

QUESTION 11

1. D
EXPLANATION: 289 x 100 / 31 = 932

2. B
EXPLANATION: 208 / 289 x 100 = 71.97% rounded to the nearest whole number = 72%

3. E
EXPLANATION: 21 / 121 x 100 = 17.35% rounded to the nearest whole number = 17%

4. D
EXPLANATION: 83 / 100 x 11 = 9

5. B
EXPLANATION: 932 / 100 x 27 = 251

QUESTION 12

1. B
EXPLANATION: 32 / 93 x 100 = 34.40% rounded to the nearest whole number = 34%

2. D
EXPLANATION: 516 / 100 x 23 = 118

3. A
EXPLANATION: 93 x 100 / 18 = 516

4. C
EXPLANATION: 61 / 100 x 19 = 11

5. B
EXPLANATION: 17 / 36 x 100 = 47.22% rounded to the nearest whole number = 47%

QUESTION 13

1. C

EXPLANATION: 298 x 100 / 26 = 1146

2. A

EXPLANATION: 174 / 298 x 100 = 58.38% rounded to the nearest whole number = 58%

3. B

EXPLANATION: 64 / 160 x 100 = 40%

4. C

EXPLANATION: 103 / 100 x 29 = 29

5. D

EXPLANATION: 1146 / 100 x 16 = 183

QUESTION 14

1. E

EXPLANATION: 718 x 100 / 10 = 7180

2. C

EXPLANATION: 7180 / 100 x 11 = 789

3. D

EXPLANATION: 473 / 718 x 100 = 65.87% rounded to the nearest whole number = 66%

4. A

EXPLANATION: 103 / 2225 x 100 = 4.62% rounded to the nearest whole number = 5%

5. B

EXPLANATION: 502 / 100 x 33 = 165

PART 4   131

QUESTION 15

1. A
EXPLANATION: 66 / 458 x 100 = 14.41% rounded to the nearest whole number = 14%

2. C
EXPLANATION: 458 x 100 / 14 = 3271

3. B
EXPLANATION: 556 / 100 x 31 = 172

4. D
EXPLANATION: 103 / 588 x 100 = 17.51% rounded to the nearest whole number = 18%

5. C
EXPLANATION: 3271 / 100 x 14 = 457

QUESTION 16

1. E
EXPLANATION: 5952 / 100 x 16 = 952

2. C
EXPLANATION: 1369 x 100 / 23 = 5952

3. B
EXPLANATION: 244 / 1369 x 100 = 17.82% rounded to the nearest whole number = 18%

4. A
EXPLANATION: 64 / 773 x 100 = 8.27% rounded to the nearest whole number = 8%

5. B
EXPLANATION: 714 / 100 x 27 = 192

DATA INTERPRETATION TESTS

QUESTION 17

1. B
EXPLANATION: 917 x 100 / 20 = 4585

2. D
EXPLANATION: 4585 / 100 x 23 = 1054

3. B
EXPLANATION: 1329 / 100 x 41 = 544

4. A
EXPLANATION: 31 / 229 x 100 = 13.53% rounded to the nearest whole number = 14%

5. E
EXPLANATION: 332 / 917 x 100 = 36.20% rounded to the nearest whole number = 36%

QUESTION 18

1. D
EXPLANATION: 15760 / 100 x 13 = 2048

2. C
EXPLANATION: 441 / 1576 x 100 = 27.98% rounded to the nearest whole number = 28%

3. D
EXPLANATION: 1576 x 100 / 10 = 15,760

4. C
EXPLANATION: 108 / 3467 x 100 = 3.11% rounded to the nearest whole number = 3%

5. E
EXPLANATION: 2836 / 100 x 22 = 623

PART 4   133

QUESTION 19

1. C

EXPLANATION: 508 x 100 / 8 = 6350

2. B

EXPLANATION: 1714 / 100 x 33 = 565

3. D

EXPLANATION: 217 / 1397 x 100 = 15.53% rounded to the nearest whole number = 16%

4. E

EXPLANATION: 328 / 508 x 100 = 64.56% rounded to the nearest whole number = 65%

5. B

EXPLANATION: 6350 / 100 x 6 = 381

QUESTION 20

1. E

EXPLANATION: 889 x 100 / 9 = 9877

2. C

EXPLANATION: 178 / 889 x 100 = 20.02% rounded to the nearest whole number = 20%

3. D

EXPLANATION: 9877 / 100 x 25 = 2469

4. B

EXPLANATION: 790 / 100 x 14 = 110

5. E

EXPLANATION: 364 / 1481 x 100 = 24.57% rounded to the nearest whole number = 25%

Now move on to the next section of the guide.

DATA INTERPRETATION TESTS

PART 5

DATA INTERPRETATION TESTS PART 5

Q1.

Determine the correct code using the table provided. Orders are coded as follows:
ORDER – COST – SHIPPING METHOD.

ORDER	CODE	COST	CODE	SHIPPING METHOD	CODE
Nails	789	Less than $100	RR	UPS	20
Screws	654	$100-$250	SS	Emery Worldwide	30
Paint	123	$251-$350	TT	DHL	40
Saw	912	$351-$450	UU	Federal Express	50
Wood	829	$451-$550	VV	Airborne Express	60
Telephone	296	$551-$650	WW	Standard Mail	70
Clock	328	$651-$750	XX	Customer Walk-In	80

1. What would be the code for an order of paint that cost $120.75 and shipped by standard mail?

   A – 789-TT-70
   B – 829-SS-70
   C – 123-SS-70
   D – 123-SS-80

   Answer [ ]

2. The code 829-UU-50 is CORRECT for an order of?

   A – Wood costing $375.50 and shipped via federal express
   B – Paint costing $375.50 and shipped via federal express
   C – Wood costing $120.75 and shipped via airborne mail
   D – Paint costing $375.25 and shipped via airborne mail

   Answer [ ]

DATA INTERPRETATION TESTS

3. An order of screws arrived that cost $125.50. If the order is shipped via DHL, it would be coded?

   A – 654-SS-40

   B – 654-TT-40

   C – 789-SS-40

   D – 789-TT-50

   Answer [ ]

4. An order of saws costing $514.25 shipped via Emery Worldwide was coded 829-WW-30 in error. Of the following, which is the CORRECT code for this order?

   A – 912-WW-30

   B – 912-VV-30

   C – 123-XX-50

   D – 296-VV-40

   Answer [ ]

5. An order of clocks costing $325.00 was sold to a walk-in customer. What is the CORRECT code for this transaction?

   A – 296-RR-20

   B – 654-RR-50

   C – 328-SS-70

   D – 328-TT-80

   Answer [ ]

Q2.

Determine the correct code using the table provided. Orders are coded as follows: ORDER – COST – SHIPPING METHOD.

ORDER	CODE	COST	CODE	SHIPPING METHOD	CODE
Windows	368	Less than $100	DD	UPS	30
Doors	147	$100-$250	EE	Emery Worldwide	40
Paint	123	$251-$350	FF	DHL	50
Cupboards	315	$351-$450	GG	Federal Express	60
Tiles	619	$451-$550	HH	Airborne Express	70
Sofa	972	$551-$650	II	Standard Mail	80
Table and chairs	146	$651-$750	JJ	Customer Walk-In	90

1. An order of doors arrived that cost $515.60. If the order is shipped via Federal Express, it would be coded?

   A – 619-II-50
   B – 147-DD-90
   C – 147-HH-60
   D – 146-HH-70

Answer

2. The code 972-II-70 is CORRECT for an order of?

   A – Sofa costing $275.50 and shipped via standard mail
   B – Tiles costing $558.99 and shipped via airborne mail
   C – Sofa costing $558.99 and shipped via airborne mail
   D – Cupboards costing $485.75 and shipped via federal express

Answer

DATA INTERPRETATION TESTS

3. What would be the code for an order of tiles that cost $325.60 and shipped by standard mail?

   A – 619-FF-80
   B – 315-GG-50
   C – 315-FF - 80
   D – 146-DD-30

   Answer [ ]

4. An order of doors costing $351.50 shipped via UPS was coded 315-DD-60 in error. Of the following, which is the CORRECT code for this order?

   A – 146-GG-30
   B – 147-GG-30
   C – 972-EE-70
   D – 619-JJ-80

   Answer [ ]

5. An order of windows costing $720.90 was sold to a customer who requested it to be delivered by federal express. What is the CORRECT code for this transaction?

   A – 368-EE-50
   B – 147-JJ-80
   C – 368-JJ-60
   D – 147-HH-60

   Answer [ ]

Q3.

Determine the correct code using the table provided. Orders are coded as follows: ORDER – COST – SHIPPING METHOD.

ORDER	CODE	COST	CODE	SHIPPING METHOD	CODE
iPhone	213	Less than $100	PP	UPS	30
42" Plasma TV	149	$100-$150	QQ	Emery Worldwide	40
Laptop	379	$151-$250	RR	DHL	50
Computer	415	$251-$350	SS	Federal Express	60
Kindle	621	$351-$450	TT	Airborne Express	70
Headphones	472	$451-$550	UU	Standard Mail	80
iPod	781	$551-$650	VV	Customer Walk-In	90

1. An order for a computer costing $490 was sold to a walk-in customer. What is the CORRECT code for this transaction?

   A – 379-UU-80
   B – 415-UU-90
   C – 149-TT-70
   D – 149-SS-50

   Answer [ ]

2. An order of kindles arrived that cost $621.30. If the order is shipped via standard mail, it would be coded?

   A – 621-VV-80
   B – 415-VV-30
   C – 213-VV-80
   D – 415-TT-50

   Answer [ ]

DATA INTERPRETATION TESTS

3. An order of laptops costing $375.85 was sold to a customer who requested it to be delivered by airborne express. What is the CORRECT code for this transaction?

   A – 621-TT-70
   B – 379-TT-70
   C – 149-SS-30
   D – 213-QQ-60

Answer [ ]

4. The code 149-TT-80 is CORRECT for an order of?

   A – Kindle costing $315.99 and shipped via Emery Worldwide
   B – IPhone costing $215.50 and sold to a walk-in customer
   C – 42" Plasma TV costing $415.50 and shipped via standard mail
   D – 42" Plasma TV costing $275.95 and shipped via airborne express

Answer [ ]

5. What would be the code for an order of iPods that cost less than $100 and shipped by standard mail?

   A – 213-VV-30
   B – 781-TT-60
   C – 213-PP-80
   D – 781-PP-80

Answer [ ]

PART 5   141

Q4.

Determine the correct code using the table provided. Orders are coded as follows:
ORDER – COST – SHIPPING METHOD.

ORDER	CODE	COST	CODE	SHIPPING METHOD	CODE
Carpet	419	Less than $100	PP	UPS	30
Tiles	245	$100-$150	QQ	Emery Worldwide	40
Rug	195	$151-$250	RR	DHL	50
Wood flooring	174	$251-$350	SS	Federal Express	60
Laminated flooring	185	$351-$450	TT	Airborne Express	70
Underlay	375	$451-$550	UU	Standard Mail	80
Gripper rods	372	$551-$650	VV	Customer Walk-In	90

1. An order of laminated flooring costing $215.95 was sold to a customer who requested it to be delivered by airborne express. They have also ordered a rug costing $124.50 to be delivered at the same time. What is the CORRECT codes for this transaction?

   A – 185-RR-70 and 419-QQ-70

   B – 185-RR-70 and 195-QQ-70

   C – 375-TT-60 and 372-PP-60

   D – 419-RR-70 and 195-RR-70

Answer

2. An order of tiles arrived that cost $451. If the order is shipped via Emery Worldwide it would be coded?

   A – 245-UU-40

   B – 245-SS-40

   C – 419-VV-30

   D – 372-QQ-60

Answer

DATA INTERPRETATION TESTS

3. What would be the code for an order of carpet that cost $281.50 and shipped via federal express?

A – 419-SS-60

B – 245-TT-30

C – 245-VV-70

D – 372-RR-80

Answer [   ]

4. The code 174-RR-50 is CORRECT for an order of?

A – Laminated flooring costing $215.75 and shipped via DHL

B – Tiles costing $375 and shipped via DHL

C – Wood flooring costing $215.75 and shipped via DHL

D – Gripper rods costing $105 and shipped via airborne express

Answer [   ]

5. An order of wood flooring costing $195.95 shipped via UPS was coded 185-RR-50 in error. Of the following, which is the CORRECT code for this order?

A – 195-SS-30

B – 174-RR-30

C – 245-SS-50

D – 195-VV-40

Answer [   ]

Q5.

Determine the correct code using the table provided. Orders are coded as follows:
ORDER – COST – SHIPPING METHOD.

ORDER	CODE	COST	CODE	SHIPPING METHOD	CODE
Loft Insulation	629	Less than £100	PP	UPS	20
Roof felt	518	£100-£150	QQ	Emery Worldwide	30
Plasterboard	475	£151-£250	RR	DHL	40
Roof shingles	691	£251-£350	SS	Federal Express	50
Vinyl flooring	895	£351-£450	TT	Airborne Express	60
Spotlights	965	£451-£550	UU	Standard Mail	70
Air Vents	872	£551-£650	VV	Customer Walk-In	80

1. What would be the code for an order of vinyl flooring that costs £265.50 and shipped via DHL?

   A – 518-QQ-20
   B – 629-PP-60
   C – 965-SS-40
   D – 895-SS-40

   Answer ☐

2. An order of air vents costing £595.85 shipped via Emery Worldwide was coded 475-UU-50 in error. Of the following, which is the CORRECT code for this order?

   A – 895-QQ-50
   B – 629-UU-20
   C – 872-VV-30
   D – 691-TT-60

   Answer ☐

DATA INTERPRETATION TESTS

3. The code 629-TT-50 is CORRECT for an order of?

    A – Loft insulation costing £385 and shipped via federal express
    B – Plasterboard costing $415 and shipped via DHL
    C – Loft insulation costing £195 and shipped via UPS
    D – Roof felt costing £297.76 and shipped via Emery Worldwide

Answer [ ]

4. An order of plasterboard arrived that cost £121.85. If the order is shipped via DHL it would be coded?

    A – 872-SS-20
    B – 475-QQ-40
    C – 475-PP-20
    D – 872-UU-60

Answer [ ]

5. An order for a roof felt costing £286.75 was sold to a walk-in customer. What is the CORRECT code for this transaction?

    A – 475-TT-60
    B – 518-SS-80
    C – 518-QQ-40
    D – 475-UU-30

Answer [ ]

PART 5

Q6.

Determine the correct code using the table provided. Orders are coded as follows: ORDER – COST – SHIPPING METHOD.

ORDER	CODE	COST	CODE	SHIPPING METHOD	CODE
Paddling pool	134	Less than £50	PP	UPS	20
Trampoline	971	£50-£100	QQ	Emery Worldwide	30
Kids swing set	375	£101-£150	RR	DHL	40
Kids kitchen set	386	£151-£200	SS	Federal Express	50
Doll house	741	£201-£250	TT	Airborne Express	60
Outdoor playhouse	591	£251-£300	UU	Standard Mail	70
Beanie chair set	370	£301-£350	VV	Customer Walk-In	80

1. The code 971-RR-80 is CORRECT for an order of?

    A – Kids swing set costing £312 and shipped via standard mail
    B – Paddling pool costing £58 and shipped via UPS
    C – Trampoline costing £108 and sold to a walk-in customer
    D – Kids swing set costing £128 and sold to a walk-in customer

Answer [ ]

2. An order of beanie chairs costing £80.90 shipped via standard mail was coded 370-UU-20 in error. Of the following, which is the CORRECT code for this order?

    A – 134-QQ-70
    B – 370-QQ-70
    C – 134-TT-40
    D – 386-RR-50

Answer [ ]

3. An order for a doll house costing £105.80 was sold to a walk-in customer. What is the CORRECT code for this transaction?

   A – 741-RR-80
   B – 971-RR-70
   C – 971-RR-80
   D – 741-SS-50

   Answer [   ]

4. An order for an outdoor playhouse arrived that cost £328.75. If the order is shipped via Emery Worldwide it would be coded?

   A – 134-SS-40
   B – 591-VV-30
   C – 386-VV-30
   D – 375-TT-40

   Answer [   ]

5. What would be the code for an order of paddling pools that costs £145.50 and shipped via UPS?

   A – 386-QQ-50
   B – 971-SS-20
   C – 134-RR-20
   D – 134-TT-20

   Answer [   ]

Q7.

Determine the correct code using the table provided. Orders are coded as follows:
ORDER – COST – SHIPPING METHOD.

ORDER	CODE	COST	CODE	SHIPPING METHOD	CODE
4 person tent	585	Less than £50	PP	UPS	20
Gas bottle	431	£50-£100	QQ	Emery Worldwide	30
Hiking boots	138	£101-£150	RR	DHL	40
Winter thermal jacket	761	£151-£200	SS	Federal Express	50
Winter thermal trousers	439	£201-£250	TT	Airborne Express	60
Rucksack	963	£251-£300	UU	Standard Mail	70
Cooking set	694	£301-£350	VV	Customer Walk-In	80

1. An order for winter thermal jackets costing £216.80 was sold and is shipped via Emery Worldwide. What is the CORRECT code for this transaction?

    A – 761-TT-30

    B – 431-SS-40

    C – 138-UU-80

    D – 431-VV-60

Answer [ ]

2. An order of gas bottles costing £110.20 shipped via DHL was coded 138-RR-50 in error. Of the following, which is the CORRECT code for this order?

    A – 963-RR-20

    B – 585-RR-40

    C – 431-RR-40

    D – 694-RR-40

Answer [ ]

DATA INTERPRETATION TESTS

3. The code 694-QQ-50 is CORRECT for an order of?

    A – Cooking set costing £215.50 and shipped via federal express

    B – Cooking set costing £150.50 and shipped via federal express.

    C – Rucksack costing £105.80 and shipped via federal express

    D – Cooking set costing £80.85 and shipped via federal express

    Answer [ ]

4. What would be the code for an order of hiking boots that costs £90.99 and shipped via airborne express?

    A – 138-QQ-60

    B – 138-TT-20

    C –138-RR-40

    D – 138-QQ-20

    Answer [ ]

5. An order for a 4 person tent arrived that cost £212.50. If the order is shipped via standard mail it would be coded?

    A – 431-VV-20

    B – 431-TT-70

    C – 585-TT-70

    D –585-UU-70

    Answer [ ]

PART 5

Q8.

Determine the correct code using the table provided. Orders are coded as follows: ORDER – COST – SHIPPING METHOD.

ORDER	CODE	COST	CODE	SHIPPING METHOD	CODE
Microwave	623	Less than £50	DD	UPS	20
Washing machine	125	£50-£150	EE	Emery Worldwide	30
Tumble dryer	425	£151-£250	FF	DHL	40
Dishwasher	921	£251-£350	GG	Federal Express	50
Fridge	428	£351-£450	HH	Airborne Express	60
Freezer	429	£451-£550	II	Standard Mail	70
Dining table and chairs	550	Greater than £551	JJ	Customer Walk-In	80

1. An order for a washing machine arrived that cost £258.89. If the order is shipped via federal express it would be coded?

A – 125-EE-20

B – 125-GG-50

C – 921-GG-50

D – 550-JJ-60

Answer [   ]

2. The code 921-HH-60 is CORRECT for an order of?

A – Dishwasher costing £250 and shipped via DHL

B – Dishwasher costing £120.50 and shipped via federal express

C – Tumble dryer costing £260 and shipped via airborne express

D – Dishwasher costing £355 and shipped via airborne express

Answer [   ]

3. An order of freezers costing £120.20 shipped via Emery Worldwide was coded 428-FF-30 in error. Of the following, which is the CORRECT code for this order?

A – 428-EE-30

B – 429-EE-30

C – 623-DD-50

D – 623-FF-70

Answer

4. An order for a dining table and chairs costing £450.80 was sold and is shipped via UPS. What is the CORRECT code for this transaction?

A – 550-DD-20

B – 550-HH-20

C – 550-II-40

D – 550-HH-70

Answer

5. What would be the code for an order of microwaves that costs £49.99 and sold to a walk-in customer?

A – 623-EE-70

B – 125-DD-80

C – 623-DD-80

D – 125-EE-50

Answer

PART 5   151

Q9.

Determine the correct code using the table provided. Orders are coded as follows:
ORDER – COST – SHIPPING METHOD.

ORDER	CODE	COST	CODE	SHIPPING METHOD	CODE
Hammers	471	Less than £50	DD	UPS	20
Drills	950	£50-£150	EE	Emery Worldwide	30
Screwdrivers	139	£151-£250	FF	DHL	40
Chainsaw	456	£251-£350	GG	Federal Express	50
Steel toe boots	795	£351-£450	HH	Airborne Express	60
Glass	366	£451-£550	II	Standard Mail	70
Wood	467	Greater than £551	JJ	Customer Walk-In	80

1. An order of steel toe boots costing £85.50 shipped via standard mail was coded 795-II-40 in error. Of the following, which is the CORRECT code for this order?

   A – 795-EE-70
   B – 950-EE-50
   C – 950-DD-80
   D – 795-GG-20

   Answer

2. An order for a chainsaw arrived that cost £168.50. If the order is shipped via airborne express it would be coded?

   A – 456-DD-20
   B – 456-FF-60
   C – 456-II-80
   D –456-FF-70

   Answer

DATA INTERPRETATION TESTS

3. What would be the code for an order of wood that costs £210.90 and shipped via UPS?

A – 795-II-80

B – 369-DD-30

C – 467-FF-20

D – 471-JJ-60

Answer [ ]

4. An order for glass costing £110.60 was sold and is shipped via standard mail. What is the CORRECT code for this transaction?

A – 366-JJ-20

B – 471-GG-60

C – 366-EE-70

D – 366-FF-70

Answer [ ]

5. The code 950-DD-80 is CORRECT for an order of?

A – Drills costing £39.99 and sold to a walk-in customer

B – Hammers costing £39.99 and sold a walk-in customer

C – Screwdrivers costing £39.99 and shipped via federal express

D – Screwdrivers costing £59.99 and shipped via airborne express

Answer [ ]

PART 5

Q10.

Determine the correct code using the table provided. Orders are coded as follows: ORDER – COST – SHIPPING METHOD.

ORDER	CODE	COST	CODE	SHIPPING METHOD	CODE
Telephone	454	Less than £50	PP	UPS	20
Clock	136	£50-£150	QQ	Emery Worldwide	30
Book case	746	£151-£250	RR	DHL	40
Lawnmower	339	£251-£350	SS	Federal Express	50
Shed	387	£351-£450	TT	Airborne Express	60
Necklace	002	£451-£550	UU	Standard Mail	70
Trainers	103	Greater than £551	VV	Customer Walk-In	80

1. What would be the code for an order for a book case that costs £80.99 and shipped via Emery Worldwide?

   A – 746-VV-50

   B – 746-QQ-80

   C – 746-TT-20

   D – 746-QQ-30

   Answer [ ]

2. An order for a shed arrived that cost £189.80. If the order is shipped via federal express it would be coded?

   A – 746-SS-20

   B – 387-RR-50

   C – 002-UU-60

   D – 136-VV-20

   Answer [ ]

DATA INTERPRETATION TESTS

3. An order for a clock costing £110.75 shipped via standard mail was coded 136-TT-40 in error. Of the following, which is the CORRECT code for this order?

   A – 136-QQ-70

   B – 136-RR-80

   C – 136-TT-60

   D –136-QQ-20

   Answer

4. The code 002-PP-80 is CORRECT for an order of?

   A – Trainers costing £79.99 and shipped via UPS

   B – Necklace costing £150 and sold to a walk-in customer

   C – Necklace costing £49.99 and sold to a walk-in customer

   D – Trainers costing £39.99 and shipped via Emery Worldwide

   Answer

5. An order for trainers costing £75 was sold and is shipped via standard mail. What is the CORRECT code for this transaction?

   A – 103-SS-70

   B – 103-QQ-70

   C – 103-UU-20

   D – 103-UU-80

   Answer

Q11.

Determine the correct code using the table provided. Orders are coded as follows:
ORDER – COST – SHIPPING METHOD.

ORDER	CODE	COST	CODE	SHIPPING METHOD	CODE
Nails	789	Less than $100	RR	UPS	20
Hammer	654	$100-$250	SS	Emery Worldwide	30
Paint	123	$251-$350	TT	DHL	40
Saw	912	$351-$450	UU	Federal Express	50
Wood	829	$451-$550	VV	Airborne Express	60
Chainsaw	296	$551-$650	WW	Standard Mail	70
Super glue	328	$651-$750	XX	Customer Walk-In	80

1. What would be the code for an order of wood that cost $120.75 and shipped by standard mail?

   A – 789-TT-70

   B – 829-TT-70

   C – 829-SS-70

   D – 123-SS-80

Answer

2. The code 654-RR-70 is CORRECT for an order of?

   A – Hammer costing $85.85 and shipped via standard mail

   B – Chainsaw costing $375.50 and shipped via federal express

   C – Hammer costing $185.85 and shipped via standard mail

   D – Paint costing $375.25 and shipped via airborne mail

Answer

DATA INTERPRETATION TESTS

3. An order of nails arrived that cost $125.50. If the order is shipped via DHL, it would be coded?

A – 789-SS-40
B – 654-TT-40
C – 789-UU-40
D – 789-TT-50

Answer [ ]

4. An order of super glue costing $38.50 shipped via Emery Worldwide was coded 328-TT-30 in error. Of the following, which is the CORRECT code for this order?

A – 328-WW-30
B – 328-RR-30
C – 328-XX-50
D – 328-VV-40

Answer [ ]

5. An order of paint costing $95.75 was sold to a walk-in customer. What is the CORRECT code for this transaction?

A – 296-RR-20
B – 123-RR-50
C – 328-SS-70
D – 123-RR-80

Answer [ ]

Q12.

Determine the correct code using the table provided. Orders are coded as follows: ORDER – COST – SHIPPING METHOD.

ORDER	CODE	COST	CODE	SHIPPING METHOD	CODE
Single bed	368	Less than $100	DD	UPS	30
Tiles	147	$100-$250	EE	Emery Worldwide	40
Paint	123	$251-$350	FF	DHL	50
Wardrobe	315	$351-$450	GG	Federal Express	60
Curtains	619	$451-$550	HH	Airborne Express	70
Duvet set	972	$551-$650	II	Standard Mail	80
King size bed	146	$651-$750	JJ	Customer Walk-In	90

1. An order of wardrobes arrived that cost $515.60. If the order is shipped via Federal Express, it would be coded?

    A – 315-II-50

    B – 147-DD-90

    C – 315-HH-60

    D – 146-HH-70

Answer [   ]

2. The code 972-DD-70 is CORRECT for an order of?

    A – Duvet set costing $45 and shipped via standard mail

    B – Tiles costing $558.99 and shipped via airborne mail

    C – Duvet set costing $45 and shipped via airborne mail

    D – Duvet set costing $120 and shipped via airborne mail

Answer [   ]

DATA INTERPRETATION TESTS

3. What would be the code for an order of curtains that cost $70.50 and shipped by standard mail?

A – 619-DD-80

B – 315-GG-50

C – 315-FF - 80

D – 146-DD-30

Answer [ ]

4. An order of tiles costing $351.50 shipped via UPS was coded 315-DD-60 in error. Of the following, which is the CORRECT code for this order?

A – 146-GG-30

B – 147-GG-30

C – 972-EE-70

D – 619-JJ-80

Answer [ ]

5. An order for a single bed costing $120.90 was sold to a customer who requested it to be delivered by federal express. What is the CORRECT code for this transaction?

A – 368-EE-50

B – 147-JJ-80

C – 368-EE-60

D – 147-HH-60

Answer [ ]

Q13.

Determine the correct code using the table provided. Orders are coded as follows:
ORDER – COST – SHIPPING METHOD.

ORDER	CODE	COST	CODE	SHIPPING METHOD	CODE
Sofa	419	Less than $100	PP	UPS	30
Cooker	245	$100-$150	QQ	Emery Worldwide	40
Kettle	195	$151-$250	RR	DHL	50
Laminated flooring	174	$251-$350	SS	Federal Express	60
Spa bath	185	$351-$450	TT	Airborne Express	70
Walk in wardrobe	375	$451-$550	UU	Standard Mail	80
Dressing table	372	$551-$650	VV	Customer Walk-In	90

1. An order for a dressing table costing $215.95 was sold to a customer who requested it to be delivered by airborne express. What is the CORRECT codes for this transaction?

   A – 185-RR-70
   B – 372-RR-70
   C – 372-TT-60
   D – 419-RR-70

   Answer [ ]

2. An order for a sofa arrived that cost $451. If the order is shipped via Emery Worldwide it would be coded?

   A – 419-UU-40
   B – 245-SS-40
   C – 419-VV-30
   D – 372-QQ-60

   Answer [ ]

DATA INTERPRETATION TESTS

3. What would be the code for an order for a spa bath that cost $620.99 and shipped via federal express?

A – 185-VV-60

B – 245-TT-30

C – 245-VV-70

D – 372-RR-80

Answer [ ]

4. The code 245-RR-50 is CORRECT for an order of??

A – Laminated flooring costing $215.75 and shipped via DHL

B – Cooker costing $375 and shipped via DHL

C – Cooker costing $215.75 and shipped via DHL

D – Cooker costing $105 and shipped via airborne express

Answer [ ]

5. An order of laminated flooring costing $195.95 shipped via UPS was coded 185-RR-50 in error. Of the following, which is the CORRECT code for this order?

A – 195-SS-30

B – 174-RR-30

C – 245-SS-50

D – 195-VV-40

Answer [ ]

PART 5

Q14.

Determine the correct code using the table provided. Orders are coded as follows:
ORDER – COST – SHIPPING METHOD.

ORDER	CODE	COST	CODE	SHIPPING METHOD	CODE
Loft Insulation	629	Less than £100	PP	UPS	20
Wallpaper	518	£100–£150	QQ	Emery Worldwide	30
Carpet	475	£151–£250	RR	DHL	40
Sliding doors	691	£251–£350	SS	Federal Express	50
Built-in unit	895	£351–£450	TT	Airborne Express	60
Air-con	965	£451–£550	UU	Standard Mail	70
Skirting	872	£551–£650	VV	Customer Walk-In	80

1. What would be the code for an order for a built in unit that costs £265.50 and shipped via DHL?

A – 518-QQ-20

B – 629-PP-60

C – 965-SS-40

D – 895-SS-40

Answer [ ]

2. An order of air con costing £595.85 shipped via UPS was coded 475-UU-50 in error. Of the following, which is the CORRECT code for this order?

A – 965-QQ-50

B – 629-UU-20

C – 965-VV-20

D – 965-TT-60

Answer [ ]

3. The code 518-TT-30 is CORRECT for an order of?

    A – Wallpaper costing £385 and shipped via Emery Worldwide
    B – Plasterboard costing $415 and shipped via DHL
    C – Loft insulation costing £195 and shipped via UPS
    D – Roof felt costing £297.76 and shipped via Emery Worldwide

    Answer [   ]

4. An order of skirting arrived that cost £121.85. If the order is shipped via DHL it would be coded?

    A – 872-SS-20
    B – 872-QQ-40
    C – 475-PP-20
    D – 872-UU-60

    Answer [   ]

5. An order for sliding doors costing £515.50 was sold to a walk-in customer. What is the CORRECT code for this transaction?

    A – 691-TT-60
    B – 691-UU-80
    C – 518-QQ-40
    D – 475-UU-30

    Answer [   ]

PART 5

Q15.

Determine the correct code using the table provided. Orders are coded as follows: ORDER – COST – SHIPPING METHOD.

ORDER	CODE	COST	CODE	SHIPPING METHOD	CODE
Sleeping bag	134	Less than £50	PP	UPS	20
Scooter	971	£50-£100	QQ	Emery Worldwide	30
Kids swing set	375	£101-£150	RR	DHL	40
Bike	386	£151-£200	SS	Federal Express	50
Go-cart	741	£201-£250	TT	Airborne Express	60
Outdoor playhouse	591	£251-£300	UU	Standard Mail	70
Tent	370	£301-£350	VV	Customer Walk-In	80

1. The code 386-RR-70 is CORRECT for an order of?

    A – Kids swing set costing £312 and shipped via standard mail
    B – Sleeping bag costing £58 and shipped via UPS
    C – Bike costing £108 and shipped via standard mail
    D – Kids swing set costing £128 and sold to a walk-in customer

Answer [ ]

2. An order for a go-cart costing £220.75 shipped via standard mail was coded 370-UU-20 in error. Of the following, which is the CORRECT code for this order?

    A – 134-QQ-70
    B – 741-TT-70
    C – 134-TT-40
    D – 741-RR-50

Answer [ ]

DATA INTERPRETATION TESTS

3. An order for sleeping bags costing £65.85 was sold to a walk-in customer. What is the CORRECT code for this transaction?

   A – 134-QQ-80
   B – 971-RR-70
   C – 971-RR-80
   D – 741-SS-50

   Answer [ ]

4. An order for an outdoor playhouse arrived that cost £210.50. If the order is shipped via UPS it would be coded?

   A – 134-SS-40
   B – 591-TT-20
   C – 386-VV-30
   D – 375-TT-40

   Answer [ ]

5. What would be the code for an order of bikes that costs £145.50 and shipped via airborne express?

   A – 386-QQ-50
   B – 971-SS-20
   C – 386-RR-60
   D – 134-TT-20

   Answer [ ]

PART 5

Q16.

Determine the correct code using the table provided. Orders are coded as follows: ORDER – COST – SHIPPING METHOD.

ORDER	CODE	COST	CODE	SHIPPING METHOD	CODE
Pram	621	Less than £50	PP	UPS	20
Cot	456	£50-£100	QQ	Emery Worldwide	30
Moses basket	103	£101-£150	RR	DHL	40
Car seat	008	£151-£200	SS	Federal Express	50
Bouncer	010	£201-£250	TT	Airborne Express	60
Bottles	364	£251-£300	UU	Standard Mail	70
Thermometers	965	£301-£350	VV	Customer Walk-In	80

1. An order for a set of bottles costing £35.60 was sold to a walk-in customer. What is the CORRECT code for this transaction?

    A – 621-PP-20

    B – 364-PP-80

    C – 965-SS-50

    D – 965-TT-60

Answer [ ]

2. What would be the code for an order for a pram that costs £215.50 and shipped via Emery Worldwide?

    A – 621-TT-30

    B – 621-QQ-50

    C – 621-UU-30

    D – 621-VV-70

Answer [ ]

3. An order for a bouncer arrived that cost £95.75. If the order is shipped via UPS it would be coded?

   A – 008-QQ-20
   B – 965-RR-40
   C – 010-QQ-20
   D – 456-TT-30

   Answer [ ]

4. An order for a car seat costing £105.75 shipped via DHL was coded 456-TT-50 in error. Of the following, which is the CORRECT code for this order?

   A – 010-RR-40
   B – 008-RR-40
   C – 103-RR-60
   D – 621-TT-70

   Answer [ ]

5. The code 103-SS-50 is CORRECT for an order of?

   A – Moses basket costing £210.50 and shipped via Emery Worldwide
   B – Moses basket costing £165.99 and shipped via federal express
   C – Moses basket costing £165.99 and sold to a walk-in customer
   D – Moses basket costing £60.99 and shipped via federal express

   Answer [ ]

Q17.

Determine the correct code using the table provided. Orders are coded as follows:
ORDER – COST – SHIPPING METHOD.

ORDER	CODE	COST	CODE	SHIPPING METHOD	CODE
Chair	621	Less than £50	PP	UPS	20
Table	456	£50-£100	QQ	Emery Worldwide	30
Over the bed wardrobes	103	£101-£150	RR	DHL	40
Lawnmower	008	£151-£200	SS	Federal Express	50
Toaster	010	£201-£250	TT	Airborne Express	60
Fridge/Freezer	364	£251-£300	UU	Standard Mail	70
Corner sofa	965	£301-£350	VV	Customer Walk-In	80

1. An order for a table costing £75.75 shipped via airborne express was coded 456-SS-70 in error. Of the following, which is the CORRECT code for this order?

   A – 456-PP-80

   B – 456-SS-20

   C – 456-TT-40

   D – 456-QQ-60

Answer [ ]

2. An order for a lawnmower costing £105.85 was shipped via DHL. What is the CORRECT code for this transaction?

   A – 621-RR-20

   B – 010-RR-40

   C – 008-RR-40

   D – 364-SS-60

Answer [ ]

DATA INTERPRETATION TESTS

3. What would be the code for an order for a corner sofa that costs £325.75 and shipped via UPS?

   A – 965-VV-20
   B – 456-SS-30
   C – 456-RR-20
   D – 965-QQ-60

   Answer [ ]

4. The code 103-UU-70 is CORRECT for an order of?

   A – Over the bed wardrobes costing £290 and shipped via Emery Worldwide
   B – Over the bed wardrobes costing £290 and shipped via standard mail
   C – Fridge/Freezer costing £290 and shipped via standard mail
   D – Over the bed wardrobes costing £350.99 and shipped via standard mail

   Answer [ ]

5. An order for a chair arrived that cost £65.40. If the order is shipped via DHL it would be coded?

   A – 364-UU-20
   B – 364-RR-30
   C – 621-QQ-40
   D – 364-RR-80

   Answer [ ]

PART 5

Q18.

Determine the correct code using the table provided. Orders are coded as follows:
ORDER – COST – SHIPPING METHOD.

ORDER	CODE	COST	CODE	SHIPPING METHOD	CODE
Tyres	615	Less than $100	RR	UPS	20
Laptop	149	$100-$250	SS	Emery Worldwide	30
Mountain bike	582	$251-$350	TT	DHL	40
Rowing boat	786	$351-$450	UU	Federal Express	50
Life jackets	520	$451-$550	VV	Airborne Express	60
Play station	008	$551-$650	WW	Standard Mail	70
3D TV	097	$651-$750	XX	Customer Walk-In	80

1. An order for a laptop costing $385.85 was shipped via standard mail. What is the CORRECT code for this transaction?

A – 19-WW-80

B – 149-RR-30

C – 149-TT-60

D – 149-UU-70

Answer [ ]

2. An order for tyres costing $103.75 shipped via federal express was coded 615-WW-80 in error. Of the following, which is the CORRECT code for this order?

A – 615-SS-50

B – 149-RR-60

C – 520-VV-80

D – 097-WW-30

Answer [ ]

170 DATA INTERPRETATION TESTS

3. An order for a mountain bike arrived that cost $189. If the order is shipped via Emery Worldwide it would be coded?

A – 582-SS-30

B – 582-WW-20

C – 585-UU-40

D – 585-SS-70

Answer [ ]

4. The code 008-TT-80 is CORRECT for an order of?

A – Play station costing $125 and shipped via DHL

B – Play station costing $255 and sold to a walk-in customer

C – Mountain bike costing $218 and shipped via DHL

D – Mountain bike costing $175 and sold to a walk-in customer

Answer [ ]

5. What would be the code for an order for a 3D TV that costs $495 and shipped via airborne express?

A – 097-TT-30

B – 097-WW-40

C – 097-VV-60

D – 097-XX-20

Answer [ ]

PART 5 171

Q19.

Determine the correct code using the table provided. Orders are coded as follows: ORDER – COST – SHIPPING METHOD.

ORDER	CODE	COST	CODE	SHIPPING METHOD	CODE
Golf clubs	472	Less than $100	RR	UPS	20
Golf bag	409	$100-$250	SS	Emery Worldwide	30
Fishing rod	743	$251-$350	TT	DHL	40
Gas bottle	432	$351-$450	UU	Federal Express	50
Recliner chair	637	$451-$550	VV	Airborne Express	60
Chest of drawers	239	$551-$650	WW	Standard Mail	70
Booster seat	609	$651-$750	XX	Customer Walk-In	80

1. An order for golf clubs costing $175.95 shipped via UPS was coded 432-TT-50 in error. Of the following, which is the CORRECT code for this order?

   A – 472-VV-50
   B – 472-WW-80
   C – 472-SS-20
   D – 472-TT-40

   Answer [ ]

2. An order for a fishing rod arrived that cost $212.50. If the order is shipped via Emery Worldwide it would be coded?

   A – 409-SS-50
   B – 743-VV-70
   C – 637-RR-80
   D – 743-SS-30

   Answer [ ]

DATA INTERPRETATION TESTS

3. An order for a booster seat costing $35.85 was shipped via standard mail. What is the CORRECT code for this transaction?

A – 609-TT-60

B – 609-RR-70

C – 743-VV-20

D – 239-TT-30

Answer

4. What would be the code for an order for a recliner chair that costs $420 and shipped via federal express?

A – 743-TT-80

B – 637-UU-50

C – 609-VV-40

D – 239-XX-70

Answer

5. The code 409-SS-30 is CORRECT for an order of?

A – Golf bag costing $345 and shipped via Emery Worldwide

B – Golf clubs costing $130.75 and shipped via Emery Worldwide

C – Golf bag costing $130.75 and shipped via Emery Worldwide

D – Golf clubs costing $59.99 and shipped via federal express

Answer

PART 5

Q20.

Determine the correct code using the table provided. Orders are coded as follows: ORDER – COST – SHIPPING METHOD.

ORDER	CODE	COST	CODE	SHIPPING METHOD	CODE
Bricks	863	Less than $100	PP	UPS	20
Fence panels	139	$100-$250	QQ	Emery Worldwide	30
Garden tool set	723	$251-$350	RR	DHL	40
Windows	438	$351-$450	SS	Federal Express	50
Glass	698	$451-$550	TT	Airborne Express	60
Wood	009	$551-$650	UU	Standard Mail	70
Carpet	073	$651-$750	VV	Customer Walk-In	80

1. What would be the code for an order for a garden tool set that costs $125.50 and shipped via standard mail?

A – 723-VV-80

B – 723-RR-30

C – 723-TT-30

D – 723-QQ-70

Answer [ ]

2. An order for glass costing $375.95 was shipped via Emery Worldwide. What is the CORRECT code for this transaction?

A – 139-QQ-40

B – 698-SS-30

C – 073-TT-50

D – 723-PP-40

Answer [ ]

3. An order for fence panels arrived that cost $475.25. If the order is sold to a walk-in customer it would be coded?

   A – 139-PP-40
   B – 139-RR-50
   C – 139-TT-80
   D – 139-VV-70

   Answer [ ]

4. The code 863-UU-40 is CORRECT for an order of?

   A – Bricks costing $125.50 and shipped via Emery Worldwide
   B – Wood costing $635 and shipped via DHL
   C – Bricks costing $635 and shipped via DHL
   D – Wood costing $125.50 and shipped via Emery Worldwide

   Answer [ ]

5. An order for windows costing $215.85 shipped via airborne express was coded 698-RR-50 in error. Of the following, which is the CORRECT code for this order?

   A – 863-VV-20
   B – 438-QQ-60
   C – 698-TT-80
   D – 139-RR-50

   Answer [ ]

Now check your answers carefully before moving on to the next section of the guide.

DATA INTERPRETATIONS PART 5 ANSWERS

QUESTION 1

1. C

EXPLANATION = the correct answer is C. The code for paint (123) costing $120.75 (SS) and shipped by standard mail (70).

2. A

EXPLANATION = the correct answer is A. The code 829-UU-50 is correct for wood (829) costing $375.50 (UU) and shipped via federal express (50).

3. A

EXPLANATION = the correct answer is A. The entry would be coded as 654 (screws), SS (costing $125.50) and 40 (shipped via DHL).

4. B

EXPLANATION = the correct answer is B. The order should have been coded as 912 (saws), VV (costing $514.25), 30 (shipped via Emery Worldwide).

5. D

EXPLANATION = the correct answer is D. The most appropriate code for the transaction would be 328 (clocks), TT (costing $325) 80 (via customer walk-in).

QUESTION 2

1. C

EXPLANATION = the correct answer is C. The entry would be coded as 147 (doors), HH (costing $515.60) and 60 (shipped via Federal Express).

2. C

EXPLANATION = the correct answer is C. The code 972-II-70 is correct for sofa (972) costing $558.99 (II) and shipped via airborne express (70).

3. A

EXPLANATION = the correct answer is A. The code for tiles (619) costing $325.60 (FF) and shipped by standard mail (80).

4. B

EXPLANATION = the correct answer is B. The order should have been coded as 147 (doors), GG (costing $351.50), 30 (shipped via UPS).

5. C

EXPLANATION = the correct answer is C. The most appropriate code for the transaction would be 368 (windows), JJ (costing $720.90), 60 (via federal express).

QUESTION 3

1. B

EXPLANATION = the correct answer is B. The most appropriate code for the transaction would be 415 (computer), UU (costing $490), 90 (via customer walk-in).

2. A

EXPLANATION = the correct answer is A. The entry would be coded as 621 (kindles), VV (costing $621.30) and 80 (shipped via standard mail).

3. B

EXPLANATION = the correct answer is B. The most appropriate code for the transaction would be 379 (laptops), TT (costing $375.85), 70 (via airborne express).

4. C

EXPLANATION = the correct answer is C. The code 149-TT-80 is correct for 42" Plasma TV (149) costing $415.50 (TT) and shipped via standard mail (80).

5. D

EXPLANATION = the correct answer is D. The code for iPods (781) costing less than $100 (PP) and shipped by standard mail (80).

QUESTION 4

1. B

EXPLANATION = the correct answer is B. The most appropriate code for the transaction would be 185 (laminate flooring), RR (costing $215.95), 70 (via airborne express). And, 195 (rug), QQ (costing $124.50), 70 (via airborne express).

2. A

EXPLANATION = the correct answer is A. The entry would be coded as 245 (tiles), UU (costing $451) and 40 (shipped via emery worldwide).

3. A

EXPLANATION = the correct answer is A. The code for carpet (419) costing $281.50 (SS) and shipped via federal express (60).

4. C

EXPLANATION = the correct answer is C. The code 174-RR-50 is correct for wood flooring (174) costing $215.75 (RR) and shipped via DHL (50).

5. B

EXPLANATION = the correct answer is B. The order should have been coded as 174 (wood flooring), RR (costing $195.95), 30 (shipped via UPS).

PART 5

QUESTION 5

1. D

EXPLANATION = the correct answer is D. The code for vinyl flooring (895) costing £265.50 (SS) and shipped via DHL (40).

2. C

EXPLANATION = the correct answer is C. The order should have been coded as 872 (air vents), VV (costing £595.85), 30 (shipped via Emery Worldwide).

3. A

EXPLANATION = the correct answer is A. The code 629-TT-50 is correct for loft insulation (629) costing £385 (TT) and shipped via federal express (50).

4. B

EXPLANATION = the correct answer is B. The entry would be coded as 475 (plasterboard), QQ (costing £121.85) and 40 (shipped via DHL).

5. B

EXPLANATION = the correct answer is B. The most appropriate code for the transaction would be 518 (roof felt), SS (costing £286.75), 80 (via customer walk-in).

QUESTION 6

1. C

EXPLANATION = the correct answer is C. The code 971-RR-80 is correct for trampoline (971) costing £108 (RR) and sold to a customer walk-in (80).

2. B

EXPLANATION = the correct answer is B. The order should have been coded as 370 (beanie chair set), QQ (costing £80.90), 70 (shipped via standard mail).

3. A

EXPLANATION = the correct answer is A. The most appropriate code for the transaction would be 741 (doll house), RR (costing £105.80), 80 (via customer walk-in).

4. B

EXPLANATION = the correct answer is B. The entry would be coded as 591 (outdoor playhouse), VV (costing £328.75) and 30 (shipped via Emery Worldwide).

5. C

EXPLANATION = the correct answer is C. The code for paddling pools (134) costing £145.50 (RR) and shipped via UPS (20).

QUESTION 7

1. A

EXPLANATION = the correct answer is A. The most appropriate code for the transaction would be 761 (winter thermal jacket), TT (costing £216.80), 30 (via Emery Worldwide).

2. C

EXPLANATION = the correct answer is C. The order should have been coded as 431 (gas bottles), RR (costing £110.20), 40 (shipped via DHL).

3. D

EXPLANATION = the correct answer is D. The code 694-QQ-50 is correct for cooking set (694) costing £80.85 (QQ) and shipped via federal express (50).

4. A

EXPLANATION = the correct answer is A. The code for hiking boots (138) costing £90.99 (QQ) and shipped via airborne express (60).

5. C

EXPLANATION = the correct answer is C. The entry would be coded as 585 (4 person tent), TT (costing £212.50) and 70 (shipped via standard mail).

QUESTION 8

1. B

EXPLANATION = the correct answer is B. The entry would be coded as 125 (washing machine), GG (costing £258.89) and 50 (shipped via federal express).

2. D

EXPLANATION = the correct answer is D. The code 921-HH-60 is correct for a dishwasher (921) costing £355 (HH) and shipped via airborne express (60).

3. B

EXPLANATION = the correct answer is B. The order should have been coded as 429 (freezers), EE (costing £120.20), 30 (shipped via Emery Worldwide).

4. B

EXPLANATION = the correct answer is B. The most appropriate code for the transaction would be 550 (dining table and chairs), HH (costing £450.80), 20 (via UPS).

5. C

EXPLANATION = the correct answer is C. The code for microwaves (623) costing £49.99 (DD) and sold to a walk-in customer (80).

PART 5   179

QUESTION 9

1. A

EXPLANATION = the correct answer is A. The order should have been coded as 795 (steel toe boots), EE (costing £85.50), 70 (shipped via standard mail).

2. B

EXPLANATION = the correct answer is B. The entry would be coded as 456 (chainsaw), FF (costing £168.50) and 60 (shipped via airborne express).

3. C

EXPLANATION = the correct answer is C. The code for wood (467) costing £210.90 (FF) and shipped via UPS (20).

4. C

EXPLANATION = the correct answer is C. The most appropriate code for the transaction would be 366 (glass), EE (costing £110.60), 70 (via standard mail).

5. A

EXPLANATION = the correct answer is A. The code 950-DD-80 is correct for drills (950) costing £39.99 (DD) and sold to a walk-in customer (80).

QUESTION 10

1. D

EXPLANATION = the correct answer is D. The code for a book case (746) costing £80.99 (QQ) and shipped via Emery Worldwide (30).

2. B

EXPLANATION = the correct answer is B. The entry would be coded as 387 (shed), RR (costing £189.80) and 50 (shipped via federal express).

3. A

EXPLANATION = the correct answer is A. The order should have been coded as 136 (clock), QQ (costing £110.75), 70 (shipped via standard mail).

4. C

EXPLANATION = the correct answer is C. The code 002-PP-80 is correct for necklace (002) costing £49.99 (PP) and sold to a walk-in customer (80).

5. B

EXPLANATION = the correct answer is B. The most appropriate code for the transaction would be 103 (trainers), QQ (costing £75), 70 (via standard mail).

QUESTION 11

1. C

EXPLANATION = the correct answer is C. The code for wood (829) costing $120.75 (SS) and shipped by standard mail (70).

2. A

EXPLANATION = the correct answer is A. The code 829-UU-50 is correct for hammer (654) costing $85.85 (RR) and shipped via standard mail (70).

3. A

EXPLANATION = the correct answer is A. The entry would be coded as 789 (nails), SS (costing $125.50) and 40 (shipped via DHL).

4. B

EXPLANATION = the correct answer is B. The order should have been coded as 328 (super glue), RR (costing $38.50), 30 (shipped via Emery Worldwide).

5. D

EXPLANATION = the correct answer is D. The most appropriate code for the transaction would be 123 (paint), RR (costing $95.75) 80 (via customer walk-in).

QUESTION 12

1. C

EXPLANATION = the correct answer is C. The entry would be coded as 315 (wardrobes), HH (costing $515.60) and 60 (shipped via Federal Express).

2. C

EXPLANATION = the correct answer is C. The code 972-II-70 is correct for duvet set (972) costing $45 (DD) and shipped via airborne express (70).

3. A

EXPLANATION = the correct answer is A. The code for curtains (619) costing $70.50 (DD) and shipped by standard mail (80).

4. B

EXPLANATION = the correct answer is B. The order should have been coded as 147 (tiles), GG (costing $351.50), 30 (shipped via UPS).

5. C

EXPLANATION = the correct answer is C. The most appropriate code for the transaction would be 368 (single bed), EE (costing $120.90), 60 (via federal express).

PART 5   181

QUESTION 13

1. B

EXPLANATION = the correct answer is B. The most appropriate code for the transaction would be 372 (dressing table), RR (costing $215.95), 70 (via airborne express).

2. A

EXPLANATION = the correct answer is A. The entry would be coded as 419 (sofa), UU (costing $451) and 40 (shipped via emery worldwide).

3. A

EXPLANATION = the correct answer is A. The code for spa bath (185) costing $620.99 (VV) and shipped via federal express (60).

4. C

EXPLANATION = the correct answer is C. The code 245-RR-50 is correct for cooker (245) costing $215.75 (RR) and shipped via DHL (50).

5. B

EXPLANATION = the correct answer is B. The order should have been coded as 174 (wood flooring), RR (costing $195.95), 30 (shipped via UPS).

QUESTION 14

1. D

EXPLANATION = the correct answer is D. The code for a built in unit (895) costing £265.50 (SS) and shipped via DHL (40).

2. C

EXPLANATION = the correct answer is C. The order should have been coded as 965 (air con), VV (costing £595.85), 20 (shipped via UPS).

3. A

EXPLANATION = the correct answer is A. The code 518-TT-30 is correct for wallpaper (518) costing £385 (TT) and shipped via Emery Worldwide (30).

4. B

EXPLANATION = the correct answer is B. The entry would be coded as 872 (skirting), QQ (costing £121.85) and 40 (shipped via DHL).

5. B

EXPLANATION = the correct answer is B. The most appropriate code for the transaction would be 691 (sliding doors), UU (costing £515.50), 80 (via customer walk-in).

QUESTION 15

1. C

EXPLANATION = the correct answer is C. The code 386-RR-70 is correct for bike (386) costing £108 (RR) and shipped via standard mail (70).

2. B

EXPLANATION = the correct answer is B. The order should have been coded as 741 (go-cart), TT (costing £220.75), 70 (shipped via standard mail).

3. A

EXPLANATION = the correct answer is A. The most appropriate code for the transaction would be 134 (sleeping bags), QQ (costing £65.85), 80 (via customer walk-in).

4. B

EXPLANATION = the correct answer is B. The entry would be coded as 591 (outdoor playhouse), TT (costing £210.50) and 20 (shipped via UPS).

5. C

EXPLANATION = the correct answer is C. The code for bikes (386) costing £145.50 (RR) and shipped via airborne express (60).

QUESTION 16

1. B

EXPLANATION = the correct answer is B. The most appropriate code for the transaction would be 364 (bottles), PP (costing £35.60), 80 (via customer walk-in).

2. A

EXPLANATION = the correct answer is A. The code for prams (621) costing £215.50 (TT) and shipped via Emery Worldwide (30).

3. C

EXPLANATION = the correct answer is C. The entry would be coded as 010 (bouncer), QQ (costing £95.75) and 20 (shipped via UPS).

4. B

EXPLANATION = the correct answer is B. The order should have been coded as 008 (car seat), RR (costing £105.75), 40 (shipped via DHL).

5. B

EXPLANATION = the correct answer is B. The code 103-SS-50 is correct for a Moses basket (103) costing £165.99 (SS) and shipped via federal express (50).

PART 5   183

QUESTION 17

1. D

EXPLANATION = the correct answer is D. The order should have been coded as 456 (table), QQ (costing £75.75), 60 (shipped via airborne express).

2. C

EXPLANATION = the correct answer is C. The most appropriate code for the transaction would be 008 (lawnmower), RR (costing £105.85), 40 (via DHL).

3. A

EXPLANATION = the correct answer is A. The code for corner sofa (965) costing £325.75 (VV) and shipped via UPS (20).

4. B

EXPLANATION = the correct answer is B. The code 103-UU-70 is correct for over the bed wardrobes (103) costing £290 (SS) and shipped via standard mail (70).

5. C

EXPLANATION = the correct answer is C. The entry would be coded as 621 (chair), QQ (costing £65.40) and 40 (shipped via DHL).

QUESTION 18

1. D

EXPLANATION = the correct answer is D. The most appropriate code for the transaction would be 149 (laptop), UU (costing $385.85), 70 (via standard mail).

2. A

EXPLANATION = the correct answer is A. The order should have been coded as 615 (tyres), SS (costing $103.75), 50 (shipped via federal express).

3. A

EXPLANATION = the correct answer is A. The entry would be coded as 582 (mountain bike), SS (costing $189) and 30 (shipped via Emery Worldwide).

4. B

EXPLANATION = the correct answer is B. The code 008-TT-80 is correct for play station (008) costing $255 (TT) and sold to a walk-in customer (80).

5. C

EXPLANATION = the correct answer is C. The code for a 3D TV (097) costing $495 (VV) and shipped via airborne express (60).

QUESTION 19

1. C

EXPLANATION = the correct answer is C. The order should have been coded as 472 (golf clubs), SS (costing $175.95), 20 (shipped via UPS).

2. D

EXPLANATION = the correct answer is D. The entry would be coded as 743 (fishing rod), SS (costing $212.50) and 30 (shipped via Emery Worldwide).

3. B

EXPLANATION = the correct answer is B. The most appropriate code for the transaction would be 609 (booster seat), RR (costing $35.85), 70 (via standard mail).

4. B

EXPLANATION = the correct answer is B. The code for a recliner chair (637) costing $420 (UU) and shipped via federal express (50).

5. C

EXPLANATION = the correct answer is C. The code 409-SS-30 is correct for golf bag (409) costing $130.75 (SS) and shipped via Emery Worldwide (30).

QUESTION 20

1. D

EXPLANATION = the correct answer is D. The code for a garden tool set (723) costing $125.50 (QQ) and shipped via standard mail (70).

2. B

EXPLANATION = the correct answer is B. The most appropriate code for the transaction would be 698 (glass), SS (costing $375.95), 30 (via emery worldwide).

3. C

EXPLANATION = the correct answer is C. The entry would be coded as 139 (fence panels), TT (costing $475.25) and 80 (via customer walk-in).

4. C

EXPLANATION = the correct answer is C. The code 863-UU-40 is correct for bricks (863) costing $635 (UU) and shipped via DHL (40).

5. B

EXPLANATION = the correct answer is B. The order should have been coded as 438 (windows), QQ (costing $215.85), 60 (shipped via airborne express).

Now move on to the next section of the guide.

DATA INTERPRETATION TESTS

PART 6

DATA INTERPRETATION TESTS PART 6

Q1.

Determine the correct training code based on the information provided in the table.
Training instruction provided to employees is coded as:
INSTRUCTOR – TRAINING – TRAINING SITE – DATE.

INSTRUCTOR CODE	TRAINING CODE	TRAINING SITE CODE	DATE CODE
Walker 222	First Aid H	Main Library 353	June 3 AAA
Brown 555	Contracting J	Ramsay Campus 215	June 4 BBB
Powley 777	Budgeting B	Arboretum 795	June 8 CCC
Wells 888	Data Analysis T	Powell Office 635	August 7 DDD
White 999	Writing I	Hyde Garage 328	August 11 EEE
Thompson 111	Computers N	Wester Hall 701	August 18 FFF
Thomas 333	Mechanics R	Public Works 008	August 23 GGG

1. The code 777-T-215-CCC is CORRECT for?

  A – Contracting training taught by Thompson at the Main Library on August 7th
  B – Contracting training taught by Powley at the Ramsay Campus on June 8th.
  C – Data analysis training taught by Powley at the Ramsay Campus on June 8th.
  D – Contracting training taught by Thomas at the Powell Office on August 18th.

Answer [   ]

2. Walker wants to conduct writing training at the Powell Office. If the department schedules the training for the 23rd August, the code would be?

  A – 555-I-328-EEE
  B – 222-I-635-GGG

C – 111-I-635-GGG
D – 111-T-795-DDD

Answer [ ]

3. Wells received her training schedule and saw the code 888-H-353-CCC. She notified her supervisor that the training needed to be moved to Wester Hall. The training was subsequently recoded?

   A – 888-H-701-CCC
   B – 555-H-701-CCC
   C – 999-B-701-AAA
   D – 333-T-635-FFF

Answer [ ]

4. White was scheduled to conduct Mechanical training at Hyde Garage on June 4th, but Thomas had to substitute at the last minute. The revised code for the training is?

   A – 333-J-795-CCC
   B – 999-R-328-BBB
   C – 333-R-328-BBB
   D – 111-N-795-DDD

Answer [ ]

5. The code 555-B-353-FFF is CORRECT for?

   A – Budgeting training taught by Brown at the Main Library on August 18th.
   B – Contracting training taught by Wells at the Main Library on August 7th.
   C – Budgeting training taught by Wells at the Main Library on August 7th.
   D – Contracting training taught by Brown at the Main Library on August 18th.

Answer [ ]

DATA INTERPRETATION TESTS

Q2.

Determine the correct exam code based on the information provided in the table.
Exam instructions provided to candidates is coded as:
INVIGILATOR - EXAM – EXAM SITE – DATE.

INVIGILATOR CODE	EXAM CODE	EXAM SITE CODE	DATE CODE
Holmes 666	English E	Anselm Hall 238	May 3rd AAA
Edwards 222	Maths M	Sports Hall 139	May 4th BBB
West 111	Science S	Augustine Hall 331	May 5th CCC
Page 777	History H	Auditorium 229	May 7th DDD
Lewin 999	Geography G	Jackson Building 117	May 14th EEE
Newton 000	P.E P	Main Library 785	May 19th FFF
Farmer 333	Citizenship C	Ramsay Building 464	June 18th GGG

1. Newton was scheduled to supervise the Science exam at Augustine Hall on May 5th, but Page had to substitute at the last minute. The revised code for this is?

    A – 000-S-331-CCC
    B – 000-S-331-BBB
    C – 777-S-331-CCC
    D – 777-S-331-AAA

Answer [　　　]

2. Holmes received her schedule and saw the code 666-G-229-EEE. If she was the invigilator, this code would be CORRECT for?

    A – Holmes would be supervising the Science exam at Anselm Hall on May 5th.
    B – Holmes would be supervising the Citizenship exam at the Main Library on May 7th.

C – Holmes would be supervising the P.E exam at the Jackson Building on June 18th.
D – Holmes would be supervising the Geography exam at the Auditorium on May 14th.

Answer [ ]

3. The code 111-H-331-FFF is CORRECT for?

   A – Edwards would be supervising the Maths exam at Augustine Hall on May 7th.
   B – West would be supervising the History exam at Augustine Hall on May 19th.
   C – Page would be supervising the Maths exam at Jackson Building on June 18th.
   D – Lewin would be supervising the English exam at the Auditorium on May 3rd.

Answer [ ]

4. Edwards will be supervising the Citizenship exam at the Ramsay Building. If the exam board schedules the exam for the 14th May, the code would be?

   A – 111-C-464-EEE
   B – 222-C-464-EEE
   C – 222-S-331-FFF
   D – 777-H-117-CCC

Answer [ ]

5. The code 000-H-785-BBB is CORRECT for?

   A – Newton would be supervising the History exam at the Main Library on May 4th.
   B – Farmer would be supervising the English exam at the Main Library on May 4th.
   C – West would be supervising the Geography exam at the Sports Hall on May 7th.
   D – Lewin would be supervising the Science exam at the Auditorium on May 3rd.

Answer [ ]

DATA INTERPRETATION TESTS

Q3.

Determine the correct sports code based on the information provided in the table. Sports instructions provided to candidates is coded as:
INSTRUCTOR - SPORT – SPORT SITE – DATE.

INSTRUCTOR CODE	SPORT CODE	SPORT SITE CODE	DATE CODE
Richards 555	Football Y	Powell Hall 654	June 5th AAA
Smith 777	Basketball X	Anselm Hall 125	June 11th BBB
Peters 888	Gymnastics V	Augustine Hall 463	June 24th CCC
Johnson 222	Dance C	Sports Centre 367	May 19th DDD
Hampton 444	Tennis E	Grove Green 421	August 7th EEE
Grove 111	Hockey T	Mote Park 006	August 9th FFF
Perkins 999	Swimming P	Mote Park Hall 007	August 24th GGG

1. Grove wants to conduct a Football lesson at the Sports Centre. If the centre schedules the lesson for the 9th August, the code would be?

A – 111-Y-367-FFF
B – 777-Y-367-FFF
C – 111-X-463-EEE
D – 111-V-125-CCC

Answer [ ]

2. The code 888-X-654-BBB is CORRECT for?

A – Football lesson taught be Peters at Powell Hall on June 11th.
B – Football lesson taught by Johnson at Grove Green on August 9th.

C – Basketball lesson taught by Peters at Powell Hall on June 11th.
D – Basketball lesson taught by Perkins at Augustine Hall on June 11th.

Answer [ ]

3. Smith received his schedule and saw the code 777-T-367-EEE. He notified his supervisor that the lesson needed to be moved to Mote Park. The training was subsequently recoded?

A – 777-T-006-FFF
B – 777-T-006-EEE
C – 777-T-007-EEE
D – 777-T-007-GGG

Answer [ ]

4. Richards was scheduled to conduct a Gymnastics lesson at Anselm Hall on June 5th, but Hampton had to substitute at the last minute. The revised code for the training is?

A – 444-C-654-DDD
B – 999-V-125-BBB
C – 444-V-125-AAA
D – 999-C-421-EEE

Answer [ ]

5. The code 555-E-367-DDD is CORRECT for?

A – Tennis lesson taught by Hampton at Grove Green on August 9th.
B – Tennis lesson taught by Hampton at Grove Green on June 24th.
C – Hockey lesson taught by Richards at the Sports Centre on May 19th.
D – Tennis lesson taught by Richards at the Sports Centre on May 19th.

Answer [ ]

DATA INTERPRETATION TESTS

Q4.

Determine the correct book signing code based on the information provided in the table.
Book signing provided is coded as:
AUTHOR – GENRE – PLACE OF SIGNING – PUBLICATION DATE.

AUTHOR CODE	GENRE CODE	PLACE OF SIGNING CODE	DATE CODE
Boyle 111	Fiction F	Los Angeles 742	Jan 31st AAA
Bonds 222	Autobiography Y	New York 374	Feb 8th BBB
Davis 333	Crime J	Washington 116	Feb 17th CCC
Tyler 777	Romance S	California 009	March 24th DDD
Sparks 666	Sci-Fi B	New Jersey 992	April 22nd EEE
Harvey 555	Medieval M	Georgia 788	April 29th FFF
Edwards 444	Thriller O	Colorado 485	May 11th GGG

1. Tyler was scheduled to give a book signing for his Autobiography at New York on the 8th February, but due to an error his book signing has been relocated to Washington. The revised code for the book signing?

A – 777-S-485-DDD
B – 777-F-788-BBB
C – 777-Y-374-BBB
D – 777-Y-116-BBB

Answer [ ]

2. Edwards wants to have his book signing for his Thriller novel in Los Angeles in January. If Edwards gets what he wants, what would the book signing code be?

A – 444-O-742-AAA
B – 333-O-116-CCC

C – 444-F-009-EEE
D – 444-M-742-AAA

Answer [ ]

3. The code 555-J-992-GGG is CORRECT for?

A – Sparks having a book signing for his Romance novel in Washington on April 29th.
B – Harvey having a book signing for her Fiction novel in New York on May 11th.
C – Sparks having a book signing for his Crime novel in Georgia on May 11th.
D – Harvey having a book signing for her Crime novel in New Jersey on May 11th.

Answer [ ]

4. Davis received his schedule and saw the code 333-O-788-EEE. He notified his editor that the book signing needed to be moved to March 24th. The book signing was subsequently recoded?

A – 333-O-788-AAA
B – 333-O-788-FFF
C – 333-O-788-DDD
D – 333-O-788-GGG

Answer [ ]

5. The code 222-B-485-CCC is CORRECT for?

A – Boyle having a book signing for his Sci-Fi novel in Colorado on February 17th.
B – Bonds having a book signing for his Sci-Fi novel in Colorado on February 17th.
C – Bonds having a book signing for his Romance novel in Colorado on February 8th.
D – Boyle having a book signing for his Romance novel in Colorado on February 8th.

Answer [ ]

DATA INTERPRETATION TESTS

Q5.

Determine the correct training code based on the information provided in the table.
Training instruction provided to employees is coded as:
INSTRUCTOR – TRAINING – TRAINING SITE – DATE.

INSTRUCTOR CODE	TRAINING CODE	TRAINING SITE CODE	DATE CODE
Parker 777	Fitness F	Larkfield Leisure 196	June 3rd AAA
Beale 111	First Aid R	Mote Park Leisure 039	June 29th BBB
Adams 333	Lifeguarding P	Gilmore Office 774	June 30th CCC
Dyer 999	Health/Hygiene H	Richardson Office 831	July 2nd DDD
Haynes 555	Child Care X	Tyler Building 258	July 5th EEE
Matthews 666	Adult Care E	Powell Building 212	July 9th FFF
Simmons 888	Physiotherapy N	Lecture Theatre 147	July 10th GGG

1. Dyer was scheduled to conduct Fitness training at Mote Park Leisure Centre on June 3rd, Adams had to substitute at the last minute. The revised code for this is?

A – 999-F-039-AAA
B – 333-F-039-AAA
C – 999-R-196-BBB
D – 333-R-196-BBB

Answer [ ]

2. The code 777-H-147-DDD is CORRECT for?

A – Parker conducting Health and Hygiene training in the Powell Building on July 2nd.
B – Parker conducting Fitness training in the Lecture Theatre on July 2nd.

C – Parker conducting Health and Hygiene training in the Lecture Theatre on July 2nd.
D – Parker conducting First Aid training in the Powell Building on July 2nd.

Answer [ ]

3. Haynes wants to conduct First Aid training at the Tyler Building. If the department schedules the training for the June 30th, the code would be?

   A – 555-F-258-CCC
   B – 999-R-258-CCC
   C – 555-R-258-CCC
   D – 999-F-258-CCC

Answer [ ]

4. Matthews received his training schedule and saw the code 666-P-196-FFF. He notified his supervisor that the training needed to be moved to July 10th. The training was subsequently recoded?

   A – 666-P-039-GGG
   B – 666-P-039-FFF
   C – 666-P-196-GGG
   D – 666-P-831-GGG

Answer [ ]

5. The code 888-X-774-DDD is CORRECT for?

   A – Simmons conducting Adult Care training at the Gilmore Office on July 2nd.
   B – Simmons conducting Child Care training at the Richardson Office on July 2nd.
   C – Simmons conducting Adult Care training at the Richardson Office on July 2nd.
   D – Simmons conducting Child Care training at the Gilmore Office on July 2nd.

Answer [ ]

DATA INTERPRETATION TESTS

Q6.

Determine the correct exam code based on the information provided in the table.
Exam instructions provided to candidates is coded as:
INVIGILATOR - EXAM – EXAM SITE – DATE.

INVIGILATOR CODE	EXAM CODE	EXAM SITE CODE	DATE CODE
Franks 999	English A	Tyler Hall 961	June 8th AAA
Smith 222	Maths N	Sports Hall 185	June 9th BBB
Adams 333	Science E	Ramsay Hall 313	June 10th CCC
O'Neill 777	History J	Auditorium 498	June 22nd DDD
O'Brien 888	French K	Lecture Theatre 112	July 7th EEE
Redgate 000	Religious T	Main Library 698	July 8th FFF
Robinson 111	Technology O	Lindsay Building 447	July 9th GGG

1. O'Brien was scheduled to supervise the Religious Studies exam at the Lindsay Building on June 9th, but O'Neill had to substitute at the last minute. The revised code for this is?

   A – 888-T-447-BBB
   B – 777-T-447-CCC
   C – 777-T-447-BBB
   D – 888-T-185-CCC

   Answer [   ]

2. Adams will be supervising the French exam at the Auditorium. If the exam board schedules the exam for the 7th July, the code would be?

   A – 333-K-498-EEE
   B – 000-E-313-AAA

C – 222-E-185-DDD
D – 333-K-313-EEE

Answer [ ]

3. The code 999-O-698-FFF is CORRECT for?

A – Smith supervising the Technology exam at the Main Library on July 8th.
B – Franks supervising the Technology exam at the Main Library on July 8th.
C – Smith supervising the French exam at the Main Library on July 9th.
D – Franks supervising the French exam at the Main Library on July 9th.

Answer [ ]

4. Robinson received her schedule and saw the code 111-E-961-CCC. If she was the invigilator, this code would be CORRECT for?

A – Robinson supervising the English exam at Tyler Hall on June 9th.
B – Robinson supervising the Science exam at the Sports Hall on June 10th.
C – Robinson supervising the Science exam at Tyler Hall on June 10th.
D – Robinson supervising the History exam at the Lecture Theatre on July 7th.

Answer [ ]

5. The code 222-N-698-GGG is CORRECT for?

A – Smith supervising the English exam at the Auditorium on June 10th.
B – O'Neill supervising the French exam at Ramsay Hall on June 8th.
C – O'Brien supervising the Technology exam at the Sports Hall on June 22nd.
D – Smith supervising the Maths exam at the Main Library on July 9th.

Answer [ ]

DATA INTERPRETATION TESTS

Q7.

Determine the correct training code based on the information provided in the table.
Training instruction provided to employees is coded as:
INSTRUCTOR – TRAINING – TRAINING SITE – DATE.

INSTRUCTOR CODE	TRAINING CODE	TRAINING SITE CODE	DATE CODE
Jackson 222	Plastering Y	Local Garage 448	Feb 17th AAA
Abraham 555	Tiling U	Express Garage 369	March 22nd BBB
Lincoln 777	Carpenter W	Public Works 137	April 5th CCC
Peters 111	Electrician M	Kent College 185	May 19th DDD
Harrison 444	Mechanics R	Canterbury College 227	July 29th EEE
Holmes 888	Builder A	Mike's Site 974	Sept 4th FFF
Wicks 333	Contractor C	Building Site 981	Dec 2nd GGG

1. The code 777-U-185-CCC is CORRECT for?

   A – Abraham conducting Tiling training at Canterbury College on April 5th.
   B – Lincoln conducting Tiling training at Kent College on April 5th.
   C – Lincoln conducting Plastering training at Canterbury College on April 5th.
   D – Abraham conducting Plastering training at Public Works on March 22nd.

Answer [   ]

2. Peters was scheduled to conduct Electrician training at the Building Site on July 29th, but Harrison had to substitute at the last minute. The revised code for the training is?

   A – 111-M-981-EEE
   B – 111-W-981-DDD

C – 444-M-981-EEE
D – 444-W-974-EEE

Answer [   ]

3. Wicks received his training schedule and saw the 333-A-974-EEE. He notified his supervisor that the training needed to be moved to Public Works. The training was subsequently recoded?

A – 333-A-137-EEE
B – 111-M-369-GGG
C – 222-A-137-DDD
D – 222-U-369-EEE

Answer [   ]

4. Holmes wants to conduct Plastering training at Canterbury College. If the department schedules the training for the September 4th, the code would be?

A – 888-M-448-FFF
B – 888-Y-974-FFF
C – 888-Y-227-FFF
D – 888-Y-227-GGG

Answer [   ]

5. The code 555-W-137-BBB is CORRECT for?

A – Lincoln conducting Carpenter training at the Public Works on March 22nd.
B – Abraham conducting Carpenter training at the Public Works on March 22nd.
C – Holmes conducting Mechanical training at Mike's Site on September 4th.
D – Holmes conducting Tiling training at Mike's Site on September 4th.

Answer [   ]

Q8.

Determine the correct sports code based on the information provided in the table. Sports instructions provided to candidates is coded as:
INSTRUCTOR - SPORT – SPORT SITE – DATE.

INSTRUCTOR CODE	SPORT CODE	SPORT SITE CODE	DATE CODE
Nelson 777	Ice Hockey I	Cricket Ground 632	May 4th AAA
Cameron 111	Ice Skating K	Maidstone Stadium 147	May 11th BBB
Barlow 333	Gymnastics R	Kent Stadium 232	June 3rd CCC
James 999	Football S	Harlow Centre 972	June 18th DDD
Madison 222	Rugby B	Local Ice Rink 009	July 17th EEE
Webster 666	Running W	Bewl Water Grounds 910	July 22nd FFF
Phillips 444	Cricket Q	Kent Field/Track 744	July 28th GGG

1. The code 333-B-232-CCC is CORRECT for?

   A – Barlow conducting a Football lesson at Kent Stadium on June 3rd.
   B – Barlow conducting a Rugby lesson at Maidstone Stadium on June 18th.
   C – Barlow conducting a Rugby lesson at Kent Stadium on June 3rd.
   D – Barlow conducting a Football lesson at Maidstone Stadium on June 18th.

Answer [   ]

2. Cameron was scheduled to conduct an Ice Hockey lesson at the Local Ice Rink on May 11th, but Nelson had to substitute at the last minute. The revised code for the training is?

   A – 111-I-009-BBB
   B – 777-K-009-AAA

C – 777-K-009-BBB
D – 777-I-009-BBB

Answer [ ]

3. Madison received his schedule and saw the code 222-R-972-AAA. He notified his supervisor that the lesson needed to be moved to May 11th. The training was subsequently recoded?

   A – 222-R-232-AAA
   B – 222-R-972-BBB
   C – 222-R-972-CCC
   D – 222-S-972-CCC

Answer [ ]

4. The code 666-K-009-EEE is CORRECT for?

   A – Webster conducting an Ice Skating lesson at the Local Ice Rink on July 17th.
   B – James conducting an Ice Hockey lesson at the Local Ice Rink on July 22nd.
   C – Webster conducting a Football lesson at Kent Stadium on July 28th.
   D – James conducting a Running lesson at Kent Field and Track on May 11th.

Answer [ ]

5. Phillips wants to conduct a Cricket lesson at the Cricket Grounds. If the centre schedules the lesson for the 4th May, the code would be?

   A – 333-Q-632-AAA
   B – 444-Q-147-AAA
   C – 444-Q-632-AAA
   D – 444-W-632-AAA

Answer [ ]

Q9.

Determine the correct book signing code based on the information provided in the table.
Book signing provided is coded as:
DIRECTOR – GENRE – LOCATION – PREMIERE DATE.

DIRECTOR CODE	GENRE CODE	LOCATION CODE	DATE CODE
Williams 111	Romance W	London 258	April 8th AAA
Johnson 222	Thriller A	Paris 771	April 19th BBB
Adams 333	Drama E	Rome 339	May 2nd CCC
Richards 444	Comedy P	Los Angeles 009	May 9th DDD
Edwards 555	Documentary M	New York 020	June 23rd EEE
Fowler 666	Horror L	California 053	July 14th FFF
Tyler 777	Fantasy F	Berlin 964	June 28th GGG

1. Tyler wants to have his premiere for his Drama film in Los Angeles. The only date that is available is 19th April. What would the code be?

A – 777-A-771-AAA
B – 777-E-009-EEE
C – 777-E-009-BBB
D – 777-P-020-EEE

Answer [ ]

2. Edwards was scheduled to have his premiere for his Horror film in London on the 8th April, but due to an error his premiere is now on the 2nd May. The revised code for the book signing?

A – 555-L-258-CCC
B – 111-L-258-CCC

C – 555-A-258-CCC
D – 555-L-339-CCC

Answer [ ]

3. The code 333-E-020-GGG is CORRECT for?

A – Adams' Drama film premiered in Los Angeles on July 14th.
B – Adams' Drama film premiered in New York on June 28th.
C – Richards' Drama film premiered in New York on June 28th.
D – Richard's Drama film premiered in Los Angeles on July 14th.

Answer [ ]

4. Williams received his premiere details and saw the code 111-M-771-DDD. He notified his manager that he needed to move the date to 23rd June. The premiere was subsequently recoded?

A – 111-P-771-EEE
B – 222-M-771-EEE
C – 111-M-771-EEE
D – 111-M-339-AAA

Answer [ ]

5. The code 666-P-258-GGG is CORRECT for?

A – Edwards' Horror film premiered in New York on July 14th.
B – Fowlers' Comedy film premiered in London on June 28th.
C – Fowlers' Thriller film premiered in Paris on June 28th.
D – Fowlers' Fantasy film premiered in California on May 9th.

Answer [ ]

Q10.

Determine the correct exam code based on the information provided in the table.
Exam instructions provided to candidates is coded as:
INVIGILATOR - EXAM – EXAM SITE – DATE.

INVIGILATOR CODE	EXAM CODE	EXAM SITE CODE	DATE CODE
Blackman 111	Law La	Lecture Theatre 457	May 8th AAA
Brentwood 222	Media Me	Gymnasium 136	May 10th BBB
Hazels 444	Film Fi	Sports Hall 971	May 11th CCC
Henderson 555	Physics Ph	Main Library 558	May 19th DDD
Woodman 777	Chemistry Ch	Private Library 559	May 22nd EEE
Butler 333	Environmental En	Erasmus Building 217	May 23rd FFF
Kimber 666	Spanish Sp	Invicta Building 319	June 16th GGG

1. The code 555-Ch-971-DDD is CORRECT for?

    A – Henderson supervising the Film exam in the Sports Hall on May 8th.
    B – Henderson supervising the Chemistry exam in the Sports Hall on May 11th.
    C – Henderson supervising the Chemistry exam in the Sports Hall on May 19th.
    D – Henderson supervising the Chemistry exam in the Sports Hall on May 22nd.

Answer [ ]

2. Brentwood was scheduled to supervise the Film exam at the Private Library on May 9th, but Kimber had to substitute at the last minute. The revised code for this is?

    A – 222-Fi-559-AAA
    B – 666-Fi-559-AAA

C – 666-Fi-558-AAA
D – 666-Fi-558-BBB

Answer [ ]

3. Hazels will be supervising the Law exam in the Erasmus Building. If the exam board schedules the exam for the May 22nd, the code would be?

   A – 444-La-319-EEE
   B – 111-La-217-EEE
   C – 444-La-217-EEE
   D – 111-La-319-EEE

Answer [ ]

4. The code 111-Sp-136-GGG is CORRECT for?

   A – Blackman supervising the Spanish exam in the Lecture Theatre on May 23rd
   B – Blackman supervising the Spanish exam in the Main Library on May 11th.
   C – Blackman supervising the Spanish exam, in the Invicta Building on May 22nd.
   D – Blackman supervising the Spanish exam in the Gymnasium on June 16th.

Answer [ ]

5. Woodman received her schedule and saw the code 777-En-319-CCC. If she was the invigilator, this code would be CORRECT for?

   A – Woodman supervising the Environmental exam in the Erasmus Building on May 11th.
   B – Woodman supervising the Environmental exam in the Invicta Building on May 11th.
   C – Woodman supervising the Environmental exam in the Main Library on May 10th.
   D – Woodman supervising the Environmental exam in the Invicta Building on May 10th.

Answer [ ]

DATA INTERPRETATION TESTS

Q11.

Determine the correct sports code based on the information provided in the table.
Sports instructions provided to candidates is coded as:
INSTRUCTOR - SPORT – SPORT SITE – DATE.

INSTRUCTOR CODE	SPORT CODE	SPORT SITE CODE	DATE CODE
Harley 333	Badminton K	YMCA 179	Jan 31st AAA
Sage 888	Karate O	Lloyds Gym 963	Feb 2nd BBB
Friend 555	Dance Q	Mote Park Gym 441	Feb 18th CCC
Phillips 777	Baseball S	Cornwallis Hall 821	March 3rd DDD
Hyett 999	Tennis C	Topnotch Health 759	March 19th EEE
Scott 111	Hockey Z	Leisure Centre 623	April 14th FFF
Sawyer 444	Netball I	La fitness Centre 237	April 18th GGG

1. Sawyer was scheduled to conduct a Tennis lesson at Lloyds Gym on February 18th, but Hyett had to substitute at the last minute. The revised code for the training is?

A – 444-C-441-CCC
B – 999-C-441-CCC
C – 444-C-963-CCC
D – 999-C-963-CCC

Answer [   ]

2. The code 555-K-759-GGG is CORRECT for?

A – Friend conducting a Karate lesson at Topnotch Health on April 18th.
B – Friend conducting a Tennis lesson at Topnotch Health on April 18th.

C – Friend conducting a Badminton lesson at Topnotch Health on April 18th.
D – Friend conducting a Netball lesson at Topnotch Health on April 18th.

Answer [ ]

3. Phillips wants to conduct a Karate lesson at Cornwallis Hall. If the hall schedules the lesson for March 3rd, the code would be?

   A – 999-O-821-DDD
   B – 555-Q-759-BBB
   C – 777-O-821-DDD
   D – 555-O-237-EEE

Answer [ ]

4. The code 888-Q-237-AAA is CORRECT for?

   A – Sage conducting a Karate lesson at the La Fitness Centre on January 31st.
   B – Sage conducting a Dance lesson at the La Fitness Centre on January 31st.
   C – Sage conducting a Tennis lesson at the Leisure Centre on February 2nd.
   D – Sage conducting a Netball lesson at the Leisure Centre on February 2nd.

Answer [ ]

5. Harley received his schedule and saw the code 333-Z-179-DDD. He notified his supervisor that the lesson needed to be moved to March 19th. The training was subsequently recoded?

   A – 333-S-179-EEE
   B – 333-Z-179-EEE
   C – 333-Z-179-FFF
   D – 333-Z-963-EEE

Answer [ ]

Q12.

Determine the correct book signing code based on the information provided in the table.
Book signing provided is coded as:
AUTHOR – GENRE – PLACE OF SIGNING – PUBLICATION DATE.

AUTHOR CODE	GENRE CODE	PLACE OF SIGNING CODE	DATE CODE
Harper 333	Horror J	LA Library 963	April 4th AAA
Jones 555	Thriller O	Kent Library 741	April 22nd BBB
Miller 444	Drama F	Kent Museum 239	May 13th CCC
Thomas 111	Romance V	Costa Coffee 465	June 8th DDD
Watson 666	Autobiography A	W H Smith 991	June 24th EEE
Martin 999	Action R	Waterstones 271	July 17th FFF
Lacey 777	Fiction N	NY Library 746	July 18th GGG

1. The code 555-F-239-DDD is CORRECT for?

A – Jones having a book signing for his Thriller novel at the Kent Museum on June 8th.
B – Harper having a book signing for his Drama novel at the Kent Museum on June 8th.
C – Miller having a book signing for her Autobiography at Costa Coffee on June 8th.
D – Jones having a book signing for his Drama novel at the Kent Museum on June 8th.

Answer ☐

2. Miller received her schedule and saw the code 444-A-746-FFF. She notified her editor that the book signing needed to be moved to July 18th. The book signing was subsequently recoded?

A – 444-A-746-GGG
B – 444-O-746-GGG

C – 444-A-746-CCC
D – 444-A-991-GGG

Answer [ ]

3. The code 777-N-271-CCC is CORRECT for?

A – Martin having a book signing for his Fiction novel at W H Smith on May 13th.
B – Lacey having a book signing for her Autobiography at Waterstones on May 13th.
C – Lacey having a book signing for her Fiction novel at Waterstones on May 13th.
D – Lacey having a book signing for her Fiction novel at Costa Coffee on April 4th.

Answer [ ]

4. Watson wants to have his book signing for his Action novel at the Kent Museum. If the only date available is April 22nd, what would the book signing code be?

A – 666-J-239-AAA
B – 666-R-239-BBB
C – 666-R-963-BBB
D – 666-R-239-CCC

Answer [ ]

5. Martin was scheduled to give a book signing for his Drama novel at the NY Library on the 8th June, but due to an error his book signing has been relocated to LA Library. The revised code for the book signing?

A – 444-F-963-DDD
B – 999-V-963-DDD
C – 999-F-963-DDD
D – 999-F-741-DDD

Answer [ ]

DATA INTERPRETATION TESTS

Q13.

Determine the correct sports code based on the information provided in the table.
Sports instructions provided to candidates is coded as:
INSTRUCTOR - ACTIVITY – SPORT SITE – DATE.

INSTRUCTOR CODE	ACTIVITY CODE	SPORT SITE CODE	DATE CODE
James 333	Legs D	Local Gym 967	June 7th AAA
Simon 999	Cardio J	YMCA 554	June 8th BBB
Alex 111	Abs O	Sports Hall 792	June 9th CCC
Matt 222	Arms Q	Fitness Centre 490	June 11th DDD
Carla 666	Bums and tums S	Leisure Centre 480	June 13th EEE
Rachel 888	Circuits X	Maidstone Grounds 008	June 18th FFF
Jack 444	Pilates Z	Private Gym 109	June 24th GGG

1. Alex received his schedule and saw the code 111-J-554-CCC. He notified his supervisor that the lesson needed to be moved to the Local Gym because he required more space. The training was subsequently recoded?

A – 111-J-554-AAA
B – 111-J-967-CCC
C – 111-J-554-CCC
D – 111-J-967-EEE

Answer [ ]

2. The code 888-S-490-FFF is CORRECT for?

A – Rachel conducting a Bums and Tums Workout at the YMCA on June 8th.
B – Rachel conducting an Arms Workout at the Fitness Centre on June 18th.

C – Rachel conducting a Bums and Tums Workout at the Fitness Centre on June 18th.
D – Rachel conducting an Arms Workout at the YMCA on June 8th.

Answer [ ]

3. Simon wants to conduct a Circuits training session at the Private Gym. If the gym schedules the lesson for June 9th, the code would be?

A – 999-Q-109-CCC
B – 999-Q-967-CCC
C – 999-O-008-GGG
D – 999-X-109-CCC

Answer [ ]

4. The code 222-D-792-AAA is CORRECT for?

A – Matt conducting an Abs Workout at the Sports Hall on June 8th.
B – Matt conducting a Legs Workout at the Sports Hall on June 7th.
C – Matt conducting a Legs Workout at the Sports Hall on June 11th.
D – Matt conducting a Legs Workout at the Fitness Centre on June 8th.

Answer [ ]

5. James was scheduled to conduct a Cardio Workout at the Local Gym on June 18th, but Carla had to substitute at the last minute. The revised code for the training is?

A – 666-J-967-FFF
B – 333-O-967-FFF
C – 333-J-967-FFF
D – 333-J-967-BBB

Answer [ ]

DATA INTERPRETATION TESTS

Q14.

Determine the correct training code based on the information provided in the table.
Training instruction provided to employees is coded as:
INSTRUCTOR – TRAINING – TRAINING SITE – DATE.

INSTRUCTOR CODE	TRAINING CODE	TRAINING SITE CODE	DATE CODE
Ben 555	Sailing R	Hastings 119	August 3rd AAA
Gareth 999	Wind Surfing U	Romney Marsh 316	August 10th BBB
David 333	Wakeboarding I	Ramsgate 551	August 23rd CCC
Elliott 111	Abseiling B	Broadstairs 784	Sept 2nd DDD
Josh 666	Kayaking X	Rye 418	Sept 11th EEE
Owen 888	Diving G	Eastbourne 009	Sept 19th FFF
Peter 222	Hang Gliding K	Folkestone 772	Sept 22nd GGG

1. The code 888-B-418-AAA is CORRECT for?

   A – Owen conducting an Abseiling lesson at Eastbourne on August 3rd.
   B – Owen conducting a Wind Surfing lesson at Ramsgate on August 3rd.
   C – Owen conducting an Abseiling lesson at Rye on August 3rd.
   D – Owen conducting a Wakeboarding lesson at Hastings on August 3rd.

Answer [ ]

2. David received his training schedule and saw the code 333-U-316-EEE. He notified his supervisor that the training needed to be moved to Sept 22nd. The training was subsequently recoded?

   A – 333-I-316-GGG
   B – 333-U-316-GGG

C – 333-U-784-GGG
D – 333-U-316-FFF

Answer [ ]

3. Peter was scheduled to conduct a Diving lesson at Broadstairs on August 10th, Josh had to substitute at the last minute. The revised code for this is?

   A – 666-G-784-BBB
   B – 222-G-784-BBB
   C – 666-X-784-AAA
   D – 222-X-784-FFF

Answer [ ]

4. Gareth wants to conduct a Hang Gliding lesson at Eastbourne. If the department schedules the training for the Sept 11th, the code would be?

   A – 555-K-009-BBB
   B – 333-I-316-DDD
   C – 999-K-009-EEE
   D – 999-K-418-DDD

Answer [ ]

5. The code 555-U-772-FFF is CORRECT for?

   A – Ben conducting a Kayaking lesson at Folkestone on September 11th.
   B – Ben conducting a Wind Surfing lesson at Eastbourne on September 11th.
   C – Ben conducting a Wind Surfing lesson at Folkestone on September 19th.
   D – Ben conducting a Hang Gliding lesson at Romney Marsh on September 2nd.

Answer [ ]

DATA INTERPRETATION TESTS

Q15.

Determine the correct exam code based on the information provided in the table.
Exam instructions provided to candidates is coded as:
INVIGILATOR - EXAM – EXAM SITE – DATE.

INVIGILATOR CODE	EXAM CODE	EXAM SITE CODE	DATE CODE
Jane 555	Art F	Main Library 741	May 18th AAA
Erin 333	Media E	Public Library 338	May 20th BBB
Michelle 666	English Literature T	Main Hall 415	May 29th CCC
David 111	English Language B	Powell Hall 887	June 3rd DDD
Frank 444	Science N	Lecture Theatre 157	June 7th EEE
Simon 777	P.E O	Gymnasium 551	June 17th FFF
Edward 222	Geography W	Sports Hall 007	June 18th GGG

1. The code 666-T-338-BBB is CORRECT for?

   A – Michelle supervising the English Language exam in the Private Library on May 20th.
   B – Michelle supervising the English Lit exam in the Private Library on May 20th.
   C – Michelle supervising the English Lit exam in the Public Library on May 20th.
   D – Michelle supervising the P.E exam in the Powell Hall on June 3rd.

Answer [ ]

2. The code 333-E-157-EEE is CORRECT for?

   A – David supervising the Media exam in the Lecture Theatre on June 7th.
   B – David supervising the Media exam in the Gymnasium on June 7th.

C – David supervising the Media exam in Lecture Theatre on June 17th.
D – Erin supervising the Media exam in the Lecture Theatre on June 7th.

Answer [   ]

3. Edward was scheduled to supervise the Geography exam at the Sports Hall on May 18th, but Jane had to substitute at the last minute. The revised code for this is?

   A – 555-T-007-AAA
   B – 555-W-007-AAA
   C – 555-W-007-CCC
   D – 555-W-157-AAA

Answer [   ]

4. Frank will be supervising the English Language exam in the Main Hall. If the exam board schedules the exam for the May 29th, the code would be?

   A – 444-T-415-CCC
   B – 444-T-338-DDD
   C – 444-B-415-CCC
   D – 444-B-157-EEE

Answer [   ]

5. Simon received his schedule and saw the code 777-N-551-EEE. If he was the invigilator, this code would be CORRECT for?

   A – Simon supervising the Science exam in the Gymnasium on June 7th.
   B – Erin supervising the Media exam in the Main Hall on June 3rd.
   C – Simon supervising the P.E exam in the Gymnasium on June 7th.
   D – Simon supervising the Media exam in the Main Hall on June 3rd.

Answer [   ]

Q16.

Determine the correct training code based on the information provided in the table. Training instruction provided to employees is coded as:
INSTRUCTOR – COURSE – COURSE SITE – START.

INSTRUCTOR CODE	COURSE CODE	COURSE SITE CODE	START CODE
Harley 666	Hairdressing R	Mid Kent 331	Feb 18th AAA
Matthew 444	Mechanics E	Canterbury 376	Feb 27th BBB
Jason 333	Electrician P	UCA 391	Mar 4th CCC
Ryan 777	Bricklaying V	Private Sessions 479	Mar 11th DDD
Harrison 222	Floristry U	Home Sessions 004	April 8th EEE
Elizabeth 111	Musician D	Hadlow 555	April 10th FFF
Shaun 888	Animal Welfare F	Greenwich 614	May 17th GGG

1. The code 777-V-331-CCC is CORRECT for?

    A – Ryan conducting an Electrician course at Mid Kent on March 4th.
    B – Ryan conducting a Bricklaying course at Mid Kent on March 4th.
    C – Jason conducting an Electrician course at Mid Kent on March 4th.
    D – Jason conducting a Bricklaying course at Mid Kent on March 4th.

Answer [ ]

2. Harrison wants to conduct a Mechanics course at Canterbury. If the department schedules the start date for February 18th, the code would be?

    A – 222-U-376-AAA
    B – 222-E-391-CCC

C – 222-E-391-AAA
D – 222-E-376-AAA

Answer [ ]

3. Elizabeth received her training schedule and saw the code 111-U-555-CCC. She notified her supervisor that the training needed to be moved to March 11th. The training was subsequently recoded?

A – 111-U-391-CCC
B – 111-U-391-EEE
C – 111-U-555-DDD
D – 111-U-555-AAA

Answer [ ]

4. Matthew was scheduled to conduct Mechanical training at UCA on April 8th, but Jason had to substitute at the last minute. The revised code for the training is?

A – 444-E-391-EEE
B – 333-E-391-EEE
C – 444-E-376-CCC
D – 333-E-376-DDD

Answer [ ]

5. The code 888-D-004-FFF is CORRECT for?

A – Shaun conducting Musical lessons at Private Sessions on April 10th.
B – Matthew conducting Musical lessons at UCA on February 27th.
C – Matthew conducting Musical lessons at Hadlow on April 8th.
D – Shaun conducting Musical lessons at home on April 10th.

Answer [ ]

DATA INTERPRETATION TESTS

Q17.

Determine the correct training code based on the information provided in the table.
Training instruction provided to employees is coded as:
INSTRUCTOR – TRAINING – TRAINING SITE – DATE.

INSTRUCTOR CODE	TRAINING CODE	TRAINING SITE CODE	DATE CODE
Carlos 555	Finance R	Administration 484	Oct 19th AAA
Santini 333	Analysis A	Public Works 421	Oct 25th BBB
Adams 111	Computers W	Auditorium 521	Nov 13th CCC
McManus 999	Writing Q	Business Park 673	Nov 28th DDD
Fowler 777	Contracts V	Business Centre 639	Dec 1st EEE
Miller 222	Editing C	Main Hall 153	Dec 17th FFF
Reynolds 888	Designing H	Main Library 159	Dec 18th GGG

1. The code 333-Q-673-CCC is CORRECT for?

   A – Analysis taught by Adams at the Business Centre on November 28th.
   B – Editing taught by Santini at the Business Park on November 13th.
   C – Writing taught by Santini at the Business Park on November 13th.
   D – Designing taught by Reynolds at the Business Centre on November 28th.

Answer

2. Fowler was scheduled to conduct analysis training at the Main Hall on December 1st, but Miller had to substitute at the last minute. The revised code for the training is?

   A – 222-A-153-EEE
   B – 222-W-673-AAA

C – 222-V-153-DDD
D – 222-A-639-AAA

Answer [ ]

3. Carlos received his training schedule and saw the 555-V-159-CCC. He notified his supervisor that the training needed to be moved to Administration. The training was subsequently recoded?

   A – 999-V-484-CCC
   B – 999-V-421-CCC
   C – 555-V-484-CCC
   D – 555-V-484-DDD

Answer [ ]

4. McManus wants to conduct Editing training at the Business Centre. If the department schedules the training for December 18th, the code would be?

   A – 999-C-639-GGG
   B – 999-W-639-GGG
   C – 999-C-521-AAA
   D – 999-V-153-GGG

Answer [ ]

5. The code 777-H-673-DDD is CORRECT for?

   A – Design training taught by Fowler at the Business Centre on November 28th.
   B – Design training taught by Miller at the Business Centre on November 13th.
   C – Design training taught by Miller at the Auditorium on October 25th.
   D – Design training taught by Fowler at the Business Park on November 28th.

Answer [ ]

DATA INTERPRETATION TESTS

Q18.

Determine the correct exam code based on the information provided in the table.
Exam instructions provided to candidates is coded as:
INVIGILATOR - EXAM – EXAM SITE – DATE.

INVIGILATOR CODE	EXAM CODE	EXAM SITE CODE	DATE CODE
Laura 888	Law G	Main Hall 647	May 5th AAA
Stephanie 333	Nursing B	Sports Hall 202	May 7th BBB
Lena 999	Technology T	Lecture Theatre 01 319	May 8th CCC
Neville 444	French D	Main Library 484	May 12th DDD
Harry 111	Spanish W	Private Library 475	May 23rd EEE
Ronald 555	History M	Lecture Theatre 02 320	June 2nd FFF
Percy 777	Maths L	Ramsay Office 667	June 3rd GGG

1. Lena was scheduled to supervise the Spanish exam at Lecture Theatre 01 on May 12th, but Neville had to substitute at the last minute. The revised code for this is?

    A – 444-W-319-DDD
    B – 444-T-319-DDD
    C – 444-W-320-DDD
    D – 444-W-320-CCC

Answer [ ]

2. Harry received his schedule and saw the code 111-G-202-FFF. If he was the invigilator, this code would be CORRECT for?

    A – Harry supervising the History exam at the Sports Hall on June 3rd.
    B – Harry supervising the Law exam at the Main Library on June 3rd.

C – Harry supervising the Law exam at the Sports Hall on June 2nd.
D – Harry supervising the Law exam at the Ramsay Office on May 8th.

Answer [ ]

3. The code 333-T-475-BBB is CORRECT for?

  A – Lena supervising the French exam at the Sports Hall on June 3rd.
  B – Stephanie supervising the Technology exam at the Private Library on May 7th.
  C – Laura supervising the History exam at the Main Hall on May 12th.
  D – Stephanie supervising the Technology exam at the Main Library on May 12th.

Answer [ ]

4. Ronald will be supervising the Nursing exam at the Lecture Theatre 02. If the exam board schedules the exam for the 23rd May, the code would be?

  A – 555-G-320-EEE
  B – 555-B-319-EEE
  C – 555-G-319-DDD
  D – 555-B-320-EEE

Answer [ ]

5. The code 777-W-484-AAA is CORRECT for?

  A – Ronald supervising the Spanish exam at the Main Library on May 5th.
  B – Neville supervising the French exam at the Sports Hall on May 7th.
  C – Harry supervising the Maths exam at the Main Hall on May 8th.
  D – Percy supervising the Spanish exam at the Main Library on May 5th.

Answer [ ]

DATA INTERPRETATION TESTS

Q19.

Determine the correct training code based on the information provided in the table. Training instruction provided to employees is coded as:
INSTRUCTOR – TRAINING – TRAINING SITE – DATE.

INSTRUCTOR CODE	TRAINING CODE	TRAINING SITE CODE	DATE CODE
Michael 777	Horse Riding R	Folkestone 118	Aug 17th AAA
Jordan 999	Rallying G	Eastbourne 741	Aug 28th BBB
Adrian 111	Motocross O	Ramsgate 961	Sept 5th CCC
Luke 333	Sky Diving P	Hastings 565	Sept 11th DDD
Elliott 555	Sailing E	Rye 709	Oct 18th EEE
Samuel 666	Parachuting S	Blackpool 666	Oct 20th FFF
Martin 888	Wakeboarding X	Broadstairs 744	Oct 24th GGG

1. Samuel wants to conduct a Sky Diving lesson at Folkestone. If the centre schedules the lesson for August 17th, the code would be?

    A – 666-O-118-BBB
    B – 666-P-118-AAA
    C – 666-P-741-DDD
    D – 666-P-118-BBB

Answer [   ]

2. The code 111-G-709-EEE is CORRECT for?

    A – Adrian conducting Sky Diving training at Blackpool on October 20th.
    B – Adrian conducting Rallying training at Rye on October 18th.

C – Elliott conducting Parachuting training at Blackpool on October 24th.
D – Martin conducting Sailing training at Eastbourne on August 28th.

Answer [ ]

3. Jordan received his schedule and saw the code 999-E-744-BBB. He notified his supervisor that the lesson needed to be moved to Sept 5th. The training was subsequently recoded?

   A – 999-E-741-CCC
   B – 999-R-744-BBB
   C – 999-E-744-CCC
   D – 999-E-744-GGG

Answer [ ]

4. Michael was scheduled to conduct Parachuting training at Ramsgate on Sept 11th, but Elliott had to substitute at the last minute. The revised code for the training is?

   A – 555-P-961-DDD
   B – 555-S-565-CCC
   C – 555-S-961-DDD
   D – 555-S-709-EEE

Answer [ ]

5. The code 333-O-565-CCC is CORRECT for?

   A – Luke conducting Motocross training at Hastings on September 5th.
   B – Luke conducting Sailing training at Eastbourne on September 11th.
   C – Jordan conducting Motocross training at Folkestone on September 5th.
   D – Jordan conducting Rallying training at Blackpool on October 24th.

Answer [ ]

DATA INTERPRETATION TESTS

Q20.

Determine the correct training code based on the information provided in the table.
Training instruction provided to employees is coded as:
INSTRUCTOR – TRAINING – TRAINING SITE – DATE.

INSTRUCTOR CODE	TRAINING CODE	TRAINING SITE CODE	DATE CODE
Beale 666	Electrical E	Local Care Home 741	June 9th AAA
Jackson 444	Midwifery N	Administration 319	June 15th BBB
Jones 222	Security S	Building Site 227	June 17th CCC
Daines 888	Construction B	Main Office 264	July 3rd DDD
Gilmore 111	Business I	Main Library 337	July 18th EEE
Green 333	Social Care M	Maidstone Hospital 008	July 29th FFF
Hartnell 555	Psychology P	Business Centre 101	August 2nd GGG

1. The code 888-S-101-BBB is CORRECT for?

    A – Security training taught by Daines at the Business Centre on June 15th.
    B – Construction training taught by Gilmore at the Building Site on June 17th.
    C – Security training taught by Jones at the Main Office on June 9th.
    D – Security training taught by Daines at the Main Library on July 3rd.

Answer [ ]

2. Jones was scheduled to conduct Social Care training at the Local Care Home on July 18th, but Jackson had to substitute at the last minute. The revised code for the training is?

    A – 222-M-741-EEE
    B – 444-M-741-EEE

C – 444-N-319-DDD
D – 222-N-319-AAA

Answer [ ]

3. The code 555-P-264-FFF is CORRECT for?

   A – Psychology training taught by Green at the Main Library on July 3rd.
   B – Psychology training taught by Hartnell at the Main Library on July 29th.
   C – Psychology training taught by Hartnell at the Main Office on July 29th.
   D – Psychology training taught by Hartnell at Administration on June 15th.

Answer [ ]

4. Beale wants to conduct Business training at the Business Centre. If the centre schedules the training session for August 2nd, the code would be?

   A – 666-S-101-EEE
   B – 444-I-101-GGG
   C – 666-I-101-GGG
   D – 666-S-319-DDD

Answer [ ]

5. Gilmore received her schedule and saw the code 111-N-008-CCC. She notified her supervisor that the training session needed to be moved to July 3rd. The training was subsequently recoded?

   A – 111-N-264-DDD
   B – 111-N-264-CCC
   C – 111-N-008-FFF
   D – 111-N-008-DDD

Answer [ ]

Now check your answers before moving on to the next section of the guide.

DATA INTERPRETATIONS PART 6 ANSWERS

QUESTION 1

1. C

EXPLANATION: The correct answer is C. The code 777-T-215-CCC would signify that Powley (777) taught Data analysis Training (T) at the Ramsay Campus (215) on June 8th (CCC).

2. B

EXPLANATION: The correct answer is B. The code for this training would be 222 (Walker) –I (Writing) –635 (Powell Office) –GGG (August 23rd).

3. A

EXPLANATION: The correct answer is A. The training would be recoded as 888 (Wells) –H (First Aid) –701 (Wester Hall) –CCC (June 8th).

4. C

EXPLANATION: The correct answer is C. The revised code for the training would be 333 (Thomas) –R (Mechanics) –328 (Hyde Garage) –BBB (June 4th).

5. A

EXPLANATION: The correct answer is A. This code is correct for Budgeting training (B) conducted by Brown (555) at the Main Library (353) on August 18th (FFF).

QUESTION 2

1. C

EXPLANATION: The correct answer is C. The revised code for the training would be 777 (Page) –S (Science) –331 (Augustine Hall) –CCC (May 5th).

2. D

EXPLANATION: The correct answer is D. This code is correct for Holmes (666) supervising the Geography exam (G) at the Auditorium (229) on May 14th (EEE).

3. B

EXPLANATION: The correct answer is B. This code is correct for West (111) supervising the History exam (H) at Augustine Hall (331) on May 19th (FFF).

4. B

EXPLANATION: The correct answer is B. This code is correct for Edwards (222) supervising the Citizenship exam (C) at Ramsay Building (464) on May 14th (EEE).

5. A

EXPLANATION: The correct answer is A. This code is correct for Newton (000) supervising the History exam (H) at the Main Library (785) on May 4th (BBB).

PART 6 227

QUESTION 3

1. A

EXPLANATION: The correct answer is A. The code for this lesson would be 111 (Grove) – Y (Football) –367 (Sports Centre) –FFF (August 9th).

2. C

EXPLANATION: The correct answer is C. The code 888-X-654-BBB would signify that Peters (888) teaching Basketball (X) at the Powell Hall (654) on June 11th (BBB).

3. B

EXPLANATION: The correct answer is B. The lesson would be recoded as 777 (Smith) –T (Hockey) –006 (Mote Park) –EEE (August 7th).

4. C

EXPLANATION: The correct answer is C. The revised code for the training would be 444 (Hampton) –V (Gymnastics) –125 (Anselm Hall) –AAA (June 5th).

5. D

EXPLANATION: The correct answer is D. This code is correct for a Tennis lesson (E) taught by Richards (555) at the Sports Centre (367) on May 19th (DDD).

QUESTION 4

1. D

EXPLANATION: The correct answer is D. The revised code for the book signing would be 777 (Tyler) –Y (Autobiography) –116 (Washington) –BBB (February 8th).

2. A

EXPLANATION: The correct answer is A. The code 444-O-742-AAA would signify that Edwards (444) would have his book signing for his Thriller (O) in Los Angeles (742) on January 31st (AAA).

3. D

EXPLANATION: The correct answer is D. This code is correct for Harvey (555) having a book signing for her Crime novel (J) in New Jersey (992) on May 11th (GGG).

4. C

EXPLANATION: The correct answer is C. The training would be recoded as 333 (Davis) – O (Thriller) –788 (Georgia) –DDD (March 24th).

5. B

EXPLANATION: The correct answer is B. This code is correct for Bonds (222) having a book signing for his Sci-Fi novel (B) in Colorado (485) on February 17th (CCC).

DATA INTERPRETATION TESTS

QUESTION 5

1. B

EXPLANATION: The correct answer is B. The revised code for the training would be 333 (Adams) – F (Fitness) –039 (Mote Park Leisure Centre) –AAA (June 3rd).

2. C

EXPLANATION: The correct answer is C. This code is correct for Parker (777) conducting Health and Hygiene training (H) in the Lecture Theatre (147) on July 2nd (DDD).

3. C

EXPLANATION: The correct answer is C. The code for this training would be 555 (Haynes) –R (First Aid) –258 (Tyler Building) – CCC (June 30th).

4. C

EXPLANATION: The correct answer is C. The training would be recoded as 666 (Matthews) –P (Lifeguarding) –196 (Larkfield Leisure Centre) – GGG (July 10th).

5. D

EXPLANATION: The correct answer is D. The code 888-X-774-DDD would signify that Simmons (888) would conduct Child Care Training (X) at the Gilmore Office (774) on July 2nd (DDD).

QUESTION 6

1. C

EXPLANATION: The correct answer is C. The revised code for the training would be 777 (O'Neill) – T (Religious studies) –447 (Lindsay Building) –BBB (June 9th).

2. A

EXPLANATION: The correct answer is A. This code is correct for Adams (333) supervising the French exam (K) at the Auditorium (498) on July 7th (EEE).

3. B

EXPLANATION: The correct answer is B. This code is correct for Franks (999) supervising the Technology exam (O) at the Main Library (698) on July 8th (FFF).

4. C

EXPLANATION: The correct answer is B. This code is correct for Robinson (111) supervising the Science exam (E) at Tyler Hall (961) on June 10th (CCC).

5. D

EXPLANATION: The correct answer is D. This code is correct for invigilator Smith (222) supervising the Maths exam (N) at the Main Library (698) on July 9th (GGG).

PART 6   229

QUESTION 7

1. B

EXPLANATION: The correct answer is B. This code is correct for training conducted by Lincoln (777) on Tiling (U) at the Kent College (185) on April 5th (CCC).

2. C

EXPLANATION: The correct answer is C. The revised code for the training would be 444 (Harrison) –M (Electrician) –981 (Building site) –EEE (July 29th).

3. A

EXPLANATION: The correct answer is A. The training would be recoded as 333 (Wicks) – A (Builder) – 137 (Public Works) –EEE (July 29th).

4. C

EXPLANATION: The correct answer is C. The code for this training would be 888 (Holmes) –Y (Plastering) –227 (Canterbury College) –FFF (Sept 4th).

5. B

EXPLANATION: The correct answer is B. This code is correct for Carpenter training (W) conducted by Abraham (555) at the Public Works (137) on March 22nd (BBB).

QUESTION 8

1. C

EXPLANATION: The correct answer is C. This code is correct for a Rugby lesson (B) taught by Barlow (333) at the Kent Stadium (232) on June 3rd (CCC).

2. D

EXPLANATION: The correct answer is D. The revised code for the training would be 777 (Nelson) – I (Ice Hockey) –009 (Local Ice Rink) –BBB (May 11th).

3. B

EXPLANATION: The correct answer is B. The lesson would be recoded as 222 (Madison) – R (Gymnastics) –972 (Harlow centre) –BBB (May 11th).

4. A

EXPLANATION: The correct answer is A. The code 666-K-009-EEE would signify that Webster (666) conducting an Ice Skating lesson (K) at the Local Ice Rink (009) on July 17th (EEE).

5. C

EXPLANATION: The correct answer is C. The code for this lesson would be 444 (Phillips) – Q (Cricket) –632 (cricket grounds) – AAA (May 4th).

QUESTION 9

1. C

EXPLANATION: The correct answer is C. The code for the premiere would be 777 (Tyler) –E (Drama) –009 (Los Angeles) –BBB (April 19th).

2. A

EXPLANATION: The correct answer is A. The revised code for the premiere would be 555 (Edwards) –L (Horror) –258 (London) –CCC (May 2nd).

3. B

EXPLANATION: The correct answer is B. This code is correct for Adams (333) having his premiere for his Drama film (E) in New York (020) on June 28th (GGG).

4. C

EXPLANATION: The correct answer is C. The training would be recoded as 111 (Williams) – M (Documentary) –771 (Paris) –EEE (June 23rd).

5. B

EXPLANATION: The correct answer is B. This code is correct for Fowlers 666) having his premiere for his Comedy film (P) in London (258) on June 28th (GGG).

QUESTION 10

1. C

EXPLANATION: The correct answer is C. This code is correct for Henderson (555) supervising the Chemistry exam (Ch) in the Sports Hall (971) on May 19th (DDD).

2. B

EXPLANATION: The correct answer is B. The revised code for the training would be 666 (Kimber) – Fi (Film exam) –559 (Private Library) –AAA (May 8th).

3. C

EXPLANATION: The correct answer is C. This code is correct for Hazels (444) supervising the Law exam (La) at the Erasmus Building (217) on May 22nd (EEE).

4. D

EXPLANATION: The correct answer is D. This code is correct for Blackman (111) supervising the Spanish exam (Sp) in the Gymnasium (136) on June 16th (GGG).

5. B

EXPLANATION: The correct answer is B. This code is correct for invigilator Woodman (777) supervising the Environmental Studies exam (En) at the Invicta Building (319) on May 11th (CCC).

QUESTION 11

1. D

EXPLANATION: The correct answer is D. The revised code for the training would be 999 (Hyett) –C (Tennis) –963 (Lloyds Gym) – CCC (February 18th).

2. C

EXPLANATION: The correct answer is C. This code is correct for Friend (555) conducting a Badminton lesson (K) at Topnotch Health (759) on April 18th (GGG).

3. C

EXPLANATION: The correct answer is C. The code for this lesson would be 777 (Phillips) – O (Karate) –821 (Cornwallis Hall) – DDD (March 3rd).

4. B

EXPLANATION: The correct answer is B. This code is correct for Sage (888) conducting a Dance lesson (Q) at the La fitness Centre (237) on January 31st (AAA).

5. B

EXPLANATION: The correct answer is B. The revised code for the training would be 333 (Harley) – Z (Hockey) –179 (YMCA) –EEE (March 19th).

QUESTION 12

1. D

EXPLANATION: the correct answer is D. this code is correct for Jones (555) having a book signing for his Drama novel (F) at Kent Museum (239) on June 8th (DDD).

2. A

EXPLANATION: The correct answer is A. The training would be recoded as 444 (Miller) – A (Autobiography) –746 (NY Library) –GGG (July 18th).

3. C

EXPLANATION: The correct answer is C. This code is correct for Lacey (777) having a book signing for her Fiction novel (N) at Waterstones (271) on May 13th (CCC).

4. B

EXPLANATION: The correct answer is B. The code 666-R-239-BBB would signify that Watson (666) would have his book signing for his Action novel (R) at Kent Museum (239) on April 22nd (BBB).

5. C

EXPLANATION: The correct answer is C. The revised code for the book signing would be 999 (Martin) –F (Drama) –963 (LA Library) –DDD (June 8th).

DATA INTERPRETATION TESTS

QUESTION 13

1. B

EXPLANATION: The correct answer is B. The revised code for the training would be 111 (Alex) – J (Cardio) –967 (Local Gym) - CCC (June 9th).

2. C

EXPLANATION: The correct answer is C. This code is correct for Rachel (888) conducting a Bums and Tums lesson (S) at the Fitness Centre (490) on June 18th (FFF).

3. D

EXPLANATION: The correct answer is D. The code for this lesson would be 999 (Simon) – X (Circuits) –109 (Private Gym) – CCC (June 9th).

4. B

EXPLANATION: The correct answer is B. This code is correct for Matt (222) conducting a Legs Workout (D) at the Sports Hall (792) on June 7th (AAA).

5. A

EXPLANATION: The correct answer is A. The revised code for the training would be 666 (Carla) – J (Cardio) –967 (Local Gym) –FFF (June 18th).

QUESTION 14

1. C

EXPLANATION: The correct answer is c. This code is correct for Owen (888) conducting an Abseiling lesson (B) at Rye (418) on August 3rd (AAA).

2. B

EXPLANATION: The correct answer is B. The training would be recoded as 333 (David) –U (Wind Surfing) –316 (Romney Marsh) – GGG (Sept 22nd).

3. A

EXPLANATION: The correct answer is A. The revised code for the training would be 666 (Josh) – G (Diving) –784 (Broadstairs) –BBB (August 10th).

4. C

EXPLANATION: The correct answer is C. The code for this training would be 999 (Gareth) –K (Hang Gliding) –009 (Eastbourne) – EEE (Sept 11th).

5. C

EXPLANATION: The correct answer is D. The code 555-U-772-FFF would signify that Ben (555) would conduct a Wind Surfing lesson (U) at Folkestone (772) on Sept 19th (FFF).

PART 6   233

QUESTION 15

1. C

EXPLANATION: The correct answer is C. The code 666-T-338-BBB would signify that Michelle (666) would supervise the English Lit exam (T) at the Public Library (338) on May 20th (BBB).

2. D

EXPLANATION: The correct answer is D. The code 333-E-157-EEE would signify that Erin (333) would supervise the Media exam (E) at the Lecture Theatre (157) on June 7th (EEE).

3. B

EXPLANATION: The correct answer is B. The revised code for the training would be 555 (Erin) – W (Geography) –007 (Sports Hall) –AAA (May 18th).

4. C

EXPLANATION: The correct answer is C. This code is correct for Frank (444) supervising the English Language exam (B) at the Main Hall (415) on May 29th (CCC).

5. A

EXPLANATION: The correct answer is A. This code is correct for invigilator Simon (777) supervising the Science exam (N) in the Gymnasium (551) on June 7th (EEE).

QUESTION 16

1. B

EXPLANATION: The correct answer is B. The code 777-V-331-CCC would signify that Ryan (777) is conducting a Bricklaying course (V) at Mid Kent (331) on March 4th (CCC).

2. D

EXPLANATION: The correct answer is D. The code for this training would be 222 (Harrison) –E (Mechanics) –376 (Canterbury) –AAA (February 18th).

3. C

EXPLANATION: The correct answer is C. The training would be recoded as 111 (Elizabeth) –U (Floristry) –555 (Hadlow) –DDD (March 11th).

4. B

EXPLANATION: The correct answer is B. The revised code for the training would be 333 (Jason) –E (Mechanics) –391 (UCA) –EEE (April 8th).

5. D

EXPLANATION: The correct answer is D. This code is correct for training conducted by Shaun (888) for Musician lessons (D) at Home (004) on April 10th (FFF).

QUESTION 17

1. C

EXPLANATION: The correct answer is C. This code is correct for Writing training (Q) conducted by Santini (333) at the Business Park (673) on November 13th (CCC).

2. A

EXPLANATION: The correct answer is A. The revised code for the training would be 222 (Miller) –A (Analysis) –153 (Main Hall) –EEE (December 1st).

3. C

EXPLANATION: The correct answer is C. The training would be recoded as 555 (Carlos) – V (Contracts) – 484 (Administration) –CCC (November 13th).

4. A

EXPLANATION: The correct answer is A. The code for this training would be 999 (McManus) –C (Editing) –639 (Business Centre) –GGG (December 18th).

5. D

EXPLANATION: The correct answer is D. This code is correct for Design training (H) conducted by Fowler (777) at the Business Park (673) on November 28th (DDD).

QUESTION 18

1. A

EXPLANATION: The correct answer is A. The revised code for the training would be 444 (Neville) – W (Spanish) –319 (Lecture Theatre 01) – DDD (May 12th).

2. C

EXPLANATION: The correct answer is C. This code is correct for Harry (111) supervising the Law exam (G) at the Sports Hall (202) on June 2nd (FFF).

3. B

EXPLANATION: The correct answer is B. This code is correct for Stephanie (333) supervising the Technology exam (T) at the Private Library (475) on May 7th (BBB).

4. D

EXPLANATION: The correct answer is D. This code is correct for Ronald (555) supervising the Nursing exam (B) at the Lecture Theatre 02 (320) on May 23rd (EEE).

5. D

EXPLANATION: The correct answer is D. This code is correct for Percy (777) supervising the Spanish exam (W) at the Main Library (484) on May 5th (AAA).

PART 6   235

QUESTION 19

1. B

EXPLANATION: The correct answer is B. The code for this lesson would be 666 (Samuel) – P (Sky diving) – 118 (Folkestone) –AAA (August 17th).

2. B

EXPLANATION: The correct answer is B. The code 111-G-709-EEE would signify that Adrian (111) teaching Rallying (G) at Rye (709) on October 18th (EEE).

3. C

EXPLANATION: The correct answer is C. The lesson would be recoded as 999 (Jordan) –E (Sailing) –744 (Broadstairs) –CCC (Sept 5th).

4. C

EXPLANATION: The correct answer is C. The revised code for the training would be 555 (Elliott) – S (Parachuting) –961 (Ramsgate) –DDD (Sept 11th).

5. A

EXPLANATION: The correct answer is A. This code is correct for Motocross training (O) taught by Luke (333) at Hastings (565) on Sept 5th (CCC).

QUESTION 20

1. A

EXPLANATION: The correct answer is A. The code 888-S-101-BBB would signify that Daines (888) teaching Security training (S) at Business Centre (101) on June 15th (BBB).

2. B

EXPLANATION: The correct answer is B. The revised code for the training would be 444 (Jackson) – M (Social Care) –741 (Local Care Home) –EEE (July 18th).

3. C

EXPLANATION: The correct answer is C. The code 555-P-264-FFF would signify that Hartnell (555) teaching Psychology training (P) at the Main Office (264) on July 29th (FFF).

4. C

EXPLANATION: The correct answer is C. The code for the session would be 666 (Beale) – I (Business) – 101 (Business Centre) –GGG (August 2nd).

5. D

EXPLANATION: The correct answer is D. The lesson would be recoded as 111 (Gilmore) – N (Midwifery) –008 (Maidstone Hospital) –DDD (July 3rd).

Now move on to the next section of the guide.

DATA INTERPRETATION TESTS

PART 7

DATA INTERPRETATION TESTS PART 7

Q1.

Study the following graph carefully and answer the questions given below.

Distribution of candidates who were enrolled for a Master's Degree and the candidates (out of those enrolled) who passed the selection process in different institutes.

Candidates Enrolled = 9500

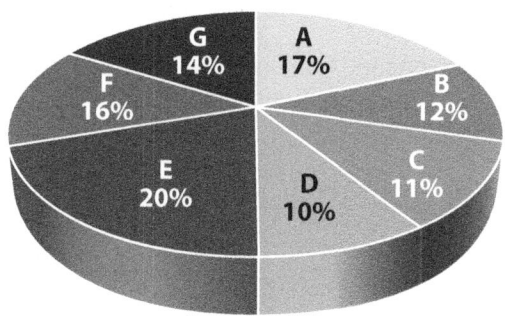

Candidates who passed the selection process = 6250

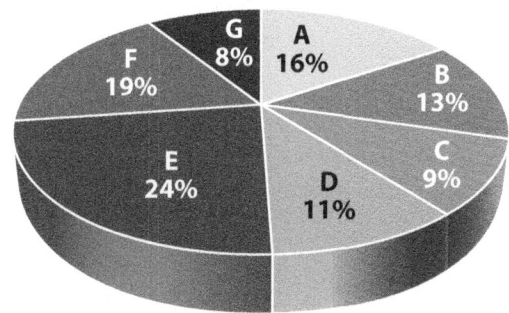

1. What percentage of candidates passed the selection process from institute C out of the total number of candidates enrolled from the same institute? Round it to the nearest whole number.

   A – 11%
   B – 62%
   C – 54%
   D – 37%

Answer

2. Which institute has the highest percentage of candidates passing the selection process to candidates enrolled?

A – C
B – E
C – G
D – F

Answer

3. The number of candidates passed from institutes A and E together exceeds the number of candidates that enrolled from institutes C and D by:

A – 675
B – 295
C – 345
D – 505

Answer

4. What is the ratio of candidates passed to the candidates enrolled from institute E?

A – 22 : 50
B – 5 : 9
C – 15 : 19
D – 15 : 30

Answer

5. What is the percentage of candidates passed to the candidates enrolled for institutes B and F together? Round it to the nearest whole number.

A – 75%
B – 62%
C – 45%
D – 54%

Answer

Q2.

Study the following graph carefully and answer the questions given below.

Distribution of candidates who were enrolled for a PHD and the candidates (out of those enrolled) who passed the selection process in different institutes.

Candidates Enrolled = 4800

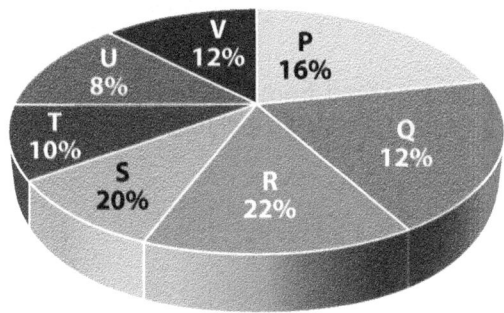

Candidates who passed the selection process = 1600

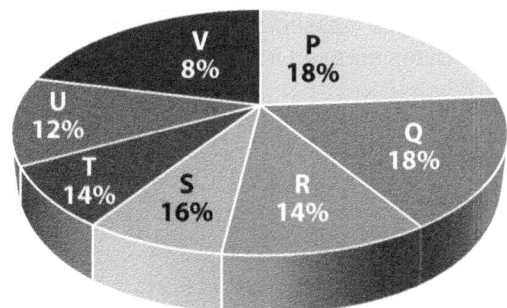

1. What is the ratio of candidates who passed the selection process to the candidates that enrolled from institute V?

   A – 1 : 3
   B – 2 : 9
   C – 11 : 13
   D – 4 : 5

Answer

DATA INTERPRETATION TESTS

2. What is the percentage of candidates passed to the candidates enrolled for institutes P and Q together? Round it to the nearest whole number.

    A – 11%
    B – 56%
    C – 43%
    D – 49%

    Answer

3. The number of candidates passed from institutes R and S together is less than the number of candidates that enrolled from institutes U and T by:

    A – 384
    B – 264
    C – 184
    D – 394

    Answer

4. What percentage of candidates passed the selection process from institute U out of the total number of candidates enrolled from the same institute? Round it to the nearest whole number.

    A – 65%
    B – 75%
    C – 25%
    D – 50%

    Answer

5. What is the difference between the percentage of candidates who passed the selection process from institute P and the percentage of candidates who were enrolled from institute T?

    A – 192
    B – 312
    C – 246
    D – 391

    Answer

Q3.

Study the following graph carefully and answer the questions given below.

Distribution of candidates who were enrolled for the 11 + and the candidates (out of those enrolled) who passed the exam in different institutes.

Candidates Enrolled = 1100

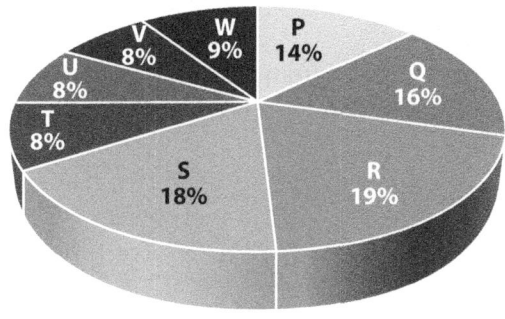

Candidates who passed the exam = 710

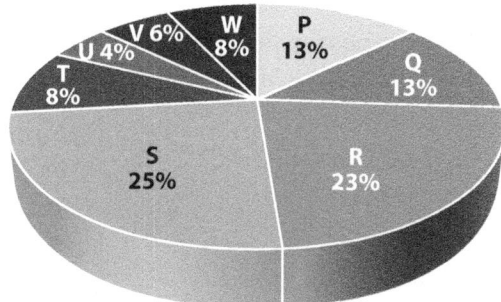

1. What is the difference between the percentage of candidates who enrolled for the exam from institute S and the percentage of candidates who enrolled for the exam from institute P?

   A – 21
   B – 44
   C – 103
   D – 87

Answer

2. What is the percentage of candidates passed to the candidates enrolled for institutes V and U together? Round up all numbers to the nearest whole number.

   A – 30%
   B – 25%
   C – 40%
   D – 70%

   Answer [ ]

3. The number of candidates passed from institutes W and U together is less than the number of candidates that enrolled from institute S by: (Round up all numbers to the nearest whole number).

   A – 92
   B – 128
   C – 65
   D – 113

   Answer [ ]

4. What percentage of candidates passed the exam from institute T out of the total number of candidates enrolled from the same institute? Round it to the nearest whole number.

   A – 65%
   B – 72%
   C – 12%
   D – 34%

   Answer [ ]

5. What is the percentage of candidates who passed the exam to the candidates that enrolled from institute V? Rounded to the nearest whole number.

   A – 21%
   B – 43%
   C – 48%
   D – 51%

   Answer [ ]

Q4.

Study the following graph carefully and answer the questions given below.

Distribution of candidates who were enrolled for a musical theatre audition and the candidates (out of those enrolled) who passed the selection process in different institutes.

Candidates Enrolled = 8550

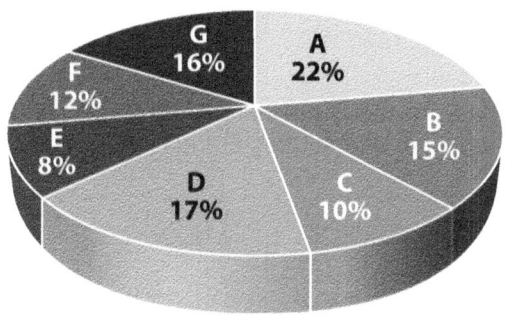

Candidates who passed the selection process = 5700

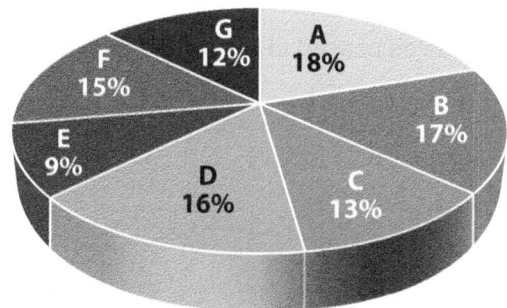

1. What percentage of candidates passed the selection process from institute D out of the total number of candidates enrolled from the same institute? Round it to the nearest whole number.

   A – 21%
   B – 85%
   C – 52%
   D – 63%

Answer

DATA INTERPRETATION TESTS

2. Which institute has the highest percentage of candidates passing the selection process to candidates enrolled?

A – B
B – F
C – C
D – A

Answer [ ]

3. The number of candidates passed from institutes B and C together exceeds the number of candidates that enrolled from institutes E and F by:

A – 20
B – 101
C – 0
D – 50

Answer [ ]

4. What is the ratio of candidates passed to the candidates enrolled from institute A?

A – 6 : 11
B – 1 : 8
C – 22 : 48
D – 101 : 186

Answer [ ]

5. What is the percentage of candidates passed to the candidates enrolled for institutes B and C together? Round it to the nearest whole number.

A – 60%
B – 50%
C – 20%
D – 80%

Answer [ ]

Q5.

Study the following graph carefully and answer the questions given below.

Distribution of candidates who were enrolled for a dance competition and the candidates (out of those enrolled) who passed the selection process to proceed to the next stage in different institutes.

Dancers enrolled = 1600

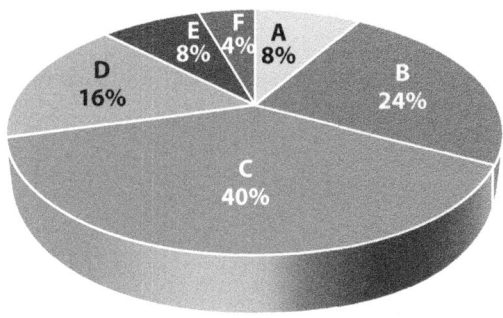

Dancers who passed the selection process = 900

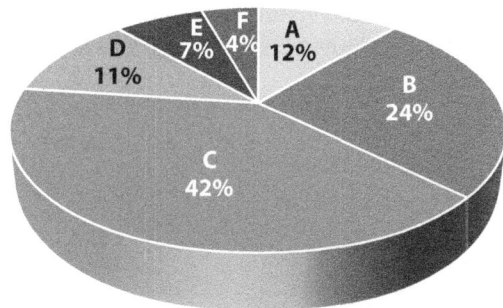

1. What percentage of dancers passed the exam from institute D out of the total number of dancers enrolled from the same institute? Round it to the nearest whole number.

   A – 46%
   B – 39%
   C – 45%
   D – 31%

Answer

DATA INTERPRETATION TESTS

2. Which institute has the highest percentage of dancers passing the selection process to candidates enrolled?

A – C
B – F
C – A
D – E

Answer

3. What is the percentage of dancers passed to the dancers enrolled for institutes A and B together? Round it to the nearest whole number.

A – 71%
B – 55%
C – 42%
D – 63%

Answer

4. The number of dancers passed from institutes C and B together is more than the number of dancers that enrolled from institutes E and F by: (Round up all numbers to the nearest whole number).

A – 368
B – 136
C – 285
D – 402

Answer

5. What is the difference between the percentage of dancers who passed the exam from institute D and the percentage of dancers who passed the exam from institute E?

A – 36
B – 32
C – 42
D – 46

Answer

Q6.

Study the following graph carefully and answer the questions given below.

Distribution of candidates who applied for a singing competition and the candidates (out of those who applied) who were selected for an audition in different institutions.

Candidates who applied = 9000

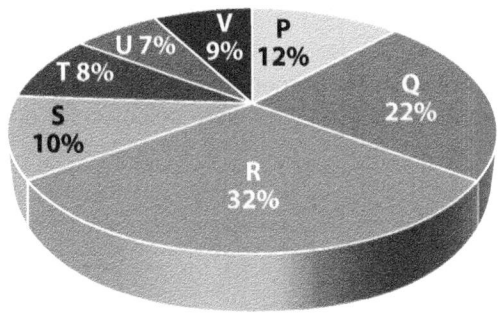

Candidates who were selected for an audition = 4500

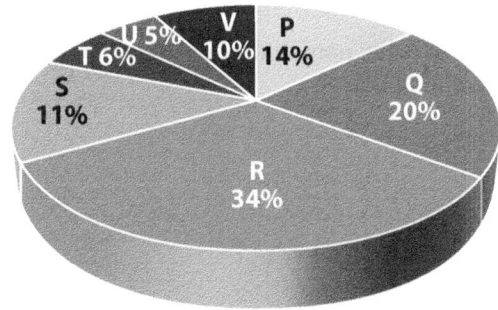

1. What is the ratio of candidates who were selected for an audition to the candidates that applied from institute T?

    A – 1 : 4
    B – 11 : 15
    C – 3 : 8
    D – 7 : 9

Answer

DATA INTERPRETATION TESTS

2. The number of candidates who were selected for an audition from institutes Q and U together is less than the number of candidates that applied from institutes P and S by:

   A – 858
   B – 855
   C – 585
   D – 558

   Answer

3. What is the difference between the percentage of candidates who applied from institute P and the percentage of candidates who were selected for an institute from the same institute?

   A – 860
   B – 250
   C – 450
   D – 220

   Answer

4. Which institute has the highest percentage of candidates who were selected for an audition to candidates who applied?

   A – S
   B – P
   C – U
   D – T

   Answer

5. What is the percentage of candidates who were selected to the candidates who applied from institutes V and R together? Round it to the nearest whole number.

   A – 31%
   B – 22%
   C – 54%
   D – 86%

   Answer

Q7.

Study the following graph carefully and answer the questions given below.

Distribution of candidates who applied to go to university and the candidates (out of those who applied) who were accepted to their first choice of university in different institutions.

Candidates who applied for university = 9900

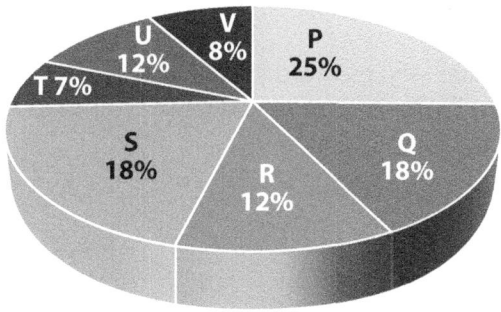

Candidates who received their first choice of university = 7800

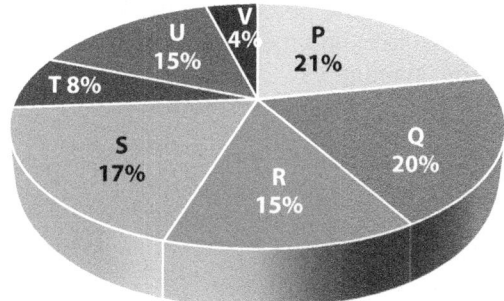

1. Which institute has the highest percentage of candidates who were received their first choice to those who applied?

   A – P and U
   B – R and S
   C – P and S
   D – R and U

Answer

DATA INTERPRETATION TESTS

2. What is the percentage of candidates who were selected to the candidates who applied from institutes Q and U together? Round it to the nearest whole number.

   A – 88%
   B – 92%
   C – 71%
   D – 35%

   Answer

3. The number of candidates who received their first university choice from institutes P and S together is more than the number of candidates who applied from institutes T and V by:

   A – 1487
   B – 1794
   C – 1479
   D – 1847

   Answer

4. What is the difference between the percentage of candidates who received their first university choice from institute R and the percentage of candidates who received their first university choice from institute V?

   A – 858
   B – 458
   C – 758
   D – 888

   Answer

5. What is the ratio of candidates who received their first university choice to the candidates that applied from institute Q?

   A – 11 :31
   B – 1 : 4
   C – 132 : 186
   D – 260 : 297

   Answer

Q8.

Study the following graph carefully and answer the questions given below.

Distribution of candidates who were enrolled for a Health and Safety exam and the candidates (out of those enrolled) who passed the exam in different institutes.

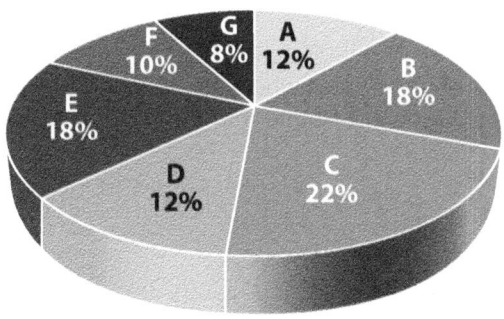

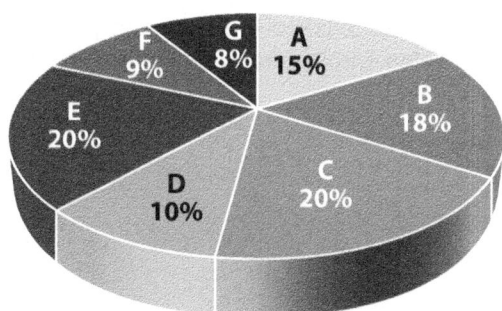

1. What is the difference between the percentage of candidates who passed the exam from institute C and the percentage of candidates who passed their exam from institute F?

   A – 184
   B – 125
   C – 176
   D – 201

Answer

DATA INTERPRETATION TESTS

2. What is the ratio of candidates who passed their exam to the candidates that enrolled from institute E?

   A – 16 : 27
   B – 3 : 4
   C – 1 : 6
   D – 5 : 29

   Answer [ ]

3. What is the percentage of candidates who were selected to the candidates who applied from institutes B and D together? Round it to the nearest whole number.

   A – 50%
   B – 75%
   C – 45%
   D – 85%

   Answer [ ]

4. What percentage of candidates passed the selection process from institute C out of the total number of candidates enrolled from the same institute? Round it to the nearest whole number.

   A – 71%
   B – 22%
   C – 48%
   D – 55%

   Answer [ ]

5. The number of candidates who passed from institutes E and B together is more than the number of candidates that enrolled from institutes A and G by:

   A – 108
   B – 45
   C – 28
   D – 8

   Answer [ ]

Q9.

Study the following graph carefully and answer the questions given below.

Distribution of candidates who were enrolled for an advanced driving course and the candidates (out of those enrolled) who passed the exam in different institutes.

Candidates enrolled = 4550

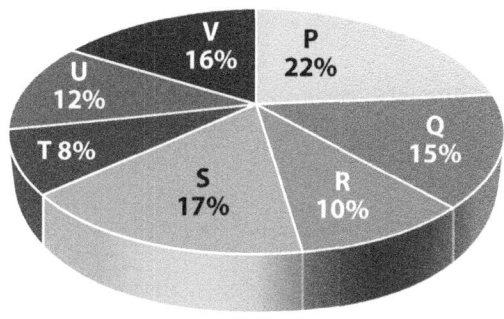

Candidates passed = 2275

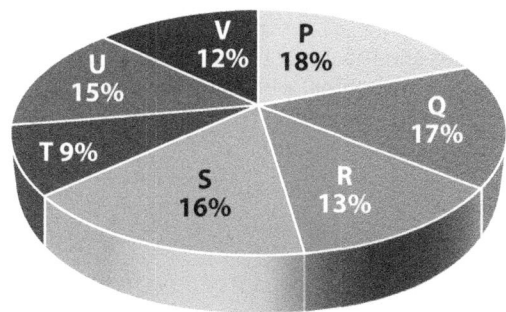

1. What is the percentage of candidates who passed to the candidates who enrolled from institutes S and V together? Round it to the nearest whole number.

   A – 18%
   B – 42%
   C – 33%
   D – 66%

Answer

2. What is the percentage of candidates who passed their exam to the candidates that enrolled from institute P?

   A – 39%
   B – 41%
   C – 72%
   D – 36%

   Answer

3. The number of candidates who passed the exam from institutes P and U together is more than the number of candidates that enrolled from institutes R and T by: Rounded to the nearest whole number.

   A – 22
   B – 11
   C – 68
   D – 38

   Answer

4. What is the difference between the percentage of candidates who enrolled from institute R and the percentage of candidates who passed the exam from the same institute? Rounded to the nearest whole number.

   A – 159
   B – 128
   C – 195
   D – 180

   Answer

5. What is the percentage of candidates who passed to the candidates who enrolled from institutes P and Q together? Round it to the nearest whole number.

   A – 47%
   B – 58%
   C – 55%
   D – 64%

   Answer

Q10.

Study the following graph carefully and answer the questions given below.

Distribution of candidates who were enrolled for a fitness course and the candidates (out of those enrolled) who passed the course in different institutes.

Candidates enrolled = 1500

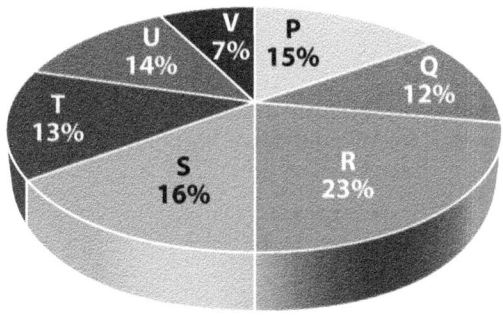

Candidates passed = 920

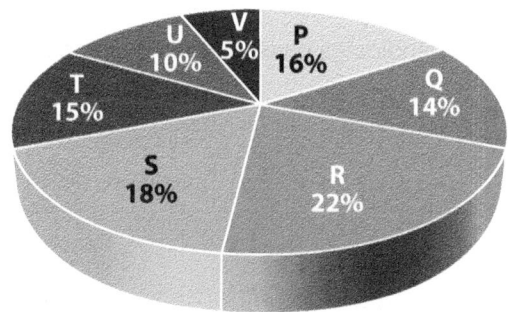

1. What percentage of candidates passed the course from institute R out of the total number of candidates enrolled from the same institute? Round it to the nearest whole number.

   A – 22%
   B – 59%
   C – 64%
   D – 81%

Answer

DATA INTERPRETATION TESTS

2. Which institute has the highest percentage of candidates passing the selection process to candidates enrolled?

    A – P
    B – Q
    C – T
    D – V

    Answer [   ]

3. The number of candidates passed from institutes R and S together exceeds the number of candidates that enrolled from institutes V and Q by:

    A – 92
    B – 83
    C – 54
    D – 61

    Answer [   ]

4. What is the percentage of candidates passed to the candidates enrolled from institute S?

    A – 69
    B – 33
    C – 71
    D – 73

    Answer [   ]

5. What is the percentage of candidates passed to the candidates enrolled for institutes P and Q together? Round it to the nearest whole number.

    A – 68%
    B – 55%
    C – 32%
    D – 78%

    Answer [   ]

Now check your ansers before moving on to the next section of the guide.

DATA INTERPRETATIONS PART 7 ANSWERS

QUESTION 1

1. C

EXPLANATION $= \left(\dfrac{9\% \text{ of } 6250}{11\% \text{ of } 9500} \times 100\right)\% = \left(\dfrac{9 \times 6250}{11 \times 9500} \times 100\right)\% = 54\%$.

2. B – E

EXPLANATION =

$A = \left[\left(\dfrac{16\% \text{ of } 6250}{17\% \text{ of } 9500}\right) \times 100\right]\% = \left[\dfrac{16 \times 6250}{17 \times 9500} \times 100\right]\% = 61.91\%$.

$B = \left[\left(\dfrac{13\% \text{ of } 6250}{12\% \text{ of } 9500}\right) \times 100\right]\% = 71.27\%$.

$C = \left[\left(\dfrac{9\% \text{ of } 6250}{11\% \text{ of } 9500}\right) \times 100\right]\% = 53.82\%$.

$D = \left[\left(\dfrac{11\% \text{ of } 6250}{10\% \text{ of } 9500}\right) \times 100\right]\% = 72.36\%$.

$E = \left[\left(\dfrac{24\% \text{ of } 6250}{20\% \text{ of } 9500}\right) \times 100\right]\% = 78.94\%$.

$F = \left[\left(\dfrac{19\% \text{ of } 6250}{16\% \text{ of } 9500}\right) \times 100\right]\% = 78.12\%$.

$G = \left[\left(\dfrac{8\% \text{ of } 6250}{14\% \text{ of } 9500}\right) \times 100\right]\% = 37.59\%$.

3. D

EXPLANATION = [(16% + 24%) of 6250] - [(10% + 11%) of 9500]
[(40% of 6250) - (21% of 9500)] = 2500 – 1995 = 505

4. C

EXPLANATION $= \left(\dfrac{24\% \text{ of } 6250}{20\% \text{ of } 9500}\right) = \left(\dfrac{24 \times 6250}{20 \times 9500}\right) = \dfrac{15}{19}$

5. A

EXPLANATION =

Candidates passed from institutes B and F together = [(13% + 19%) of 6250]
Candidates enrolled from institutes B and F together = [(12% + 16%) of 9500]

$\left(\dfrac{32\% \times 6250}{28\% \times 9500} \times 100\right)\% = 75\%$

QUESTION 2

1. B
EXPLANATION = $\left(\dfrac{8\% \text{ of } 1600}{12\% \text{ of } 4800}\right) = \left(\dfrac{8 \times 1600}{12 \times 4800}\right) = \dfrac{2}{9}$

2. C
EXPLANATION =
Candidates passed from institutes P and Q together = [(18% + 18%) of 1600]
Candidates enrolled from institutes P and Q together = [(16% + 12%) of 4800]
$\left(\dfrac{36 \times 1600}{28 \times 4800} \times 100\right)\% = 42.85\%$

3. A
EXPLANATION = [(14% + 16%) of 1600] - [(10% + 8%) of 4800]
[(30% of 1600) - (18% of 4800)] = 480 - 864 = So institutes R and S is less than U and T by 384

4. D
EXPLANATION = $\left(\dfrac{12\% \text{ of } 1600}{8\% \text{ of } 4800} \times 100\right)\% = \left(\dfrac{12 \times 1600}{8\% \times 4800} \times 100\right)\% = 50\%.$

5. A
EXPLANATION = [(18% of 1600)] - [(10% of 4800] = 288 – 480 = So the difference would be 192

QUESTION 3

1. B
EXPLANATION = [(18% of 1100)] - [(14% of 1100] = 198 –154 = 44

2. C
EXPLANATION: Candidates passed from institutes U and V together = [(4% + 6%) of 710]
Candidates enrolled from institutes U and V together = [(8% + 8%) of 1100]
$= \left(\dfrac{10 \times 710}{16 \times 1100} \times 100\right)\% = 40\%$

3. D
EXPLANATION = [(8% + 4%) of 710] - [(18% of 1100]
= [(12% of 710) - (18% of 1100)] = 113

4. A
EXPLANATION = $\left(\dfrac{8\% \text{ of } 710}{8\% \text{ of } 1100} \times 100\right)\% = \left(\dfrac{8 \times 710}{8 \times 1100} \times 100\right)\% = 65\%.$

5. C
EXPLANATION = $\left(\dfrac{6\% \text{ of } 710}{8\% \text{ of } 1100}\right) = \left(\dfrac{6 \times 710}{8 \times 1100}\right) \times 100 = 48\%$

QUESTION 4

1. D
EXPLANATION = $\left(\dfrac{16\% \text{ of } 5700}{17\% \text{ of } 8550} \times 100\right)\% = \left(\dfrac{16 \times 5700}{17 \times 8550} \times 100\right)\% = 63\%.$

2. C – C
EXPLANATION =

$A = \left[\left(\dfrac{18\% \text{ of } 5700}{22\% \text{ of } 8550}\right) \times 100\right]\% = \left[\dfrac{18 \times 5700}{22 \times 8550} \times 100\right]\% = 54.55\%.$

$B = \left[\left(\dfrac{17\% \text{ of } 5700}{15\% \text{ of } 8550}\right) \times 100\right]\% = 75.56\%.$

$C = \left[\left(\dfrac{13\% \text{ of } 5700}{10\% \text{ of } 8550}\right) \times 100\right]\% = 86.67\%.$

$D = \left[\left(\dfrac{16\% \text{ of } 5700}{17\% \text{ of } 8550}\right) \times 100\right]\% = 62.75\%.$

$E = \left[\left(\dfrac{9\% \text{ of } 5700}{8\% \text{ of } 8550}\right) \times 100\right]\% = 75\%.$

$F = \left[\left(\dfrac{15\% \text{ of } 5700}{12\% \text{ of } 8550}\right) \times 100\right]\% = 83.33\%.$

$G = \left[\left(\dfrac{12\% \text{ of } 5700}{16\% \text{ of } 8550}\right) \times 100\right]\% = 50\%.$

3. C
EXPLANATION = [(17% + 13%) of 5700] - [(8% + 12%) of 8550]
[(30% of 5700) - (20% of 8550)] = 1710 – 1710 = 0

4. A
EXPLANATION = $\left(\dfrac{18\% \text{ of } 5700}{22\% \text{ of } 8550}\right) = \left(\dfrac{18 \times 5700}{22 \times 8550}\right) = \dfrac{6}{11}$

5. D

EXPLANATION: Candidates passed from institutes B and C together = [(17% + 13%) of 5700]
Candidates enrolled from institutes B and F together = [(15% + 10%) of 8550]

$$= \left(\frac{30 \times 5700}{25 \times 8550} \times 100\right)\% = 80\%$$

QUESTION 5

1. B

EXPLANATION $= \left(\frac{11\% \text{ of } 900}{16\% \text{ of } 1600} \times 100\right)\% = \left(\frac{11 \times 900}{16 \times 1600} \times 100\right)\% = 39\%$.

2. C – A

EXPLANATION =

$A = \left[\left(\frac{12\% \text{ of } 900}{8\% \text{ of } 1600}\right) \times 100\right]\% = \left[\frac{12 \times 900}{8 \times 1600} \times 100\right]\% = 84.375\%$.

$B = \left[\left(\frac{24\% \text{ of } 900}{24\% \text{ of } 1600}\right) \times 100\right]\% = 56.25\%$.

$C = \left[\left(\frac{42\% \text{ of } 900}{40\% \text{ of } 1600}\right) \times 100\right]\% = 59.06\%$.

$D = \left[\left(\frac{11\% \text{ of } 900}{16\% \text{ of } 1600}\right) \times 100\right]\% = 38.67\%$.

$E = \left[\left(\frac{7\% \text{ of } 900}{8\% \text{ of } 1600}\right) \times 100\right]\% = 49.21\%$.

$F = \left[\left(\frac{4\% \text{ of } 900}{4\% \text{ of } 1600}\right) \times 100\right]\% = 56.25\%$.

3. D

EXPLANATION = Candidates passed from institutes A and B together = [(12% + 24%) of 900]
Candidates enrolled from institutes A and B together = [(8% + 24%) of 1600]

$$= \left(\frac{36 \times 900}{32 \times 1600} \times 100\right)\% = 63\%$$

4. D

EXPLANATION = [(42% + 24%) of 900] - [(8% + 4%) of 1600]
= [(66% of 900) - (12% of 1600)] = 492

5. A

EXPLANATION = [(11% of 900)] - [(7% of 900] = 99 – 63 = 36

QUESTION 6

1. C
EXPLANATION = $\left(\dfrac{6\% \text{ of } 4500}{8\% \text{ of } 9000}\right) = \left(\dfrac{6 \times 4500}{8 \times 9000}\right) = \dfrac{3}{8}$

2. B
EXPLANATION = [(20% + 5%) of 4500] - [(12% + 10%) of 9000]
[(25% of 4500) - (22% of 9000)] = 1125 – 1980 = -855

3. C
EXPLANATION = [(12% of 9000] - [(14% of 4500)] = 1080 –630 = 450

4. B – P
EXPLANATION =

$P = \left[\left(\dfrac{14\% \text{ of } 4500}{12\% \text{ of } 9000}\right) \times 100\right]\% = \left[\dfrac{14 \times 4500}{12 \times 9000} \times 100\right]\% = 58.33\%.$

$Q = \left[\left(\dfrac{20\% \text{ of } 4500}{22\% \text{ of } 9000}\right) \times 100\right]\% = 45.45\%.$

$R = \left[\left(\dfrac{34\% \text{ of } 4500}{32\% \text{ of } 9000}\right) \times 100\right]\% = 53.125\%.$

$S = \left[\left(\dfrac{11\% \text{ of } 4500}{10\% \text{ of } 9000}\right) \times 100\right]\% = 55\%.$

$T = \left[\left(\dfrac{6\% \text{ of } 4500}{8\% \text{ of } 9000}\right) \times 100\right]\% = 37.5\%.$

$U = \left[\left(\dfrac{5\% \text{ of } 4500}{7\% \text{ of } 9000}\right) \times 100\right]\% = 35.71\%.$

$V = \left[\left(\dfrac{10\% \text{ of } 4500}{9\% \text{ of } 9000}\right) \times 100\right]\% = 55.55\%.$

5. C
EXPLANATION = Candidates selected from institutes R and V together = [(10% + 34%) of 4500]
Candidates applied from institutes R and V together = [(9% + 32%) of 9000]

$= \left(\dfrac{44 \times 4500}{41 \times 9000} \times 100\right)\% = 54\%$

DATA INTERPRETATION TESTS

QUESTION 7

1. D – R + U

EXPLANATION =

$P = \left[\left(\dfrac{21\% \text{ of } 7800}{25\% \text{ of } 9900}\right) \times 100\right]\% = \left[\dfrac{21 \times 7800}{25 \times 9900} \times 100\right]\% = 66.18\%.$

$Q = \left[\left(\dfrac{20\% \text{ of } 7800}{18\% \text{ of } 9900}\right) \times 100\right]\% = 87.54\%.$

$R = \left[\left(\dfrac{15\% \text{ of } 7800}{12\% \text{ of } 9900}\right) \times 100\right]\% = 98.48\%.$

$S = \left[\left(\dfrac{17\% \text{ of } 7800}{18\% \text{ of } 9900}\right) \times 100\right]\% = 74.41\%.$

$T = \left[\left(\dfrac{8\% \text{ of } 7800}{7\% \text{ of } 9900}\right) \times 100\right]\% = 90.04\%.$

$U = \left[\left(\dfrac{15\% \text{ of } 7800}{12\% \text{ of } 9900}\right) \times 100\right]\% = 98.48\%.$

$V = \left[\left(\dfrac{4\% \text{ of } 7800}{8\% \text{ of } 9900}\right) \times 100\right]\% = 39.39\%.$

2. B

EXPLANATION = Candidates who received their first university choice from institutes Q and U together = [(20% + 15%) of 7800]

Candidates enrolled from institutes Q and R together = [(18% + 12%) of 9900]

$= \left(\dfrac{35 \times 7800}{30 \times 9900} \times 100\right)\% = 92\%$

3. C

EXPLANATION = [(21% + 17%) of 7800] – [(7% + 8%) of 9900]

[(38% of 7800) – (15% of 9900)] = 2964 – 1485 = 1479

4. A

EXPLANATION = [(15% of 7800)] – [(4% of 7800] = 1170 – 312 = 858

5. D

EXPLANATION = $\left(\dfrac{20\% \text{ of } 7800}{18\% \text{ of } 9900}\right) = \left(\dfrac{20 \times 7800}{18 \times 9900}\right) = \dfrac{260}{297}$

QUESTION 8

1. C
EXPLANATION = [(20% of 1600)] - [(9% of 1600] = 320 − 144 = 176

2. A
EXPLANATION = $\left(\dfrac{20\% \text{ of } 1600}{18\% \text{ of } 3000}\right) = \left(\dfrac{20 \times 1600}{18 \times 3000}\right) = \dfrac{16}{27}$

3. A
EXPLANATION = Candidates who passed from institutes B and D together = [(18% + 10%) of 1600]
Candidates enrolled from institutes B and D together = [(18% + 12%) of 3000]

$= \left(\dfrac{28 \times 1600}{30 \times 3000} \times 100\right)\% = 50\%$

4. C
EXPLANATION = $\left(\dfrac{20\% \text{ of } 1600}{22\% \text{ of } 3000} \times 100\right)\% = \left(\dfrac{20 \times 1600}{22 \times 3000} \times 100\right)\% = 48\%$.

5. D
EXPLANATION = [(20% + 18%) of 1600] - [(8% + 12%) of 3000]
[(38% of 1600) - (20% of 3000)] = 608 − 600 = 8

QUESTION 9

1. B
EXPLANATION = Candidates who passed from institutes S and V together = [(16% + 12%) of 2275]
Candidates enrolled from institutes S and V together = [(17% + 16%) of 4550]

$= \left(\dfrac{28 \times 2275}{33 \times 4550} \times 100\right)\% = 42\%$

2. B
EXPLANATION = $\left(\dfrac{18\% \text{ of } 2275}{22\% \text{ of } 4550}\right) = \left(\dfrac{18 \times 2275}{22 \times 4550}\right) \times 100 = 41\%$

3. C

EXPLANATION = [(20% + 18%) of 2275] - [(10% + 8%) of 4550]
[(33% of 2275) - (18% of 4550)] = 819 − 750.75 = 68.25 = 68

4. A

EXPLANATION = [(10% of 4550)] - [(13% of 2275] = 455 − 295.75 = 159.25

5. A

EXPLANATION = Candidates who passed from institutes P and Q together = [(18% + 17%) of 2275]
Candidates enrolled from institutes P and Q together = [(22% + 15%) of 4550]

$$= \left(\frac{35 \times 2275}{37 \times 4550} \times 100\right)\% = 47\%$$

QUESTION 10

1. B

EXPLANATION = $\left(\frac{22\% \text{ of } 920}{23\% \text{ of } 1500} \times 100\right)\% = \left(\frac{22 \times 920}{23 \times 1500} \times 100\right)\% = 59\%$.

2. B – Q

EXPLANATION =

$P = \left[\left(\frac{16\% \text{ of } 920}{15\% \text{ of } 1500}\right) \times 100\right]\% = \left[\frac{16 \times 920}{15 \times 1500} \times 100\right]\% = 65.42\%$.

$Q = \left[\left(\frac{14\% \text{ of } 920}{12\% \text{ of } 1500}\right) \times 100\right]\% = 71.56\%$.

$R = \left[\left(\frac{22\% \text{ of } 920}{23\% \text{ of } 1500}\right) \times 100\right]\% = 58.67\%$.

$S = \left[\left(\frac{18\% \text{ of } 920}{16\% \text{ of } 1500}\right) \times 100\right]\% = 69\%$.

$T = \left[\left(\frac{15\% \text{ of } 920}{13\% \text{ of } 1500}\right) \times 100\right]\% = 70.77\%$.

$U = \left[\left(\frac{10\% \text{ of } 920}{14\% \text{ of } 1500}\right) \times 100\right]\% = 43.81\%$.

$V = \left[\left(\frac{5\% \text{ of } 920}{7\% \text{ of } 1500}\right) \times 100\right]\% = 43.81\%$.

3. B

EXPLANATION = [(18% + 22%) of 920] - [(7% + 12%) of 1500]

[(40% of 920) - (19% of 1500)] = 368 – 285 = 83

4. A

EXPLANATION = $\left(\dfrac{18\% \text{ of } 920}{16\% \text{ of } 1500}\right) = \left(\dfrac{18 \times 920}{16 \times 1500}\right) \times 100 = 69\%$

5. A

EXPLANATION = Candidates passed from institutes P and Q together = [(16% + 14%) of 920]

Candidates enrolled from institutes P and Q together = [(15% + 12%) of 1500]

$= \left(\dfrac{30 \times 920}{27 \times 1500} \times 100\right) \% = 68\%$

Now move on to the next section of the guide.

DATA INTERPRETATION TESTS

PART 8

DATA INTERPRETATION TESTS PART 8

Q1.

ANNUAL PERCENT CHANGE IN DOLLAR AMOUNT OF SALES
AT FIVE RETAIL STORES FROM 2005 TO 2007

STORE	PERCENT CHANGE FROM 2005 TO 2006	PERCENT CHANGE FROM 2006 TO 2007
P	-20	8
Q	-10	10
R	6	10
S	-9	-14
T	16	-6

1. If the dollar amount of sales at Store Q was $600,000 for 2005, what was the dollar amount of sales at that store for 2007?

    A – $625,000
    B – $594,000
    C – $660,000
    D – $315,000
    E - $543,000

Answer

2. At store T, the dollar amount of sales for 2006 was what percent of the dollar amount of sales for 2007? Give your answer to the nearest 0.1 percent.

Answer

3. Based on the information given, which of the following statements must be true? Indicate all true statements.

    A – For 2007, the dollar amount of sales at store S was greater than that at each of the other four stores.

    B – The dollar amount of sales at store S for 2007 was more than 21 percent less than that for 2005.

    C – The dollar amount of sales at store R for 2007 was more than 16 percent greater than that for 2005.

Answer/s

Q2. ANNUAL PERCENT CHANGE IN DOLLAR AMOUNT OF SALES AT FIVE SUPERMARKETS FROM 2000 TO 2002

STORE	PERCENT CHANGE FROM 2000 TO 2001	PERCENT CHANGE FROM 2001 TO 2002
A	8	12
B	14	-14
C	-10	10
D	6	18
E	-5	-11

1. At supermarket E, the dollar amount of sales for 2001 was what percent of the dollar amount of sales for 2002? Give your answer to the nearest 0.1 percent.

   Answer [112.4]

2. Based on the information given, which of the following statements must be true? Indicate all true statements.

   A – The dollar amount of sales at supermarkets A for 2002 was more than 20 percent greater than that for 2000.

   B – For 2002, the dollar amount of sales at supermarket D was greater than that at each of the other four supermarkets.

   C – The dollar amount of sales at supermarkets D for 2002 was more than 26 percent less than that for 2000.

   Answer/s [A]

3. If the dollar amount of sales at supermarket B was $700,000 for 2000, what was the dollar amount of sales at that supermarket for 2002?

   A – $668,820
   B – $626,250
   C – $686,280
   D – $666,880
   E – $860,250

   Answer [C]

PART 8   269

Q3. ANNUAL PERCENT CHANGE IN DOLLAR AMOUNT OF SALES
AT FIVE BOOK STORES FROM 2008 TO 2010

STORE	PERCENT CHANGE FROM 2008 TO 2009	PERCENT CHANGE FROM 2009 TO 2010
L	8	15
M	-11	10
N	-8	-6
O	10	-10
P	20	10

1. Based on the information given, which of the following statements must be true? Indicate all true statements.

    A – The dollar amount of sales at book store L for 2010 was more than 25 percent greater than that for 2008.

    B – For 2010, the dollar amount of sales at book store N was greater than that at each of the other four supermarkets.

    C – The dollar amount of sales at book store P for 2010 was 32 percent more than that for 2008.

Answer/s [ ]

2. At store O, the dollar amount of sales for 2009 was what percent of the dollar amount of sales for 2010? Give your answer to the nearest 0.1 percent.

Answer [ ]

3. If the dollar amount of sales at store L was $590,000 for 2008, what was the dollar amount of sales at that store for 2010?

    A – $722,550
    B – $732,870
    C – $742,650
    D – $774,250
    E – $732,780

Answer [ ]

DATA INTERPRETATION TESTS

Q4. ANNUAL PERCENT CHANGE IN DOLLAR AMOUNT OF SALES AT FIVE GROCERY STORES FROM 2010 TO 2012

STORE	PERCENT CHANGE FROM 2010 TO 2011	PERCENT CHANGE FROM 2011 TO 2012
Q	10	-20
R	18	8
S	-4	-16
T	4	-4
U	-20	15

1. For store T, the dollar amount of sales for 2010 are the same as the dollar amount of sales for 2012. True or false?

   Answer [ ]

2. If the dollar amount of sales at store R was $395,000 for 2010, what was the dollar amount of sales at that store for 2011?

   A – $466,100
   B – $503,388
   C – $450,500
   D – $505,838
   E – $600,000

   Answer [ ]

3. Based on the information given, which of the following statements must be true? Indicate all true statements.

   A – For 2012 the dollar amount of sales at Store T was greater than that at each of the other four stores.

   B – The dollar amount of sales at Store R for 2012 was more than 27 percent greater than that for 2010.

   C – The dollar amount of sales at Store S for 2012 was more than 19 percent less than that for 2010.

   Answer/s [ ]

Q5. ANNUAL PERCENT CHANGE IN DOLLAR AMOUNT OF SALES
AT FIVE FASHION STORES FROM 2011 TO 2013

STORE	PERCENT CHANGE FROM 2011 TO 2012	PERCENT CHANGE FROM 2012 TO 2013
U	18	-10
V	17	-7
W	16	6
X	20	-5
Y	-15	-8

1. If the dollar amount of sales at Store X was $575,850 for 2011, what was the dollar amount of sales at that store for 2013?

    A – $565,590
    B – $656,469
    C – $665,550
    D – $556,964
    E – $600,600

Answer [ ]

2. At store V, the dollar amount of sales for 2012 was what percent of the dollar amount of sales for 2013? Give your answer to the nearest 0.1 percent.

Answer [ ]

3. Based on the information given, which of the following statements must be true? Indicate all true statements.

    A – For 2013, the dollar amount of sales at store U was greater than that at each of the other four stores.

    B – The dollar amount of sales at store Y for 2011 was more than 21 percent less than that for 2013.

    C – The dollar amount of sales at store W for 2013 was more than 20 percent greater than that for 2011.

Answer/s [ ]

DATA INTERPRETATION TESTS

Q6. *ANNUAL PERCENT CHANGE IN DOLLAR AMOUNT OF SALES AT FIVE COMPANIES FROM 2004 TO 2006*

STORE	PERCENT CHANGE FROM 2004 TO 2005	PERCENT CHANGE FROM 2005 TO 2006
Q	17	10
R	-3	-11
S	10	-21
T	-13	26
U	15	-15

1. Both company S and company T make $350,000 in 2004. what is the difference between the dollar amounts of sales both companies make in 2006?

   A – $304,150
   B – $383,670
   C – $34,500
   D – $79,520
   E – $85,000

   Answer [   ]

2. At store U, the dollar amount of sales for 2005 was what percent of the dollar amount of sales for 2006? Give your answer to the nearest 0.1 percent.

   Answer [   ]

3. If the dollar amount of sales at Store Q was $125,000 for 2004, what was the dollar amount of sales at that store for 2006?

   A – $160,875
   B – $187,550
   C – $160,750
   D – $60,857
   E – $157,850

   Answer [   ]

Q7.

ANNUAL PERCENT CHANGE IN DOLLAR AMOUNT OF SALES AT FIVE WAREHOUSES FROM 2001 TO 2003

WAREHOUSE	PERCENT CHANGE FROM 2001 TO 2002	PERCENT CHANGE FROM 2002 TO 2003
H	14	-9
I	13	7
J	-6	-11
K	15	10
L	19	-29

1. The dollar amount of sales Warehouse K makes in 2001 is $265,500. What is the difference between the dollar amounts of sales in 2002 compared to the amount of sales in 2003? Rounded to the nearest whole numbers.

A – $305,325
B – $60,875
C – $30,533
D – $335,858
E – $105,875

Answer [ ]

2. At store H, the dollar amount of sales for 2002 was what percent of the dollar amount of sales for 2003? Give your answer to the nearest 0.1 percent.

Answer [ ]

3. If the dollar amount of sales at Store L was $180,000 for 2001, what was the dollar amount of sales at that store for 2003?

A – $214,200
B – $220,150
C – $152,082
D – $156,306
E – $220,745

Answer [ ]

DATA INTERPRETATION TESTS

Q8. ANNUAL PERCENT CHANGE IN DOLLAR AMOUNT OF SALES
AT FIVE BOOK BUSINESSES FROM 2007 TO 2009

STORE	PERCENT CHANGE FROM 2007 TO 2008	PERCENT CHANGE FROM 2008 TO 2009
U	10	-11
V	9	9
W	18	-17
X	-12	17
Y	8	19

1. Based on the information given, which of the following statements must be true? Indicate all true statements.

    A – For 2009, the dollar amount of sales at business V was greater than that at each of the other four businesses.

    B – The dollar amount of sales at business V for 2008 was the same amount of dollar sales for 2009.

    C – The dollar amount of sales at store Y for 2009 was more than 28 percent greater than that for 2007

    Answer/s [   ]

2. At store U, the dollar amount of sales for 2008 was what percent of the dollar amount of sales for 2009? Give your answer to the nearest 0.1 percent.

    Answer [   ]

3. If the dollar amount of sales at Store X was $150,500 for 2007, what was the dollar amount of sales at that store for 2009? Rounded to the nearest whole number.

    A – $132,440
    B – $158,695
    C – $124,450
    D – $154,955
    E – $139,850

    Answer [   ]

Q9.

ANNUAL PERCENT CHANGE IN DOLLAR AMOUNT OF SALES
AT FIVE RETAIL STORES FROM 2010 TO 2012

STORE	PERCENT CHANGE FROM 2010 TO 2011	PERCENT CHANGE FROM 2011 TO 2012
P	-20	8
Q	10	20
R	6	13
S	17	-16
T	-3	-9

1. If the dollar amount of sales at Store P was $500,000 for 2010, what was the dollar amount of sales at that store for 2012?

   A – $459,000
   B – $413,000
   C – $478,000
   D – $432,000
   E – $440,000

Answer [ ]

2. Based on the information given, which of the following statements must be true? Indicate all true statements.

   A – For 2011, the dollar amount of sales at store Q was greater than that at each of the other four stores.

   B – The dollar amount of sales at store T for 2012 was more than 11 percent less than that for 2010.

   C – The dollar amount of sales at store R for 2012 was more than 19 percent greater than that for 2010.

Answer/s [ ]

3. At store S, the dollar amount of sales for 2011 was what percent of the dollar amount of sales for 2012? Give your answer to the nearest 0.1 percent.

Answer [ ]

Q10. *ANNUAL PERCENT CHANGE IN DOLLAR AMOUNT OF SALES AT FIVE GROCERY STORES FROM 2000 TO 2002*

STORE	PERCENT CHANGE FROM 2000 TO 2001	PERCENT CHANGE FROM 2001 TO 2002
H	20	-10
I	-5	-6
J	16	5
K	-17	-6
L	4	-13

1. Based on the information given, which of the following statements must be true? Indicate all true statements.

    A – The dollar amount of sales at store I for 2002 was more than 10 percent less than that for 2000.

    B – For 2011, the dollar amount of sales at store H was greater than that at each of the other four stores.

    C – The dollar amount of sales at store J for 2002 was more than 21 percent greater than that for 2000.

    Answer/s [   ]

2. At store H, the dollar amount of sales for 2001 was what percent of the dollar amount of sales for 2002? Give your answer to the nearest 0.1 percent.

    Answer [   ]

3. If the dollar amount of sales at Store K was $300,000 for 2000, what was the dollar amount of sales at that store for 2002?

    A – $213,789
    B – $236,940
    C – $213,940
    D – $249,490
    E – $234,060

    Answer [   ]

Now check your answers carefully.

PART 8   277

DATA INTERPRETATIONS PART 8 EXPLANATIONS AND ANSWERS

QUESTION 1

1. B

EXPLANATION: if the dollar amount of sales at Store Q was $600,000 for 2005, then it was 10% greater for 2006. So, this accounts to 110% of that amount (110% of $600,000 = $660,000). For 2007, the amount of sales was 90% of 2006. To work out the sales for 2007: (90% of $660,000 = $594,000). So, the correct answer is choice B, $594,000.

2. 106.4%

EXPLANATION: If A is the dollar amount of sales at store T, from 2006 to 2007 there was a decrease by -6. 6 divided by 100 = 0.06, which means 0.94 is the dollar amount for 2007. Therefore, you need to divide A by 0.94. So 1 divided by 0.94 = 1.06382... To work out the percentage, multiply this by 100 to give you 106.38. To 1 decimal place and thus, the correct answer is 106.4%.

3. B and C

EXPLANATION: For Choice A, since the only data given are percent changes from year to year, there is no way to compare the actual dollar amount of sales at the stores for 2007 or for any other year. The actual dollar amount of sales for 2007 may have been much smaller than that for any of the other four stores, and therefore Choice A is not necessarily true.

For Choice B, if B is the dollar amount of sales at store S for 2005, then the dollar amount for 2006 is 0.91 % of B: (100 − 9 = .91). The dollar amount for 2007 would be (100 − 14 = .86). So, 0.91 x 0.86 = 0.7826, as a percent = 78.26. So, this represents a percent decrease of 100 − 78.26 = 21.74 percent, which is more than 21 percent, so Choice B must be true.

For Choice C, if C is the dollar amount of sales at store R for 2005, then the dollar amount for 2006 is given by 1.06C and the dollar amount for 2007 is given by 1.10. So, 1.10 x 1.06 = 1.166. Note this represents a 16.6% increase, which is greater than 16%, so Choice C must be true.

QUESTION 2

1. 112.4%

EXPLANATION: If A is the dollar amount of sales at supermarket E, from 2001 to 2002 there was a decrease by -11. 11 divided by 100 = 0.11, which means 0.89 is the dollar amount for 2002. Therefore, you need to divide A by 0.89. So 1 divided by 0.89 = 1.12359... To work out the percentage, multiply this by 100 to give you 112.35. To 1 decimal place and thus, the correct answer is 112.35%.

2. A

EXPLANATION: For Choice A, if A is the dollar amount of sales at supermarket A for 2000, then the dollar amount for 2001 is given by 1.08A and the dollar amount for 2002 is given by 1.12. So, 1.08 x 1.12 = 1.2099. Note this represents a 20.99% increase, which is greater than 20%, so Choice A must be true.

For Choice B, since the only data given are percent changes from year to year, there is no way to compare the actual dollar amount of sales at the supermarkets for 2002 or for any other year. The actual dollar amount of sales for 2002 may have been much smaller than that for any of the other four supermarkets, and therefore Choice B is not necessarily true.

For Choice C, if C is the dollar amount of sales at store D for 2000, then the dollar amount for 2001 is given by 1.06C and the dollar amount for 2002 is given by 1.18. So, 1.06 x 1.18 = 1.2508. Note this represents a 25.08% increase, which is not greater than 26%, so Choice C is not true.

3. C

EXPLANATION: if the dollar amount of sales at Store B was $700,000 for 2000, then it was 14% greater for 2001. So, this accounts to 114% of that amount (114% of $700,000 = $798,000). For 2002, the amount of sales was 86% of 2001. To work out the sales for 2002: (86% of $798,000 = $686,280). So, the correct answer is choice C, $686,280.

QUESTION 3

1. C

EXPLANATION: For Choice A, if A is the dollar amount of sales at store L for 2008, then the dollar amount for 2009 is given by 1.08A and the dollar amount for 2010 is given by 1.15. So, 1.08 x 1.15 = 1.242. Note this represents a 24.2% increase, which is not greater than 25%, so Choice A is not true.

For Choice B, since the only data given are percent changes from year to year, there is no way to compare the actual dollar amount of sales at the stores for 2010 or for any other year. The actual dollar amount of sales for 2010 may have been much smaller than that for any of the other four stores, and therefore Choice B is not necessarily true.

For Choice C, if C is the dollar amount of sales at store P for 2008, then the dollar amount for 2009 is given by 1.20C and the dollar amount for 2010 is given by 1.10. So, 1.20 x 1.10 = 1.32. Note this represents a 32% increase, which was 32% more than that for 2008, so Choice C is true.

2. 111.1%

EXPLANATION: If A is the dollar amount of sales at store O, from 2009 to 2010 there was a decrease by -10. 10 divided by 100 = 0.1, which means 0.90 is the dollar amount for 2010. Therefore, you need to divide A by 0.90. So 1 divided by 0.90 = 1.11111... To work out the percentage, multiply this by 100 to give you 111.11. To 1 decimal place and thus, the correct answer is 111.1%.

3. E

EXPLANATION: if the dollar amount of sales at Store L was $590,000 for 2008, then it was 8% greater for 2009. So, this accounts to 108% of that amount (108% of $590,000 = $637,200). For 2010, the amount of sales was 15% of 2009. To work out the sales for 2010: (115% of $637,200 = $732,780). So, the correct answer is choice E, $732,780.

QUESTION 4

1. False

EXPLANATION: Note that an increase of 4 percent for one year and a decrease of 4 percent for the following year does not result in the same dollar amount as the original dollar amount because the base that is used in computing the percent's is for the first change would be different from the base amount for the second change.

2. A

EXPLANATION: if the dollar amount of sales at Store R was $395,000 for 2010, then it was 18% greater for 2011. So, this accounts to 118% of that amount (118% of $395,000 = $466,100).

3. B and C

EXPLANATION: For Choice A, since the only data given are percent changes from year to year, there is no way to compare the actual dollar amount of sales at the stores for 2012 or for any other year. The actual dollar amount of sales for 2012 may have been much smaller than that for any of the other four stores, and therefore Choice A is not necessarily true.

For Choice B, if B is the dollar amount of sales at store R for 2010, then the dollar amount for 2011 is given by 1.18C and the dollar amount for 2012 is given by 1.08. So, 1.18 x 1.08 = 1.2744. Note this represents a 27.44% increase, which is greater than 27%, so Choice B must be true.

For Choice C, if C is the dollar amount of sales at store S for 2010, then the dollar amount for 2011 is 0.96 % of C (100 – 4 = .96). The dollar amount for 2012 would be 0.84 (100 – 16 = .84). So, 0.96 x 0.84 = 0.8064, as a percent = 80.64. So, this represents a percent decrease of 100 – 80.64 = 19.36 percent, which is more than 19 percent, so Choice C must be true.

QUESTION 5

1. B

EXPLANATION: if the dollar amount of sales at Store X was $575,850 for 2011, then it was 20% greater for 2012. So, this accounts to 120% of that amount (120% of $575,850 = $691,020). For 2013, the amount of sales was 95% of 2012. To work out the sales for 2013: (95% of $691,020 = $656,469). So, the correct answer is choice B, $656,469.

2. 107.5%

EXPLANATION: If A is the dollar amount of sales at store V, from 2012 to 2013 there was a decrease by -7. 7 divided by 100 = 0.07, which means 0.93 is the dollar amount for 2013. Therefore, you need to divide A by 0.93. So 1 divided by 0.93 = 1.07526... To work out the percentage, multiply this by 100 to give you 107.526. To 1 decimal place and thus, the correct answer is 107.5%.

3. B and C

EXPLANATION: For Choice A, since the only data given are percent changes from year to year, there is no way to compare the actual dollar amount of sales at the stores for 2013 or for any other year. The actual dollar amount of sales for 2013 may have been much smaller than that for any of the other four stores, and therefore Choice A is not necessarily true.

For Choice B, if B is the dollar amount of sales at store Y for 2011, then the dollar amount for 2012 is 0.85% of B: (100 – 15 = 0.85). The dollar amount for 2013 would be (100 – 8 = .92). So, 0.85 x 0.92 = 0.782. As a percent = 78.2. So, this represents a percent decrease of 100 – 78.2 = 21.8 percent, which is more than 21 percent, so Choice B must be true.

For Choice C, if C is the dollar amount of sales at store W for 2011, then the dollar amount for 2012 is given by 1.16C and the dollar amount for 2013 is given by 1.06. So, 1.16 x 1.06 = 1.2296. Note this represents a 22.96% increase, which is greater than 20%, so Choice C must be true.

QUESTION 6

1. D

EXPLANATION: if the dollar amount of sales at company S was $350,000 for 2004, then it was 10% greater for 2005. So, this accounts to 110% of that amount (110% of $350,000 = $385,000). For 2006, the amount of sales was 79% of 2005. To work out the sales for 2006: (79% of $385,000 = $304,150).

For company T, the dollar amount for 2004 was $350,000. Then it was 13% decrease for 2005. So, this accounts to 87% of that amount (87% of $350,000 = $304,500). For 2006, the amount of sales was 26% of 2005. To work out the sales for 2006: (126% of $304,500 = $383,670).

So, the difference between the dollar amounts between both companies for 2006 is $79,520.

2. 117.6%

EXPLANATION: If A is the dollar amount of sales at store U, from 2005 to 2006 there was a decrease by -15. 15 divided by 100 = 0.15, which means 0.85 is the dollar amount for 2006. Therefore, you need to divide A by 0.85. So 1 divided by 0.85 = 1.17647... To work out the percentage, multiply this by 100 to give you 117.647. To 1 decimal place and thus, the correct answer is 117.6%.

3. A

EXPLANATION: if the dollar amount of sales at company Q was $125,000 for 2004, then it was 17% greater for 2005. So, this accounts to 117% of that amount (117% of $125,000 = $146,250). For 2006, the amount of sales was 110% of 2005. To work out the sales for 2006: (110% of $146,250 = $160,875). So the answer is A, $160,875.

QUESTION 7

1. C

EXPLANATION: if the dollar amount of sales at Warehouse K was $265,500 for 2001, then it was 15% greater for 2002. So, this accounts to 115% of that amount (115% of $265,500 = $302,325). For 2003, the amount of sales was 10% of 2002. To work out the sales for 2003: (110% of $302,325 = $335,857.5). To the nearest whole number = $335,858. So, the correct answer would be 335,858 – 305,325 = 30,533.

2. 109.9%

EXPLANATION: If A is the dollar amount of sales at store H, from 2002 to 2003 there was a decrease by -9. 9 divided by 100 = 0.09, which means 0.91 is the dollar amount for 2003 Therefore, you need to divide A by 0.91. So 1 divided by 0.91 = 1.09890... To work out the percentage, multiply this by 100 to give you 109.890. To 1 decimal place and thus, the correct answer is 109.9%.

3. C

EXPLANATION: if the dollar amount of sales at company L was $180,000 for 2001, then it was 19% greater for 2002. So, this accounts to 119% of that amount (119% of $180,000 = $214,200). For 2003, the amount of sales was -29%, which accounts for 71% of the total of 2002. To work out the sales for 2003: (71% of $214,200 = $152,082). So the answer is C, $152,082.

QUESTION 8

1. C

EXPLANATION: For Choice A, since the only data given are percent changes from year to year, there is no way to compare the actual dollar amount of sales at the business for 2009 or for any other year. The actual dollar amount of sales for 2009 may have been much smaller than that for any of the other four businesses, and therefore Choice A is not necessarily true.

For Choice B, despite having the same increased number for each year, the business sales for 2008 would not be the same as 2009. Note that an increase of 10 percent for one year and a decrease of 10 percent for the following year does not result in the same dollar amount as the original dollar amount because the base that is used in computing the percent is different.

For Choice C, if C is the dollar amount of sales at store Y for 2007, then the dollar amount for 2008 is given by 1.08C and the dollar amount for 2009 is given by 1.19. So, 1.08 x 1.19 = 1.2852. Note this represents a 28.52% increase, which is greater than 28%, so Choice C must be true.

2. 112.4%

EXPLANATION: If A is the dollar amount of sales at store U, from 2008 to 2009 there was a decrease by -11. 11 divided by 100 = 0.11, which means 0.89 is the dollar amount for 2009. Therefore, you need to divide A by 0.89. So 1 divided by 0.89 = 1.12359... To work out the percentage, multiply this by 100 to give you 112.359. To 1 decimal place and thus, the correct answer is 112.4%.

3. D

EXPLANATION: if the dollar amount of sales at company X was $150,500 for 2007, then it was -12% decrease for 2008. So, this accounts to 88% of that amount (88% of $150,500 = $132,440). For 2009, the amount of sales was 17% greater than that of 2008, which accounts for 117% of the total of 2008. To work out the sales for 2009: (117% of $132,440 = $54,954.8). Rounded to the nearest whole number = $154,955. So the answer is D.

QUESTION 9

1. D

EXPLANATION: if the dollar amount of sales at company P was $500,000 for 2010, then it was -20% decrease for 2011. So, this accounts to 80% of that amount (80% of $500,000 = $400,000). For 2012, the amount of sales was 8% greater than that of 2011, which accounts for 108% of the total of 2011. To work out the sales for 2012: (108% of $400,000 = $432,000). So the answer is D, $432,000.

2. B and C

EXPLANATION: For Choice A, since the only data given are percent changes from year to year, there is no way to compare the actual dollar amount of sales at the stores for 2011 or for any other year. The actual dollar amount of sales for 2011 may have been much smaller than that for any of the other four stores, and therefore Choice A is not necessarily true.

For Choice B, if B is the dollar amount of sales at store T for 2010, then the dollar amount for 2011 is 0.97 % of B: (100 – 3 = .97). The dollar amount for 2012 would be (100 – 9 = .91). So, 0.97 x 0.91 = 0.8827, as a percent = 88.27. So, this represents a percent decrease of 100 – 88.27 = 11.73 percent, which is more than 11 percent, so Choice B must be true.

For Choice C, if C is the dollar amount of sales at store R for 2010, then the dollar amount for 2011 is given by 1.06C and the dollar amount for 2012 is given by 1.13. So, 1.06 x 1.13 = 1.1978. Note this represents a 19.78% increase, which is greater than 19%, so Choice C must be true.

3. 119%

EXPLANATION: If A is the dollar amount of sales at store S, from 2011 to 2012 there was a decrease by -16. 16 divided by 100 = 0.16, which means 0.84 is the dollar amount for 2012. Therefore, you need to divide A by 0.84. So 1 divided by 0.84 = 1.19047... To work out the percentage, multiply this by 100 to give you 119.047. To 1 decimal place and thus, the correct answer is 119%.

PART 8   283

QUESTION 10

1. A and C

EXPLANATION: For Choice A, if A is the dollar amount of sales at store I for 2000, then the dollar amount for 2001 is 0.95 % of B: (100 – 5 = .95). The dollar amount for 2002 would be (100 – 6 = .94). So, 00.95 x 0.94 = 0.893, as a percent = 89.3. So, this represents a percent decrease of 100 – 89.3 = 10.7 percent, which is more than 10 percent, so Choice A must be true.

For Choice B, since the only data given are percent changes from year to year, there is no way to compare the actual dollar amount of sales at the stores for 2011 or for any other year. The actual dollar amount of sales for 2011 may have been much smaller than that for any of the other four stores, and therefore Choice B is not necessarily true.

For Choice C, if C is the dollar amount of sales at store J for 2000, then the dollar amount for 2001 is given by 1.16C and the dollar amount for 2002 is given by 1.05. So, 1.16 x 1.05 = 1.218. Note this represents a 21.8% increase, which is greater than 21%, so Choice C must be true.

2. 111.1%

EXPLANATION: If A is the dollar amount of sales at store H, from 2001 to 2002 there was a decrease by -10. 10 divided by 100 = 0.10, which means 0.90 is the dollar amount for 2002. Therefore, you need to divide A by 0.90. So 1 divided by 0.90 = 1.1111… To work out the percentage, multiply this by 100 to give you 111.111. To 1 decimal place and thus, the correct answer is 111.1%.

3. E

EXPLANATION: if the dollar amount of sales at company K was $300,000 for 2000, then it was -17% decrease for 2001. So, this accounts to 83% of that amount (73% of $300,000 = $219,000). For 2002, the amount of sales was 6% greater than that of 2001, which accounts for 106% of the total of 2001. To work out the sales for 2002: (94% of $249,000 = $219,000). So the answer is E, $234,060.

A FEW FINAL WORDS

You have now reached the end of the testing guide and no doubt you will be ready to take your test.

The majority of candidates who pass the selection process for their chosen career have a number of common attributes. These are as follows:

1. They believe in themselves.

The first factor is self-belief. Regardless of what anyone tells you, you can pass your tests and get the job that you really want. Just like any test, interview or selection process, you have to be prepared to work hard in order to be successful. Make sure you have the self-belief to pass the test with high scores and fill your mind with positive thoughts.

2. They prepare fully.

The second factor is preparation. Those people who achieve in life prepare fully for every eventuality and that is what you must do when you prepare for your test. Work very hard and especially concentrate on your weak areas.

3. They persevere.

Perseverance is a fantastic word. Everybody comes across obstacles or setbacks in their life, but it is what you do about those setbacks that is important. If you fail at something, then ask yourself 'why' you have failed. This will allow you to improve for next time and if you keep improving and trying, success will eventually follow. Apply this same method of thinking when you prepare for your test.

4. They are self-motivated.

How much do you want this job? Do you want it, or do you really want it?

When you apply for any job you should want it more than anything in the world. Your levels of self-motivation will shine through on your application, whilst sitting the test and also during your interview. For the weeks and months leading up to the selection process, be motivated as best you can and always keep your fitness levels up as this will serve to increase your levels of motivation.

Work hard, stay focused and be what you want…

Richard McMunn

P.S. Don't forget, you can get FREE access to more tests online at:

www.PsychometricTestsOnline.co.uk

Get more books, manuals,
online tests and training courses at:

www.How2Become.com

Printed and bound by CPI Group (UK) Ltd, Croydon, CR0 4YY